JUL -- 2002

COUNSELING AND PSYCHOLOGY IN
ELEMENTARY SCHOOLS

COUNSELING AND PSYCHOLOGY IN ELEMENTARY SCHOOLS

By

HENRY KACZKOWSKI

and

C. H. PATTERSON

University of Illinois
College of Education
Urbana-Champaign

CHARLES C THOMAS • PUBLISHER
Springfield • Illinois • U.S.A.

Published and Distributed Throughout the World by
CHARLES C THOMAS • PUBLISHER
Bannerstone House
301-327 East Lawrence Avenue, Springfield, Illinois, U.S.A.

© 1975, by CHARLES C THOMAS • PUBLISHER
ISBN 0-398-03218-1
Library of Congress Catalog Card Number: 74-8973

Printed in the United States of America
Q-1

Library of Congress Cataloging in Publication Data

Kaezkowski, Henry.
  Counseling and psychology in elementary schools.

  1. Personnel service in elementary education.
 I. Patterson, Cecil Holden, 1912-   joint author.
II. Title. (DNLM: 1. Child guidance. 2. Counseling.
3. Education. 4. Psychology, Educational. LB1027.5 K11c)
LB102715.K26 1974   372.1'4   74-8973
ISBN 0-398-03218-1

PREFACE

With the increasing interest and expansion of counseling in the elementary school, textbooks in elementary school counseling have been proliferating. The question, "Why another?" is a legitimate one.

The reason for this text is a simple one. The authors have found no existing text adequate for their needs, or the needs of their students as they see them. The lacks of existing books are fundamentally two: (1) they lack a point of view or an integrative focus and (2) while they cover a wide variety of things (some often trivial), they omit consideration of a number of important things. For example, they do not recognize developments in psychology, such as the use of behavior modification in classroom management, and the work with learning disabilities.

Most books attempt to be encyclopedic, and become little more than comments on a long list of topics. They get bogged down in detail, and long lists of items (such as tests that *might* be used). The reader can't see the forest for the trees. There is no focus or integration. The reader is left wondering what is fundamental and what is peripheral, what is important and what is trivial, and the student—since he perhaps rightly expects to be examined on them—ends up trying to memorize endless details and lists of items.

As a result, he is left in a forest of confusion about the role of the counselor in the elementary school—what he should or should not do, how or when he is to perform the endless lists of duties, how he is to meet all the demands upon him. The demands upon and the responsibilities of the counselor as pictured are overwhelming. There are just too many responsibilities and too many things to do, too many choices and decisions to make. Worse, there are no clear ways to meet his responsibilities, no pathways to the many goals or objectives he is urged to achieve, no criteria or principles on the basis of which he is to make

v

choices and decisions. The focus is, on the one hand, upon highly specific activities, and on the other hand, on vague distant goals —helping students work toward citizenship and civic responsibility, improved international relationships, global changes in society, etc.

In contrast, this book attempts a systematic, integrated approach to counseling and psychology in the elementary school. It is not simply a smorgasbord of facts and information. Following a brief history of counseling in the elementary school and a review of various approaches to counseling in elementary schools, the question of the goal of education is raised. It is proposed that the goal of education is the developing of self-actualizing persons. This is not really a new goal—it has been implicit in many of the educational developments and reforms since the development of progressive education. The Educational Policies Commission, over 30 years ago, included self-realization and the development of good human relationships in its statement of the goals of education.[1] Unfortunately, these goals have been lost sight of in the concern about improving subject matter achievement, through the development of new curriculums and the use of technology. The current interest in humanistic education brings these goals to the fore. It seems to be appropriate now to make the goal of developing self-actualizing persons explicit, since it appears to be possible to begin to operationalize and implement it in the schools.

The acceptance of this goal for education moves counseling and psychology from a peripheral activity, or a "service" in helping education achieve its traditional and limited goal of intellectual and cognitive achievement, to the center of the educational process. Counseling and psychology have always been concerned with the development of the individual's potentials, beyond those of the intellect alone.

The remaining chapters of the book are concerned with how counseling and student personnel services work toward this goal, both directly and indirectly. This goal does not eliminate con-

---

[1]Educational Policies Commission. *The purposes of education in American democracy.* (Washington, National Education Association, 1938).

cern with skills and subject matter—the standard curriculum—since these are viewed as necessary or desirable subgoals in the development of self-actualizing persons. But the focus is upon the more central aspects of the self-actualizing person—his affective or emotional development as a person, and his relationships with others, so important—indeed essential—to his development as a person.

The achievement of the other general goals with which writers are sometimes concerned—citizenship, peaceable international relationships, etc.—is attained by developing self-actualizing individuals, who, as responsible, fully functioning persons will be able to resolve the problems related to these goals for man and society. In fact, the only effective way in which these problems can be attacked and resolved is through the development of self-actualizing persons.

The focus and responsibility of the counselor is thus clear and simple—in form and conceptualization if not in achievement: to facilitate the development of self-actualizing persons. The book indicates the ways in which this can be done.

The emphasis is upon the core essentials, since space is limited. There is no attempt at encyclopedic coverage, to the extent of simply listing activities, names, references, etc. There is little attention to a number of things covered in the usual text: student records, individual inventory, methods of collecting data and information on students, general testing programs, computer scheduling. Such things are at the same time the result, and a cause of, the focus on *guidance* of the individual. The new approach represented in this book is a move from this sterile and obsolete concept which has held counselors in a straitjacket for so long. It moves from the concept of guidance to that of facilitation. The counselor is freed from an impossible task—and a morally or ethically indefensible one—of *guiding the development of the child,* to become *a facilitator of human development.*

Henry Kaczkowski
C. H. Patterson

CONTENTS

COUNSELING AND PSYCHOLOGY IN ELEMENTARY SCHOOLS

PART I

INTRODUCTION

Chapter 1

THE DEVELOPMENT OF ELEMENTARY SCHOOL COUNSELING

IT IS AN INTERESTING FACT in the history of education that counseling began not in elementary schools as one might expect but in secondary schools. This is explained by the nature of the counseling movement which became incorporated in the school. It was vocationally oriented, developing from the work of Frank Parsons, who in the first decade of this century began to work with out-of-school youth in Boston. Although there were a few schools that offered some counseling to students, the first formal public school counseling department was apparently the Vocational Information Department established in Boston in 1913.

It was to be half a century before the importance of counseling in the elementary school was recognized. If, as was the case for several decades, counseling was limited to vocational counseling, it becomes understandable why counseling did not enter the elementary school. Vocational counseling simply did not appear to be relevant to elementary school students.

THE SCHOOL PSYCHOLOGIST

Although the need for counselors in the elementary school was not recognized until very recently, the need for psychological services was felt much earlier. The date when the first psychologist entered the schools is unknown. In the report of a conference on school psychology held in the 1950s, a reference is made to the

5

appointment of a psychologist in Connecticut in 1915 to examine backward children.[1] In the 1920s persons designated as school psychologists appeared in school systems.

The development of school psychology has been related to two concerns in education. The first is special education. Although special education for the mentally retarded began early in this century, its expansion came in the 1930s. School psychologists were required to evaluate children for special classes, essentially by means of intelligence tests. They became, and remain in many if not most school systems, psychometrists, administering endless tests to endless lines of children, never able to catch up with the referrals.

The second concern in education relating to the development of school psychology is the interest in the child with learning problems, or emotional-psychological problems. Although this concern dates back many years (to the beginning of clinical psychology in the first psychological clinic founded by Witmer at the University of Pennsylvania in 1896), it has only been since World War II that it has received anywhere near adequate attention. The school psychologist who functions in remedial work with learning and emotional problems becomes a clinical psychologist and psychotherapist. Not only do relatively few psychologists function in this way, but there is disagreement among school psychologists about whether this is an appropriate role. Practicing psychotherapy particularly is not accepted by many as a legitimate function of the school psychologist. The Thayer Conference on School Psychology in 1954 could not agree upon the appropriate role and functions of the school psychologist,[2] and little essential agreement has been reached since then.

THE ELEMENTARY SCHOOL COUNSELOR

Early Beginnings. Counselors in elementary schools began to appear in the 1920s. However, they were few in number. In 1928, a survey found that only 16 of the 75 cities covered had elementary school counselors in their systems, and only six re-

[1]Norma E. Cutts Ed., *School psychologists at mid-century* (Washington, American Psychological Association, 1955), p. 24.
[2]*Ibid.*

ported counselors assigned to individual schools. Several years later another survey found only 23 of 62 elementary schools reporting with guidance services.[3]

Faust, in his history of elementary school counseling has nothing to say about the nature of programs or services in the period prior to the fifties.

The Middle Period. It was in the 1950s that any noticeable growth in elementary school counseling occurred. A survey of 611 "typical" schools in 19 states by the National Association of Guidance Supervisors and Counselor Trainers found about one-third of them with some form of guidance services, about the same proportion as those having school psychologists. About 25 per cent desired more counselors, compared to 46 per cent desiring more school psychologists.[4] Most of these schools had less than the services of a full-time counselor, and a fourth had less than half-time services. The National Education Association found that in 1959 only 15.4 per cent of the schools in districts with a population over 500,000 had no elementary school guidance services. However, 61.5 per cent reported only limited services; the trend was toward expansion rather than reduction of services.

Some publications on elementary school counseling began to appear during this decade. During the 30s and 40s a number of articles with titles such as "Guidance in the Elementary School" had appeared in various education journals. These were brief, general, and descriptive. The articles in the 50s began to become concerned about the role and functions of the counselor. However, the general focus was upon the teacher as a counselor or guidance worker.[5] Probably the first text was that of Hatch.[6]

---

[3]Reported in Ruth Martenson & Harry Smallenburg, *Guidance in elementary schools* (Englewood Cliffs, Prentice-Hall, 1968), pp. 12-13.

[4]*Ibid.,* pp. 13-14.

[5]See Ira Gordon, *The teacher as a guidance worker* (New York, Harper & Row, 1956); John Barr, *The elementary teacher and guidance* (New York, Holt, Rinehart & Winston, 1958); Edgar Johnston, Mildred Peters and William Evraiff, *The role of the teacher in guidance* (Englewood Cliffs, Prentice-Hall, 1959); Gerald Kowitz & Norma Kowitz, *Guidance in the elementary classroom* (New York, McGraw-Hill, 1959).

[6]Raymond Hatch, *Guidance services in the elementary schools* (Dubuque, William C. Brown, 1951).

The Los Angeles County Schools had published a "Guidance Handbook in Elementary Schools" in 1948, and in 1951 the U.S. Office of Education published a circular on "Pupil Personnel Services in Elementary and Secondary Schools." Hatch's book was followed by several others.[7]

The approach to counseling in the elementary school during most of this decade was still what Faust designates as the traditional approach. The traditional approach is heavily influenced by secondary school counseling and guidance. Thus, the counselor is involved in testing, including tests of aptitudes and interests as well as achievement, in "analysis of the individual" (actually the collection of nonstandardized or nontest data on the individual), in individual counseling, and in consultation with parents and administrators. There is little emphasis on consulting with teachers or inservice training of teachers, and practically no emphasis on counseling parents, teachers and administrators. The orientation is problem and crisis centered, focusing on special children.

The Transitional Sixties. Beginning in the early sixties elementary school counseling became the focus of attention of counselor educators and professional associations. Educators had also become more interested in providing counseling at the elementary level. And students began appearing in counselor education programs with a desire to work in elementary schools rather than in secondary schools.

This emphasis on elementary school counseling and beginning demand for counselors produced a need for programs for the

---

[7]Ervin Detjen and Mary Detjen, *Elementary school guidance* (New York, McGraw-Hill, 1952); Roy Willey, *Guidance in elementary education* (New York, Harper & Row, 1952); Harold Bernard, James Evans, and Franklin Zeran, *Guidance services in the elementary school* (New York, Chartwell House, 1954); Harold Cottingham, *Guidance in elementary schools: principles and practices* (Bloomington, McKnight & McKnight, 1956); Ruth Martenson & Harry Smallenburg, *Guidance in elementary schools* (Englewood Cliffs, Prentice-Hall, 1958); Harold Cottingham, *Guidance and elementary schools: principles and practices* (Bloomington, McKnight & McKnight, 1959); Robert Knapp, *Guidance in the elementary school* (Boston, Allyn & Bacon, 1959).

preparation of counselors to work at the elementary school level. Yet counselor education programs were almost entirely oriented toward the preparation of secondary school counselors.[8] This focus was encouraged by the support of counselor education by the National Defense Education Act of 1958 (Public Law 85-864). This legislation, passed following the first launching of a space vehicle by Russia, was designed to expand programs in counseling and guidance in secondary schools in order to provide testing programs "to identify students with outstanding aptitudes and ability," and counseling "to advise students of courses of study best suited to their ability, aptitudes and skills," and "to encourage students with outstanding aptitude and ability to complete their secondary school education, take the necessary courses for admission to institutions of higher education, and enter such institutions."

In 1964 an amendment to the National Defense Education Act to extend support to elementary school counseling was proposed. The extension was supported and justified on the bases that federal support had been successful in significantly increasing the number of counselors in secondary schools, and that support now should be given to elementary school counseling to provide for the early identification of able students and potential dropouts. Such identification could lead to the prevention of dropouts and the resolving of problems before they become too serious. Testimony indicated that less than 15 per cent of elementary schools had counseling available on more than a one day a week basis.

The amendment was passed, but too late for the Office of Education to announce a program for soliciting proposals on a national scale for the academic year 1965-66. However, rather than wait a year, the Office of Education selected three institutions and invited them to present proposals. These were the University of

---

[8]Dale Nitzschke and George Hill, *The elementary school counselor; preparation and functions* (Athens, Center for Educational Research and Services, College of Education, Ohio University, 1964) found that of 575 colleges and universities offering master's degrees, less than 8 per cent claimed to have a master's degree program in elementary school guidance.

Illinois, the University of Missouri, and Arizona State University.

Following the recommendation of the American Personnel and Guidance Association that adequately prepared counselors should have two years of graduate work, the University of Illinois proposed a three-semester program (a summer, two semesters, and a summer) which, with prerequisites, would provide two years of training. This proposal was reduced, however, by the Office of Education to a summer and two semesters. Arizona State developed a 60 semester hour program including two summers and an academic year. The University of Missouri program was an academic year in length.

Thus the development of programs for the preparation of elementary school counselors got underway. NDEA support continued for three years (the support of the University of Illinois program was continued for only two years). Federal funds were made available in 1965 to school districts for the employment of elementary school counselors.

Faust sees the sixties as witnessing a change from the traditionalist approach, through a neotraditionalist phase, to a developmentalist approach to counseling in the elementary school. The neotraditionalist approach continues the emphasis on individual counseling of special children, and parent, teacher and administrator consultation. There is less emphasis on educational program planning, career and occupational exploration, and testing. There is still little concern with counseling parents, teachers and administrators. Group counseling is added to individual counseling, however. The crisis orientation continues, but there is some concern with prevention.

The developmental elementary school counselor, according to Faust is not crisis oriented, but focuses on the learning climate of the school or classroom as it impinges on all children. In addition to individual and group counseling of children, he engages in counseling teachers (but not parents or administrators). He engages in consultation with teachers and administrators, but, in contrast with the traditional and neotraditional counselor, not with parents.

THE FUTURE

The sixties, as indicated above, saw the beginning of elementary school counseling as a field in its own right. But the period did not result in the development of a unified, generally accepted concept, or model, for the counselor in the elementary school. The period was one of ferment and competing ideas. One line of development seemed to be a move, supported by the Office of Education, to develop separate and distinct programs of education for elementary and secondary school counselors.

It was, of course, too much to expect that the development and general acceptance of a model for elementary school counseling could occur in a few years. It was only in the sixties that secondary school counseling reached a stage where there was general agreement on the role and functions and preparation of the counselor, and, of course changes are still occurring here. It is, of course, to be expected that the process of developing a generally accepted model for elementary school counseling will not take the long period of time required in the case of secondary school counseling. The professional status of secondary school counseling has barely been achieved at the present time, but such status for elementary school counseling should be achieved almost simultaneously with that of secondary school counseling.

This decade will be one of achieving some agreement upon a model for elementary school counseling. Probably no one of the current models will be accepted or adopted in its entirety. Elements of all of the apparently divergent models will probably be incorporated in a new model. A major focus of this book will be the examination of current models, and the development of a tentative integration of them into a general model or approach to elementary school counseling.

A major aspect of the currently developing situation in education, which has not been adequately related to elementary school counseling, is the involvement of psychologists in problems of learning and of children's classroom behavior, particularly through the application of techniques of behavior modification. It is essential that this movement be related to, or even incorporated into, counseling. Hence, the inclusion of the term psychology in the title of this book.

SUMMARY

Elementary school counseling is essentially a development of the decade of the sixties, although a few schools had some counseling services as early as the twenties. The paradox that counseling first developed in the secondary school is a consequence of the fact that counseling as applied or incorporated in the schools was restricted to vocational counseling.

Psychologists were involved in the schools chiefly because of the need to evaluate students for acceptance into special classes, mainly for the mentally retarded. Some psychologists moved beyond functioning as psychometricians and became clinical counselors, engaging in counseling or psychotherapy with children. But school psychology has not generally adopted this role.

Elementary school counseling was slow to develop because, even with the recognition of the mental health needs of elementary school children, counselors were not seen as being able to contribute to meeting these needs. It has only been recently, in the last decade or two, that school counseling has moved beyond guidance and concern with educational-vocational problems to counseling involving personal-emotional-social problems.

At present there is no general agreement on the role and functions of the counselor in the elementary school. Several models or approaches have been proposed, most of them overlapping. The next few years will no doubt result in the crystallization and acceptance of an approach incorporating aspects of the several existing models.

SUGGESTED READING

Faust, V.: *History of elementary school counseling: overview and critique,* Boston, Houghton-Mifflin, 1968. The only historical survey of the development of elementary school counseling; it is however a highly biased interpretation, whose chief purpose is to propagate the model of the author.

Chapter 2

MODELS FOR ELEMENTARY SCHOOL COUNSELING

THERE HAVE BEEN INNUMERABLE PROPOSALS for defining the role and functions of elementary school counselors. The journals are full of articles, many repetitious, devoted to this topic. While most writers do not restrict the counselor to a single function, they often emphasize or focus upon a major function, with others peripheral. For purposes of discussion this approach will be used here in the description of single-function models as a basis for moving to a more complex or comprehensive model.

COUNSELOR AS DATA HANDLER

One of the earliest concepts of the counselor is of a collector and dispenser of information. In the services orientation to counseling or pupil personnel work, the term which designates this approach is the individual inventory service, or the pupil inventory service. The counselor spends most of his time accumulating and recording information about students, using a variety of methods and techniques. These methods include such things as the autobiography, the questionnaire, sociometric tests, and standardized tests of ability and achievement. Sometimes case studies are made or compiled by the counselor. The approach may be dignified by the term child study.

In addition to collecting and recording information about students, the counselor selects, collects, organizes and maintains information of an occupational and social nature. This information is then dispensed or disseminated to individual students and groups of students.

The emphasis in the preparation of counselors is upon methods and techniques of gathering information, the development and maintenance of records and forms, and the organization of procedures for filing, storing, and retrieving records. Perhaps the major illustration of this approach is represented by the Hatch and Costar text.[1] It appears, however, that there are few if any who accept or support an approach to elementary school counseling in which this activity is the major or central activity of the counselor.

COUNSELOR AS COORDINATOR

A major function of the counselor is seen by some writers as that of coordination. This approach tends to view guidance as a general or decentralized function, or as being mainly a function of teachers. A specialist is not assumed to be necessary. This is particularly the case where a psychologist and a social worker are available. The counselor serves as a coordinator of the services of these and other specialists (visiting teacher, nurse, speech therapist), and as a referral agent to them, and/or to other community resources or services. He may conduct or serve as chairman of group meetings or case conferences on individual children who pose problems.

The concept of the teacher as the major provider of guidance services, or the key to the guidance program, is apparently being abandoned. It never was clear just what the guidance activities of the teacher are, or should be, apart from being a good teacher, being interested in the child as an individual, and recognizing the importance of the child's feelings and emotions in the learning process. There seems to be general acceptance at present of the need for a specialist in pupil personnel work in addition to the psychologist and the social worker.

---

[1] Raymond N. Hatch and James W. Costar, *Guidance services in the elementary school* (Dubuque, William C. Brown, 1961).

THE CHILD DEVELOPMENT SPECIALIST

In 1965 a bill was introduced into Congress (House of Representatives Bill 11322) by Sam Gibbons of Florida entitled the "Elementary and Preschool Child Development Act." As amended in 1966, the bill was intended to develop "a program embodying early identification and prevention" of "the school dropout, disruptive behavior, delinquency, crime, and serious emotional handicap." To do this the bill provided for the training of "highly skilled child development specialists for work through all schools, with children, their families, and community personnel." Training would consist of at least two years of graduate work consisting of courses preparing the student to "assist elementary school personnel with the individual learning or behavior problems of elementary school children, as well as with the educational progress of such children," to "assist school personnel in the recognition of elementary school children who have or who are developing serious emotional, learning, or behavior problems," and to "assist teachers, parents, and school staff to become knowledgeable about community and other resources for the use of such children and families requiring assistance in the solution of such problems of elementary school children." Thirty thousand fellowships were to be provided over a five-year period, which would produce an estimated 21,000 specialists. The institutions providing the training would receive $2,500 per year for each student.

In addition, the States were to be given grants to be used to employ child development specialists to work in the first three grades of elementary schools with responsibility for no more than 350 children each, and to pay institutions of higher education "for conducting training, demonstrations, and short-term workshops for the purpose of familiarizing teachers, principals, and other personnel in the elementary schools . . . and community agencies with the coordination and effective utilization of child development specialists . . . ."

Large numbers of counselor educators supported the bill in written statements or testimony, motivated no doubt by the laudable goals of the legislation, but also perhaps by the money which would become available. It was also supported by the National Institute of Mental Health, the National Education Association, counselors, psychiatrists, special educators, sociologists, teachers, and others. Nevertheless, the bill did not pass the House, even though it was recommended by the Committee on Education and Labor.

There were a number of problems with the legislation. One was that there was no assurance that child development specialists would receive any preparation in counseling. In fact, child development departments in colleges of home economics were prepared to engage in the education of these persons. Thus, the child development specialist might not be prepared to work with children in a counseling relationship. Now this might not be considered a problem if counselors were also available. But it would probably be unlikely that a school or school system would employ counselors *and* child development specialists. Since the salaries of the latter would be subsidized, they would be employed *instead of* counselors. If they were not prepared or qualified to engage in counseling, then children would be deprived of the opportunity for counseling.

Thus, the just beginning profession of elementary school counseling, also stimulated by federal funds for education under NDEA, would die aborning. The American Personnel and Guidance Association, which did not have an opportunity to testify before the Committee on Education and Labor, opposed the bill because of this overlap with NDEA and the developing profession of elementary school counseling. The Association felt there was no need for a new specialist in addition to counselors, psychologists and social workers. Well-prepared counselors should be trained in child development, and able to do anything that a child development specialist could do, and also could engage in counseling as well. APGA felt that direct assistance to children should receive as much emphasis in the elementary school as consultation for teachers and others. It also objected to the restriction of child development specialists to working with only the first three grades.

A further question about the child development specialist

model relates to the preparation and competencies of teachers. The need for a child development specialist is in inverse proportion to the preparation and competence of teachers in child development. It could be argued that, rather than having child development specialists in the schools, we should give teachers better preparation in child development.

Some of those who supported the Gibbons bill apparently felt that its ultimate form could be influenced, perhaps to assure preparation in counseling, and had visions of the child development specialist actually being, and being designated as, a counselor, and also, on the basis of two years of graduate training, assuming many of the functions of the psychologist and social worker.[2]

COUNSELOR AS CONSULTANT

The concept of the counselor as a consultant has received considerable support from writers in the field. The counselor as a child development specialist would function primarily as a consultant to teachers and administrators.

There appear to be two major bases for the model of the counselor as consultant. The first is the contention that, because of the current shortage of elementary school counselors, and the improbability of any immediate large increase in their numbers, the counselor could never meet the needs of individual students for direct services, mainly individual and group counseling. Therefore, to avoid the counselor spending all his time with a few students, and thus neglecting all the others, he should avoid getting involved in the time-consuming counseling relationship, and instead spend his time as a consultant, thereby reaching and helping all students.

The second basis is the argument against counseling as being appropriate for elementary school age children. It is claimed that counseling is inappropriate or infeasible with elementary school children because they are not verbal, or not capable of conceptualizing and verbalizing their problems. Smith and Eckerson, for example, state that "only a limited number of children in ele-

[2]Richard H. Byrne, Personal communication, May 19, 1967.

mentary grades have the maturity for the self-analysis and under-standing needed for counseling on personal problems."[3] They cite no evidence for this statement. It is not supported by either experience or experiment. Any mother or teacher will disagree with the idea that children are not verbal. There are of course wide individual differences in verbal ability among children, as there are among adults. The readiness and willingness of children to verbalize to adults also varies, and is related to the situation. If, as is usually the case, verbalization is discouraged, even pun-ished, in the classroom, and in the halls and corridors of the school, most children will not talk. Our schools reduce the ver-balization of children, particularly of those from minority groups, whose different speech habits—pronunciation, accents, and gram-mar—are criticized or ridiculed. Further, if the conceptual ability of children is so low that they cannot benefit from counseling, then it would follow that they cannot benefit from classroom teaching, since classroom learning is highly conceptual in nature. Children have been counseled in child guidance clinics for fifty years or more. For those children who for some reason are unable or unwilling to verbalize with the counselor, play therapy is available.

The value and quality of consultation which is based solely upon a theoretical or book knowledge of children are question-able. Consultation should be based upon a knowledge of children through association and experience with them. Moreover, the consultant should know the particular child in the case of con-sultation about a specific student. Observation of children or the child in the classroom is insufficient. The most valuable and use-ful experience with children as a basis for consultation is obtained in the actual counseling of children.

One of the difficulties with the consultation model is the prob-lem of when the counselor is going to engage in teacher consul-tation when the teacher in the elementary school is in charge of a self-contained classroom for the entire day. It is unfortunate, but true, that the teacher has little if any time for consultation,

<hr>

[3]H. M. Smith and Louise O. Eckerson, *Guidance for children in elementary schools* (Washington, U. S. Government Printing Office, 1963), p. 14.

and the counselor who is a consultant will find himself sitting alone in his office most of the day.

THE DEVELOPMENTAL COUNSELOR

Child psychology and child development have been discovered, or rediscovered, by a number of writers and counselor educators. As a result we have seen the coining of a new term, developmental counseling.

The developmental counselor is not the same as the child development specialist. He actually engages in counseling. Presumably, however, this is a new kind of counseling. It focuses upon the needs of children as they pass through various "life stages" and face certain "developmental tasks." It is difficult to see how any competent counselor working with children could avoid or fail to deal with these needs, tasks, or developmental problems if they are real and are presented to him by students. Nevertheless, there is a newness about the concept which is appealing and serves as the basis for a lot of writing about developmental counseling.[4] Faust refers to the "new" elementary counselor, as opposed to the traditionalist and the neotraditionalist, as a developmentalist.[5]

This model serves as the basis for drawing distinctions between two contrasting approaches, expressed as dichotomies. Thus the developmental approach is concerned with "normal" children rather than "problem" children, with "all" children rather than specific deviant children. It is preventive rather than remedial, "non-crisis oriented," non-problem centered. It is non-clinical, non-therapy oriented. Children with problems, children in crisis situations, are referred to psychologists, social workers, and psychiatrists. Thus, there is a distinction between the counselor and these other specialists.

These distinctions are artificial rather than real. There is no clear distinction or separation between "normal" or "problem" children, between difficulty in proceeding through a develop-

---

[4]Donald H. Blocher, *Developmental counseling* (New York, Ronald, 1966).
[5]Verne Faust, *History of elementary school counseling* (Boston, Houghton-Mifflin, 1968), pp. 4-10.

mental stage or in handling a developmental task and a crisis situation or problem. Prevention and remediation cannot be easily separated. What is curative or remedial in terms of an existing problem or crisis is preventive for the future. Counseling children with problems in the elementary school may be preventive of problems at the secondary level. While we may be interested in prevention, we cannot ignore those who need help in the present. It is not usually possible to refer all children with problems to psychologists, social workers or psychiatrists. There are not enough of them available to work with all those children who are in need of help. Many of them do not need a psychiatrist, but simply a counselor. Faust seems to suggest that even when these other specialists are not available, the counselor avoids counseling in favor of engaging in other activities. "The community's refusal or inability to employ psychologists or social workers does not justify the new counselor's jeopardizing his own roles or objectives for all children by turning much of his attention to the kind of work which psychologists and social workers have been historically charged to undertake."[6] Such a position borders on the unethical. For a professionally trained counselor to withhold his services from students who need help with serious problems verges on criminal negligence. One cannot ignore those who have problems while we spend all our time on trying to prevent problems. As Arbuckle points out, "We may stress the need to take action so that future accidents will not occur, but we cannot in the meantime ignore the victims of the latest accidents."[7] No matter how much we are concerned about preventing automobile accidents, we do not leave victims lying in the street.

So-called developmental counseling is simply counseling in the context of knowledge and understanding of the psychological and psychosocial development of the student and the society in which he lives. Its apparent newness is perhaps a reflection of the recognition by secondary school counselors that much of what has

---

[6]Verne Faust, *The counselor-consultant in the elementary school* (Boston, Houghton-Mifflin, 1968), p. 37.

[7]Dugald S. Arbuckle, A Semantic Excursion (Letters and Comments), *Personnel and Guidance Journal*, Vol. 41 (1962), pp. 64-66.

been called counseling at the secondary school level has ignored the student as a developing person, and has focused upon the narrow context of the educational system.

THE COUNSELOR AS SOCIAL ENGINEER

The concern with all children, and the recognition that many problems in our society originate not in the individual but in the society or social environment, have led some counselors and psychologists to focus upon the environment rather than upon the individual. Stewart and Warnath focus upon this approach in their book, in which the counselor is presented as a changer of the social environment.[8]

At the elementary school level, the argument has been advanced that children's problems more often originate in the environment, the family or the school, than in the child, and therefore the persons in his environment must be changed rather than the child. Moreover, it is assumed that young children are helpless to change their own environments, so that counseling having this objective is ineffective.

There is, of course, much merit in this point of view. Certainly we do not live in the best of possible worlds, and changes are needed to make it more livable and more conducive to the optimum development of the individual. But, while the counselor, both as a citizen and as a professional, has some responsibility for improving his society, it is not his responsibility alone, nor is it his only or major responsibility. Aspects of this problem have been discussed in recent papers of one of the authors.[9] The counselor in the school certainly has some responsibility for the psychological environment of the school. But while it is true that young children cannot control their environments, they are not helpless, and can initiate changes. Moreover, changes in the environment may not be possible, and the counselor has some

[8]Lawrence H. Stewart and Charles F. Warnath, *The counselor and society: a cultural approach* (Boston, Houghton-Mifflin, 1965).

[9]C. H. Patterson, "The social responsibility of psychologists," *The Counseling Psychologist*, Vol. 1 (1969), (4), pp. 97-100, and "Psychology and social responsibility," *Professional Psychology*, Vol. 3, (1972), pp. 1-10.

responsibility in working with students who are victims of a bad environment.

A recent development in environmental intervention is the activity known as behavior modification. Here the principles of conditioning, particularly operant conditioning, are applied in the classroom, by a psychologist or by the teacher under the instruction and supervision of a psychologist.[10] Counselors have not yet become involved to any great extent in behavior modification as yet. The approach is a useful and effective one for certain situations, however, and will be considered in more detail later in this book.

THE COUNSELOR AS COUNSELOR

One of the models for the elementary school counselor insists that the counselor is a counselor, whose time should be spent in individual and group counseling with children. There is clearly a need for counseling, for someone with whom individual and small groups of children can talk, relate to, or work with in play therapy. Parents, teachers and administrators all seem to recognize this need and to want a counselor who will counsel children.[11] Elementary school children will accept counseling and can benefit from it. Counseling need not be restricted to problem children, crisis problems, or seriously disturbed children. So-called "normal" children, with "developmental" problems, can be helped. Group counseling particularly can be useful in relation to the latter.

---

[10]See, e.g., Robert H. Woody, *Behavioral problem children in the schools* (New York, Appleton-Century-Crofts, 1969); Garth J. Blackman and Adolph Silberman, *Modification of child behavior: principles and procedures* (Belmont, Wadsworth, 1971); J. M. Ackermann, *Operant conditioning techniques for the classroom teacher* (Chicago, Scott, Foresman, 1972).

[11]See, e.g., William P. McDougall and H. M. Reitan, "The elementary counselor as perceived by elementary principals," *Personnel and Guidance Journal*, Vol. 42, (1963), pp. 348-354; James J. Muro and Merritt C. Oelke. "Guidance needs in the elementary school—cue to preparation of counselors," *Personnel and Guidance Journal*, Vol. 7, (1967), pp. 7-12; Buff Oldridge, "Two roles for elementary school guidance personnel," *Counselor Education and Supervision*, Vol. 43, (1964), pp. 367-370; H. M. Smith and Louise O. Eckerson, *Guidance services in elementary schools: a national survey* (Washington, U. S. Government Printing Office, 1966).

It took a long time—several decades—before counseling became recognized and accepted as the major function of the counselor in the secondary school, although even now it is far from actually being the major function in many schools. But this recognition has provided a positive atmosphere for the acceptance of counseling in the elementary school. It would seem to be unfortunate, and a disservice to those children who need the personal relationship of counseling, to abandon counseling for indirect impersonal services to children in the elementary school.

THE COUNSELOR AS A PSYCHOLOGICAL EDUCATOR

A recent development in education is the concern with affective education as well as cognitive education, that is, with the understanding and development of feelings and emotions as well as with thoughts and ideas. The term humanistic education has been used to cover this development, as well as to include education in human relations. Several books directed to teachers have appeared.[12]

Mosher and Sprinthal report on a project in psychological education in the secondary school.[13] Counselors have not yet been involved in psychological education in the schools. But certainly this is an area in which counselors should be involved, at all levels of education. If all children were educated in the emotional realm as well as in the cognitive realm, and in human relations, so that parents and teachers provided a relationship to children which included the conditions for adequate personal development, then few students would need intensive counseling or psychotherapy. There is some evidence, also, that the direct teach-

---

[12]See, e.g., Gerald Weinstein and Mario D. Fantini, *Toward humanistic education: a curriculum of affect* (New York, Praeger, 1970); George I. Brown, *Human teaching for human learning* (New York, Viking, 1971); C. H. Patterson, *Humanistic education* (Englewood Cliffs, Prentice-Hall, 1973).

[13]Ralph L. Mosher and Norman A. Sprinthal, "Psychological education in secondary schools," *American Psychologist*, Vol. 25, (1970), pp. 911-924; Ralph L. Mosher, Normal A. Sprinthal, et al., "Psychological education: a means to promote personal development during adolescence," *The Counseling Psychologist*, Vol. 2(4), (1971), pp. 3-74. See also James J. Pancrazio, "The counselor in psychological education and human relations training." In H. A. Moses (ed.) *Student personnel work in general education.* (Springfield, Illinois, Charles C Thomas, 1974).

ing of the basic principles of facilitative interpersonal relations can be as effective as counseling or psychotherapy for individuals with problems.[14] This is, perhaps, for the long run, the most promising approach to counseling and psychology in the schools.

COMPREHENSIVE MODELS

No one of the models which have been discussed proposes that the elementary school counselor limit himself to one function, that is, the function which is the focus of the model. All accept other functions or duties. There is thus overlap among all the models. No single-function model is seriously proposed for acceptance, to the exclusion of the functions emphasized by the other models. But, although most writers propose a more comprehensive model, they differ in the function which they consider central, and in the order of importance of the other functions which they include. The brief consideration of the pros and cons of the single function models indicates the difficulty of developing a generally acceptable model.

Each one of the functions and duties listed above, as well as dozens of more specific duties, can be defended as necessary or important. Each would find someone to insist that it be included in a model for elementary school counseling on the basis that every elementary school counselor should perform it. In addition, there are numerous other duties or activities performed by some elementary counselor which can be considered useful or desirable. For example, in one conference a participant defended, as a legitimate function of the counselor, her providing an extracurricular course in grooming and personal care for junior high school girls. While this might be desirable and helpful, probably few would insist that it should be an activity of every counselor. But what is an essential function? What criterion, or criteria, should be applied to determine what functions should be included in a comprehensive model of elementary school counseling? And how is the order of importance of these functions to be determined? Too often writers are satisfied to list as many duties and

---

[14]C. H. Patterson, "Education and training as the preferred mode of treatment," *The Counseling Psychologist*, Vol. 3(1), (1971), pp. 77-79.

functions as they can think of, with no attempt to select or restrict or to order them in terms of importance. Such a list does not constitute a model.

A comprehensive model of elementary school counseling must be based upon some philosophical, theoretical, or systematic position regarding the purpose or goal of counseling and psychological services in the elementary school. There seems to have been little thinking or writing of this nature beyond the slogan that "guidance is a good thing." The Preliminary Statement of the Joint ACES-ASCA Committee on the Elementary School Counselor stated: "We believe that guidance for all children is an essential component of the total educational experience in the elementary school."[15] But that is the end of any justification for an elementary school counselor.

In the next chapter, we shall present a rationale and foundation for a model for counseling in the elementary school, and a tentative comprehensive model for the role and functions of counselors and psychologists in the elementary school.

SUMMARY

There have been numerous discussions of the role and functions of elementary counselors. Little agreement appears to be present among those proposing various models. Several different models appear to be emphasized by different writers. While there has been considerable discussion of the counselor versus consultant models, there are other models. Two early models, the counselor as a data handler, and the counselor as a coordinator of services, appear to have few adherents at present. But other models, including those of the counselor as a child development specialist, the developmental counselor, and the counselor as a social engineer are still being advocated. A newly proposed model is that of the counselor as a psychological educator.

Few would accept a single-function model, however. These models are described as a means of presenting the pros and cons of the major functions proposed for elementary school counselors.

---

[15]"Preliminary Statement, Joint ACES-ASCA Committee on the Elementary School Counselor," *Personnel and Guidance Journal*, Vol. 44, (1966), pp. 659-661.

Most would propose a more comprehensive model consisting of the major functions, though emphasizing or focusing on different ones.

There appears to be inadequate consideration of the philosophical or theoretical basis for a comprehensive model. We turn, therefore, to an attempt to provide such a basis.

SUGGESTED READING

Patterson, C. H.: Elementary school counselor or child development consultant? *Personnel and Guidance Journal*, 46: 75-76, 1967.

Patterson, C. H.: The counselor in the elementary school. *Personnel and Guidance Journal*, 48: 979-986, 1969.

Patterson, C. H.: The counselor in the elementary school. Chapter 6 in *An introduction to counseling in the school*. New York, Harper & Row, 1971.

Chapter 3———

THE COUNSELOR:
FACILITATOR OF
PERSONAL DEVELOPMENT

T HE ROLE AND FUNCTIONS of the counselor must be related to
the educational setting, process, and goals. In this chapter
we shall consider, or reconsider, the goal of education, propose
a broader goal than that traditionally, or even currently, accepted,
and suggest the elements of a model for elementary school counseling related to this broader goal.

THE NATURE AND GOALS OF EDUCATION

Traditionally, the goal of education has been to teach the three
R's or, somewhat more broadly, to transmit the culture to the
young. The curriculum, in addition to the tools of reading, writing and arithmetic, has consisted of subject matter, which is made
up of aspects of the culture, organized or "packaged" in courses.
The concern of the school has been pretty much restricted to the
cognitive or intellectual development of its students. Education,
particularly at the advanced level, is not limited, in this approach,
to the acquisition of information or knowledge, but extends to
the development of the ability to think and to reason. The physical, social and emotional development of the student is not a
concern, except incidentally, of education.

This point of view in education has been labeled the essentialist position, referring to its concern with what it considered as
the essential, rather than the peripheral, aspects of education.

The student personnel point of view corresponding to this concept of education is the services approach. Student personnel work consists of a constellation of services to students to supplement the curriculum. In the words of one writer, it serves the function of "delivering the student to the classroom in the optimum condition for profiting from instruction."[1]

Education has been moving away from the traditional or essentialist position. The so-called "life-adjustment" approach developed in the 1940's as a move away from the narrow essentialist goal of intellectual development. In part, this was a recognition that learning is not a purely intellectual process, that what and how well a child learns is related to his physical and emotional state. But it also represented a broader view of education. Education should be for living, and living is more than thinking. Perhaps the major goal added by the life adjustment approach was that of preparation for work, or a vocation in life. It still did not concern itself directly with education in the areas of social and emotional development. These were still essentially the concerns of the family and the church.

Progress toward the concern of education with the personal-social-emotional development of the student was perhaps delayed by the criticisms of education following the launching of the first space vehicle by Russia in 1957. Demands were made for a more rigorous, scientifically oriented curriculum. "Soft" subjects and educational "frills" were attacked. The reform of the schools which was envisioned by the critics was toward a stronger subject matter orientation. The new curriculums in math and the physical sciences were an outcome of this renewed subject matter focus. The emphasis upon more efficient techniques of instruction supported the development of teaching machines and computer assisted instruction.[2]

Recently education has been subjected to an entirely different

---

[1] F. F. Bradshaw, "The scope and aim of a personnel program," *Educational Research*, Vol. 17 (1936), p. 121.

[2] For a critique of this movement, and a further development of the following discussion, see C. H. Patterson, *Humanistic education* (Englewood Cliffs, Prentice-Hall, 1973).

barrage of criticism.[3] The focus of criticism changed from subject matter and the content of the curriculum to the atmosphere of the classroom and of the school. This atmosphere, it was charged, retards rather than facilitates learning. The classroom climate is one of repression, control—in Silberman's words, a grim, joyless place. Rather than developing the potentials of children, schools often stifle their potentials. In short, schools hurt children, rather than helping them—they are not fit places for human beings.

These criticisms provide the stimulus, indeed the demand, that we reexamine the purposes and goals of education, a task that education has not engaged in since John Dewey. The introduction of technology has led to talk about a revolution in education. But technology is used in the service of the traditional goal of mastery of subject matter. A real revolution would involve a change in the basic goal of education.

Such a revolution might be termed a humanistic revolution, since it is concerned with the humanization of education. It is concerned with developing human, or humane, beings, whole persons; not simply persons who can think, but persons who can feel deeply, can love, can live with others—in short, who can utilize all their potentials as fully functioning persons. In other words, the purpose of education is to develop self-actualizing persons.

The goal of self-actualization is not an external goal, arbitrarily selected by others and imposed on students. It is not inconsistent with the nature and needs of the individual. It represents the common, basic need of all living beings; it is inherent in the organism. The striving for the development of the self is the basic human motivation. "An organism is governed by a tendency to actualize, as much as possible, its individual capacities, its 'nature in the world.'"[4] Combs and Snygg refer to the maintenance and

---

[3]See, for example, James Herndon, *The way it spozed to be* (New York, Simon & Schuster, 1965); John Holt, *How children fail* (New York, Pitman, 1964); Herbert Kohl, *36 children* (New York, American Library, 1967); Jonathan Kozol, *Death at an early age* (Boston, Houghton-Mifflin, 1967); George Leonard, *Education and ecstasy* (New York, Delacorte, 1968); and Charles E. Silberman, *Crisis in the classroom* (New York, Random House, 1970).

[4]Kurt Goldstein, *The organism* (New York, Harcourt, Brace & Jovanovich, 1939).

enhancement of the self as "the all inclusive human need which motivates all behavior at all times and in all places."[5]

Education is not alone in adopting this goal, or at odds with other institutions in our society. The production of self-actualizing persons is—or should be—the goal of our society and all of its institutions, the family, the church, political institutions and the social and economic system. Counseling and student personnel services have long been concerned with the personal development of students. As long as this concern was not the center of the educational process, student personnel work was peripheral and ancillary. But when the basic goal of education is the development of self-actualizing persons, counseling and student personnel work become central. They are no longer services appended to the educational process; they are an inherent part of education.

Counselors and personnel workers have long insisted that they are concerned with the needs of students. But it has never been too clear just what this meant, or just what needs were included. Now it is possible to define these needs in terms of the characteristics of the self-actualizing person.

THE SELF-ACTUALIZING PERSON

Combs and Snygg describe the *adequate* self or personality which characterizes the self-actualizing person. Such a person perceives himself in positive ways; that is, he accepts himself, and has a positive self-concept. The adequate person also accepts others: "we are so entirely dependent upon the good will and cooperation of others in our society that it would be impossible to achieve feelings of adequacy without some effective relationship with them. The adequate personality must be capable of living effectively and efficiently with his fellows."[6] The adequate person is open to his experiences, and is able to accept into awareness all his perceptions, without distortion, or rejection. Behaviorally, he manifests more efficient behavior, since he is not

---

[5]Arthur W. Combs & Donald Snygg, *Individual behavior*, 2nd Ed. (New York, Harper & Row, 1959), p. 38.
[6]*Ibid.*, p. 246.

handicapped by defensiveness. Being secure, he can take chances, and is spontaneous and creative. He is independent, finding that his own feelings, beliefs and attitudes are adequate guides to his behavior. Finally, according to Combs and Snygg, the adequate person is compassionate; being less defensive, he can relate closely with others without hostility and fear.

Carl Rogers accepts the existence of "one basic tendency and striving—to actualize, maintain, and enhance the organism,"[7] which is manifested by growth and maturation, differentiation, independence, and self-responsibility. The end product of this process of striving is the fully functioning person, who has three main characteristics: (1) He is open to his experience, to all stimuli, external and internal, and does not have to be defensive or distort his experience. (2) He lives existentially. He is constantly in process, flexible and adaptable. (3) His behavior is determined from within. The locus of control is internal. Since he is open to his experience, all relevant behavior is available to influence his behavior. Some relevant data may be missing so that behavior would not always be perfect, but the presence of constant feedback would lead to correction. He would be realistically socialized. "We do not need to ask who will control his aggressive impulses, for when he is open to all of his impulses, his need to be liked by others and his tendency to give affection are as strong as his impulses to strike out or to seize for himself. He will be aggressive in situations in which aggression is realistically appropriate, but there will be no runaway need for aggression.[8] The fully functioning person is a creative and self-actualizing person.

Abraham Maslow has provided perhaps the most detailed description of the self-actualizing person as a result of his research. He obtained a criterion group of persons (living and dead), selected on the basis of professional judgment as self-actualizing persons. His general definition of a self-actualizing person was one who showed "the full use and exploitation of talents, capacities, potentialities, etc. Such people seem to be fulfilling them-

---

[7]Carl R. Rogers, *Client-centered therapy* (Boston, Houghton-Mifflin, 1951), p. 487.
[8]Carl R. Rogers, *Freedom to learn* (Columbus, Merrill, 1969), p. 291.

selves and to be doing the best that they are capable of doing. They are people who have developed or are developing the full stature of which they are capable."[9]

In an intensive study of these persons, Maslow found that they could be differentiated from ordinary or "average" people on the basis of fourteen characteristics.

(1) More efficient perception of reality and more comfortable relations with it. This includes the detection of the phony and dishonest person, and the accurate perception of what exists rather than the distortion of perception by one's needs. *Self-actualizing people are more aware of their environment,* both human and non-human. They are not afraid of the unknown, and can tolerate the doubt, uncertainty and tentativeness accompanying the perception of the new and unfamiliar.

(2) Acceptance of self, others and nature. Self-actualizing persons are not ashamed or guilty about their human nature, with its shortcomings, imperfections, frailties and weaknesses. Nor are they critical of these characteristics in others. *They respect and esteem themselves and others.* Moreover, *they are open, genuine, without pose or facade.* They are not, however, self-satisfied, but are concerned about discrepancies between what is and what might be or should be, in themselves, others, and society.

(3) Spontaneity. Self-actualizing persons are not hampered by convention, but they do not flout it. *They are not conformists,* but neither are they anti-conformist for the sake of being so. They are not externally motivated, or even goal directed—rather their motivation is the internal one of growth and development, the actualization of their selves and potentialities.

(4) Problem-centering. Self-actualizing persons are not ego-centered, but focus on problems outside themselves. They are *mission oriented,* often on the basis of a *sense of responsibility,* duty, or obligation rather than of personal choice.

(5) The quality of detachment; the need for privacy. *The self-*

---

[9]Abraham H. Maslow, "Self-actualizing people: a study of psychological growth," in Clark E. Moustakas (ed.) *The self: explorations in personal growth* (New York, Harper & Row, 1956), pp. 161-162.

actualizing person enjoys solitude and privacy. It is possible for him to remain unruffled and undisturbed by much which upsets others. He may even appear to others to be asocial.

(6) Autonomy, independence of culture and environment. Self-actualizing persons, though dependent on others for the satisfaction of the basic needs of love, safety, respect, and belongingness, "are not dependent for their main satisfactions on the real world, or other people or culture or means-to-ends, or in general, on extrinsic satisfactions. *Rather they are dependent for their own development and continued growth upon their own potentialities and latent resources.*"[10]

(7) Continued freshness of appreciation. *Self-actualizing persons repeatedly* (though not continuously) *experience awe, pleasure, and wonder in their everyday world.*

(8) The "mystic experience," the "oceanic feeling." In varying degrees and with varying frequencies, *self-actualizing persons have experiences of ecstasy, awe, and wonder,* with feelings of limitless horizons opening up, followed by the conviction that the experience was important and valuable and had a carry-over into daily life.

(9) Gemeinschaftsgefühl. *Self-actualizing persons have a deep feeling of empathy, sympathy or compassion for human beings in general.* This feeling is in a sense unconditional, in that it exists along with the recognition of the existence of negative qualities in others which provoke occasional anger, impatience and disgust.

(10) Interpersonal relations. *Self-actualizing people have deep interpersonal relations with others.* They are selective, however, and the circle of friends is small, usually consisting mainly of other self-actualizing persons. They attract others to them as admirers or disciples.

(11) The democratic character structure. *The self-actualizing person does not discriminate* on the basis of class, education, race, or color. He is humble in his recognition of what he knows in comparison with what could be known, and is ready to learn from

---

[10]*Ibid.,* p. 176.

anyone. *He respects everyone* as potential contributors to his knowledge, but also just because they are human beings.

(12) Means and ends. Self-actualizing persons are highly ethical. *They clearly distinguish between means and ends, and subordinate means to ends.*

(13) *Philosophical, unhostile sense of humor.* Although all the self-actualizing subjects studied by Maslow had a sense of humor, it was not of the ordinary type. Their sense of humor was the spontaneous, thoughtful type, intrinsic to the situation. Their humor did not involve hostility, superiority, or sarcasm.

(14) Creativeness. All Maslow's subjects were judged to be creative, each in his own way. The creativity involved here is not the special-talent creativeness. It is a creativeness potentially inherent in everyone, but usually suffocated by acculturation. *It is a fresh, naive, direct way of looking at things.*

MEDIATE GOALS AND SUBGOALS

The acceptance of self-actualization as the goal of education does not rule out concern for many of the things with which the school is now concerned. Self-actualization is the ultimate goal. Other goals, which contribute toward this ultimate goal, may be termed mediate goals. One of the values of an ultimate goal is that it provides a criterion by which mediate goals, or subgoals, may be evaluated.

It can be argued that a person cannot function at his highest level in our society if he is illiterate and unable to handle simple mathematics. Certain basic skills are necessary to function at almost any level in our society. Thus, the teaching of these skills is a part of the process of developing self-actualizing persons. This is the justification for their inclusion in education, not because they are in some way good in themselves, or for society. This justification also focuses attention upon the manner in which basic skills and knowledge are taught. Methods of instruction should not, as is often the case, be inconsistent with the development of a self-actualizing person.

The acceptance of a hierarchy or of levels of goals has another value. It provides for the recognition of the single, basic common goal of all men, but it also allows for the recognition of individual differences among men in the way in which they achieve this goal. Subgoals may, to some extent at least, vary among men. Some may be able to achieve self-actualization without a high school diploma, a college degree, or advanced specialized training, but others may not. Maslow points out that, since self-actualization is the actualization of a self, and since no two selves are identical, individuals may actualize themselves in different ways.[11] The self-actualizing individual is driven to utilize his talents, he achieves satisfaction from developing his potentials and from exercising his talents which vary widely from individual to individual.

THE CONDITIONS FOR SELF-ACTUALIZATION

If we accept the goal of self-actualization for education, then we must consider how this goal is to be achieved. While it is, as indicated above, desirable or necessary that individuals have certain academic skills and certain subject matter information and knowledge, these are not sufficient for self-actualization. The individual must be helped to develop as a person, a person who has the characteristics of the self-actualizing person described above, one who accepts and respects himself and others, who understands himself and others, who is open, honest and genuine, and who thus is able to develop good interpersonal relationships with others. In short, these involve the principles of good human or interpersonal relationships.

While it is possible, and desirable, to teach these principles, it is necessary that the teaching be done in an atmosphere characterized by certain conditions. These conditions are the existence of the principles of good human relations themselves in the person who teaches, who becomes a model as well as an instructor.

Experience and research in counseling or psychotherapy have identified and defined a number of principles or conditions of good human relationships. Three in particular are basic.

----

[11]Abraham H. Maslow, *Toward a psychology of being* (New York, Van Nostrand & Reinhold, 1962), p. 196.

Empathic Understanding. Empathic understanding is an understanding from an internal frame of reference; it is understanding of another achieved by putting oneself in the place of the other, so that one sees him and the world, as closely as possible, as he does. Rogers' definition perhaps expresses it as well as any: "an accurate, empathic understanding of the [other's] world as seen from the inside. To sense the [other's] private world as if it were your own, but without losing the 'as if' quality—this is empathy . . . "[12] There seem to be no synonyms for empathic understanding. Unlike other languages, English does not have two words to designate the two kinds of understanding or knowing: knowing *about,* and the knowing which is empathy. Some American Indian languages apparently had this concept, indicated by the phrase "walk in his moccasins." The theme of the novel *To Kill a Mockingbird* is dependent on the concept of empathy. At one point the lawyer Atticus Finch, trying to help his children understand people's behavior, said: "if . . . you can learn a simple trick . . . you'll get along a lot better with all kinds of folks. You never really understand a person until you consider things from his point of view—until you climb into his skin and walk around in it."[13] However, this is not a trick, nor is it simple.

Respect or Nonpossessive Warmth. The second condition is a deep respect for another, an acceptance of him as a person of worth, as he is, without judgment or condemnation, criticism, ridicule, or depreciation. It is a respect which includes a warmth and liking for another as a person, with all his faults, deficiencies, or undesirable or unacceptable behavior. It is a deep interest and concern for him and his development. It is the warmth of a parent who may still reject, or not accept, particular behaviors of the child. Thus one may accept and respect a person as a person, but still not agree with or condone all of his behaviors.

Genuineness. Genuineness is the congruence or integration of the therapist in the relationship: "it means that within the relationship he is freely and deeply himself, with his actual experi-

---

[12]Carl R. Rogers, *On becoming a person* (Boston, Houghton-Mifflin, 1961), p. 284.

[13]Harper Lee, *To kill a mockingbird* (New York, Popular Library, 1962), p. 24.

ence accurately represented by his awareness of himself."[14] The therapist is not thinking or feeling one thing and saying another. He is open, honest, sincere. He is freely and deeply himself, without a facade, and not playing a role. He is, as the existentialists term it, authentic, or, to use Jourard's term, transparent.[15]

These conditions—and perhaps some others not yet clearly identified—are necessary for the development of the individual as a person. The individual is free to grow, to change; he is not restricted or immobilized by threat. Instead of using his energies for defense, he can use them for growth. He becomes aware of inconsistencies between his experiences and his self-concept, between his self as it is and the self he would like to be and can be. He discovers his potentialities. He becomes a self-actualizing person.

Not only do these conditions lead to personal development—they also lead to the learning of specific behaviors and subject matter. They are necessary conditions for meaningful, personal, real and persisting learning. Indeed, there is evidence that a student having difficulty in reading may, under these conditions—either in a therapy or in a natural situation,[16] learn to read without any special or remedial instruction in reading. Outcomes such as this include the mediate goals or subgoals referred to above. It appears that when we provide these conditions, the recipient—or the student—in developing his potentials for self-actualization, will determine or recognize relevant subgoals and work toward achieving them, or seeking and obtaining specific help in doing so.

THE HUMANIZATION OF EDUCATION

The absence of the conditions described above is dehumanizing. A child deprived of these conditions will not become a human being, a person. Such deprivation is more damaging psycho-

---

[14]Carl R. Rogers, "The necessary and sufficient conditions of therapeutic personality change," *Journal of Consulting Psychology*, Vol. 21, (1957), pp. 95-103.

[15]Sidney Jourard, *The transparent self* (New York, Van Nostrand & Reinhold, 1964).

[16]George Dennison, *The lives of children* (New York, Vintage Books, 1969).

logically than deprivation of material things. The lack of, or an inadequate supply of, these conditions leads to problems in learning, behavior problems, juvenile delinquency and crime, and emotional disturbances.

The presence of these conditions facilitates learning and the development of self-actualizing persons. It is the lack of them which has led to the recent criticism of schools as dehumanizing.

Society is becoming more concerned about the treatment of its members. The right to treatment of those who are emotionally disturbed or mentally retarded is being recognized in the courts. In Alabama, for example, a Federal District Court considered a case brought against Alabama officials in a class action suit in 1970. The suit charged that by failing to provide adequate staff and facilities, state mental hospitals and schools for the retarded were antitherapeutic and harmful. The judge (in 1972) ordered changes which were suggested by the amici curiae (friends of the court) in the case, which included the American Psychological Association, the American Orthopsychiatric Association, the American Association on Mental Deficiency, and the American Civil Liberties Union.

It is not too much to envision a time in the future when such action might be taken in the case of a school or school system that was determined to be harmful to children.

THE COUNSELOR AS A FACILITATOR OF PERSONAL DEVELOPMENT

With the acceptance of self-actualization as the goal of education, teachers and counselors are working toward the same goal, and, as indicated above, student personnel work becomes an integral part of education rather than a peripheral service. The basis for a model of counseling and psychology in elementary schools with an integrating focus has been created. Teachers, counselors and student personnel workers are concerned with the personal development of students. The teacher functions in the classroom setting, while counselors and student personnel workers function in the broader school setting. The latter are, however, concerned with personal development in the classroom, and cooperate with teachers in this effort.

If we are concerned with the personal development of students, we should approach the development of a model for counseling and psychology in terms of the needs of students. What do students need, that is not provided, or not adequately provided, in the classroom? Then we can consider how these needs can be met.

The basic single and common need of all children, as has already been emphasized, is the need for development, enhancement or actualization of the self. This main need can be analyzed into its parts, or subneeds.

1. *Children need to learn.* The motivation to learn is not something that has to be created; it exists. The child is a natural learner. Anyone who observes an infant or young child will become aware that he is constantly active, engaged in exploring himself and his environment. The normal child is curious and interested in his environment. He needs no encouragement to explore it. There is no problem of motivation. As Skinner notes, "no one asks how to motivate a baby. A baby naturally explores everything it can get at, unless restraining forces have been at work, and this tendency doesn't die out."[17]

Learning is the normal state of the organism. We do not need to teach in the sense of imposing something on the child or putting something into him. In an appropriate environment children learn by themselves. Young children learn most of what they do learn by themselves, without instruction. What we call play is the principal means of learning before school age. Moreover the most significant learning of many older children occurs in play outside of the school.

Why is it, then, that there is such a problem regarding learning in school, and so much concern with motivation to learn? In the first few years of school the curiosity, interest, enthusiasm and persistence in learning of many children are destroyed. They become passive, silent, bored, resistent. Leonard reports his observation of children in kindergarten and those in fourth grade classes, comparing the spontaneity, naturalness, and responsiveness of the kindergarten children with the controlled, quiet, in-

---

[17]B. F. Skinner, *Walden two* (New York, Macmillan, 1948), p. 101.

hibited behavior of the fourth graders.[18] Something happens to kill the natural learning of children. This something must be related to what goes on in the classroom. The school environment, rather than facilitating learning, retards or destroys it.

It is the function of the teacher to provide the conditions which facilitate learning. But if this is not being done, counselors and student personnel workers should be concerned. As experts in learning and development, and the conditions for such development, they should be able to provide help and assistance to teachers in the teaching-learning process. *A function of counselors, then, is to serve as a resource to the classroom teacher to assist her in making the classroom a learning environment.*

2. *Children need self-esteem.* The self-actualizing person is characterized by acceptance of himself. He feels he is somebody, a person of worth. He can respect himself. There is no great discrepancy between the self concept and the ideal self.

Self-esteem is dependent, to a great extent, at least, on being accepted, esteemed and respected by others. One cannot accept or respect himself if he feels he is considered worthless by others. The child must have the experience of being accepted as a person of worth because of *who* he is, not *what* he is. Such acceptance is unconditional—it does not depend on what he does or does not do.

Where acceptance, respect, liking or approval depend entirely, or almost entirely, on academic achievement, they are conditional. This is too often the situation in the classroom and the school. Much of the misbehavior of children is a testing of the teacher's liking and respect for them. They are asking, "Does he really like *me*, regardless of what I do or how I perform?"

Failure in academic activities together with fear of further failure is being recognized as destructive to self-esteem. If failure and the fear of failure are so harmful, then shouldn't we create a situation where no child experiences failure? This question represents a confusion between failure and how failure is regarded. Actually, failure could not be completely eliminated or avoided

---

[18]George B. Leonard, *Education and ecstasy* (New York, Delacorte, 1968), pp. 110-111.

if we tried to do so. And life outside of the school is not failure free. It is not the fact of failure but its meaning which is the problem. Failure in school is threatening because it means not simply that the child has made a mistake, or has failed a particular problem or task, but because it means that *he as a person is a failure*—total and complete. The infant and preschool child often fails, completely and miserably. But his failures do not prevent him from learning, because failure is not accompanied by derision, punishment, disgrace, shame or loss of love and respect. We expect him to fail. We learn, as is often said, by our mistakes, but only if we are permitted to learn by not being made to feel that we are no good, hopeless, *a* failure.

The counselor or psychologist is concerned about the development of self-esteem in children. *As a consultant to teachers, the counselor attempts to make the classroom a place where the child's self-esteem is developed, fostered and maintained.* In addition, where self-esteem is lacking or low, the counselor has a responsibility. The loss of self-esteem is a central factor in emotional disturbance. *Thus, in individual and group counseling the counselor attempts to restore self-esteem in those children in whom it is low and inhibiting their development as self-actualizing persons.*

3. *Children need to discover their potentials and talents.* If a person is going to actualize his potentials, he needs to have some awareness of what they are. Often a person's potentials come to light in situations where he is free to do what he wants to do. Interests are often guides to potentials.

A major problem here is that the school, traditionally, is relatively uninterested in potentials other than intellectual or cognitive potentials. Education conceived as the development of the intellect is still strong in the school, and concern with other potentials is peripheral—they are relegated, for the most part, to the "extracurricular" realm. This emphasis is apparent in the use of the term "underachievement." Underachievement never refers to anything other than academic underachievement.

As a result, the child often has little opportunity to discover or recognize potentials which he may have in other areas than the intellectual—and, perhaps, at the secondary school level, athletic potentials. Human relations potentials are particularly neglected. To be sure, "leadership" is often stressed. But this is a super-ordinate-subordinate, hierarchical relationship, rather than the interpersonal relationships of equals.

The emphasis upon competition inhibits the development of cooperative human relationships. Students are pitted against each other. To cooperate can be regarded as cheating. One student's success is another student's failure. An eighth grade girl expressed it well in a counseling interview:

> *Student:* Oh, and teachers when they start grading on the curve, ... when we have a teacher that doesn't grade on the curve, or a test that isn't being graded on the curve, if a friend makes an A I'm glad for her. "Congratulations, you made an A." If I made an A too, I can go down and congratulate her even more heartily— "You made an A—good." But if it's graded on the curve and she makes an A, I say, I think that that's bad because she made a high A and my grade might be lower because hers, because she did better on the test, you know. On that grading on a curve, you don't respect the kids who make the high grades; you're just mad at them, uh, I don't know.
>
> *Counselor:* I see. That kind of system—you can't help feeling that they're your enemy and yet it isn't their fault.[19]

The counselor who accepts self-actualization as the goal of education has a responsibility for helping children discover their potentials. *He does this by trying to move the school from its narrow preoccupation with intellectual potentials. In addition, he can work with individual students, sometimes with the use of tests, to help them discover unknown and unused potentials.*

4. Children need to overcome obstacles or blocks to the development and use of their potentials. There are many obstacles to personal development. They may exist or operate at different levels of goals as these levels were defined earlier. For example, inability to read or write constitutes an obstacle to utilizing one's intellectual or cognitive potentials. At another level, particularly applicable in the elementary school, there may be obstacles to a

---

[19]Julius Seaman, *The case of Nan*, (Record) Nashville, Tennessee: Counselor Recordings, 1963.

child's learning to read or write when he has the capabilities for doing so.

Important at this level are the obstacles which are designated as learning disabilities. These disabilities are many and varied, and constitute an area which is receiving the attention of specialists in psychology. Learning disabilities may be of neurological origin, of psychological origin, or of social origin. In any event, the counselor and other personnel specialists should be involved in identification, evaluation and treatment.

General physical condition and health problems can interfere with optimum development of the child. The school nurse becomes involved here. Speech impediments or problems also are obstacles to personal development, and are the concern of the speech therapist. Reading problems may be the concern of a remedial reading teacher or specialist.

Social or emotional problems can become serious handicaps to personal development. Depending upon their nature and severity, and the resources available, they may be dealt with by the counselor, the social worker or the psychologist.

Counselors and personnel workers therefore are involved in working with children who manifest a variety of conditions which interfere with their personal development.

5. *Children need to experience good interpersonal relationships.* Many of the problems or emotional disturbances in children are the result of the lack of, or inadequate, facilitative interpersonal relationships. A number of conditions have been identified as necessary for a good human relationship. Three of the basic, or core, conditions, discussed above, are empathy or empathic understanding, respect and warmth, and genuineness or honesty. These conditions are necessary for good interpersonal relationships in all areas of life, including the school and the family. Good interpersonal relationships are related to self-actualization as both cause and effect. They are necessary conditions for self-actualization, and they are characteristics of self-actualizing persons, resulting from the experiencing of these conditions.

If the goal of education is the developing of self-actualizing persons, and if these conditions are necessary for self-actualization, then the school, including its counselors and student personnel workers, must be concerned about the existence of these conditions in the environment of children.

The counselor assists children who have or are lacking or whose environment is deficient in these conditions in individual and group counseling. These conditions are the basis for any counseling or psychotherapy relationship. *The counselor consults with teachers and the administration to develop these conditions in the school* and the classroom. Since the family members have tremendous influence upon the child in the realm of interpersonal relationships, *counselors and personnel workers must work with parents, both individually and in groups, to help them provide an environment which consists of or includes the necessary core conditions.* In addition to these more customary ways of facilitating personal development, *the counselor should become involved, as a psychological educator, in the teaching of these conditions in the classroom,* probably more by in-service preparation of teachers than by direct instruction. As education comes to accept the developing of self-actualization as its goal, teacher education programs will prepare teachers both for offering the core conditions in the classroom and for teaching them, both didactically, and experientially by small group experiences.

THE ELEMENTS OF A MODEL

It is apparent that, adopting the developing of self-actualizing persons as the ultimate goal of education, and considering the needs of children in relation to this goal, we have arrived at a number of major functions of the counselor and other student personnel workers which are identical to those proposed by various others who have considered elementary school counseling. But we are no better off than before in terms of ordering these functions on the basis of priority or importance. All of them are necessary if we are to meet the needs of children. All are important, and it is not possible to determine any fixed order of importance.

Although perhaps not immediately apparent from the overview presented here, a consideration of the number and variety of functions with their related duties leads to the conclusion that no one person could perform all these functions adequately, even if the student-counselor ratio were reduced considerably, even to 100 to 1. It would appear to be unrealistic to expect one person to master all the areas of knowledge and skill, even if the period of preparation were doubled from the recommended two years of graduate work for counselors.

The problem is thus one of breaking up the duties among several professionals. The traditional division, with psychologists doing testing, the social worker working with the family and community and the counselor doing most of the other things is increasingly being questioned. Faust appears to accept this division because the traditional function of the psychologist avoids conflict and overlap with the counselor.[20] But this leaves uncovered the area of learning disabilities, in which neither the traditional psychologist nor counselor is prepared to function.

The Bureau of Educational Personnel of the U. S. Office of Education, in the Pupil Personnel Services Program under the Education Professions Development Act, proposes a new pupil personnel specialist, "a new (not merely an additional) professional, more versatile than his colleagues and predecessors, one who is able to relate as effectively to the individual student as to groups of either students or teachers, and who can, at the same time, see the school system as a whole while being concerned with the growth of the individual. In short, the goal of the program is to train professionals who will train others to deal with individuals as well as its administrators, teachers and students."[21] It is not clear just what the limitations of such a specialist would be. Narrowly defined roles of psychologists, social workers, nurses and counseling and guidance personnel, are rejected as artificial, yet their functions are not defined or related to those of the pupil personnel specialist. The pupil personnel specialist will work, or consult, mainly with teachers, who in turn

[20]Verne Faust, *The counselor-consultant in the elementary school* (Boston, Houghton-Mifflin, 1968), pp. 168-171.

[21]C. Patrick McGreevy, "A new design of pupil personnel service programs utilized by the U. S. Office of Education," *The Counseling Psychologist*, Vol. 2 (1971), (3), pp. 88-91.

will work with individual students. Thus apparently there would be little, if any, individual or group counseling. The functions of the proposed new specialist are too vaguely and unclearly defined to constitute a model, and there is no consideration of who would meet the needs of students not covered by this specialist.

It appears to be too early to set up a specific model at this time. The emphasis should be upon attempting to provide someone to meet the needs of students which have been considered above. The counselor should certainly be prepared to provide individual and group counseling, and consultation with teachers and administrators regarding both individual students and the psychological climate of the school and classroom. The psychologist should be qualified in evaluating handicaps and learning disabilities of children. Either the counselor or the psychologist might work with children with specific learning disabilities, often in conjunction with a remedial or special teacher or speech therapist. Counselors and psychologists might share in the psychological education of teachers, students and parents. Social workers might be involved with the latter.

Our purpose in the remainder of this book is not to be concerned so much with who does what, as with considering what should be provided in the elementary school to meet the needs of students in their development as self-actualizing persons.

SUMMARY

In this chapter we have proposed a new goal for education: the development of self-actualizing persons. When this is the function of education, then counselors and student personnel workers, who have traditionally, at least in theory, been concerned with this goal, become central rather than peripheral in the educational process.

The 1938 publication of the Educational Policies Commission stated four objectives for education. The first two were education for self-realization, and education for human relationships.[22] The goal of self-actualization for education is therefore not a new one.

---

[22]Educational Policies Commission, *The purposes of education in American democracy* (Washington, National Education Association, 1938), p. 12.

It has been recognized for a long time. But it has never been implemented, probably because to do so would require revolutionary changes in the school and the teaching-education process. We can no longer delay or put off these changes.

The major needs of students in becoming self-actualizing persons were presented, together with the ways these needs are met by counselors and personnel workers. It appears that the functions involved in meeting these needs are too numerous or varied to expect a single person to be adequately prepared and able to perform them all, even with responsibility for a relatively small number of students. Thus there appears to be a need for a number of specialists. The division of these functions among the traditional specialists, that is, counselors, school psychologists and social workers, is being challenged. Yet, with modifications to include the functions of dealing with learning disabilites and psychological education, this system would appear to be viable.

In any event, rather than consider functions in terms of who is to perform them, we shall deal with them as functions which are necessary to meet the needs of students in becoming self-actualizing persons.

These major functions of counselors and student personnel specialists may be divided into two groups. In the first, the counselor works directly with the child. This group includes individual counseling and play therapy, group counseling, speech therapy, tutoring. In the second, the counselor works indirectly to assist the child, or children. Included are consultation and counseling with teachers and administrators, consultation and counseling with parents, classroom management or behavior modification in the classroom, and inservice education of teachers in psychological education. This grouping will be used to order the discussion of major functions and activities of counselors and student personnel workers.

SUGGESTED READINGS

Patterson, C. H.: *Humanistic education.* Englewood Cliffs, Prentice-Hall, 1973.

Silberman, Charles E.: *Crisis in the classroom.* New York, Random House, 1970.

Chapter 4

THE CLASSROOM TEACHER AS A FACILITATOR

FOR MANY YEARS WRITERS in the field of elementary school guidance have reiterated that the classroom teacher is the key person in the guidance program. Without doubt the teacher is an important figure in the life of the child. But in the best school or system, there is no one key person. All staff members, teachers, administrators and pupil personnel workers, are key persons. The important factor is that they are working together toward the same goals, and not at cross-purposes.

In an earlier text, one of the authors has emphasized that the most important contribution of the teacher to the guidance or student personnel program is to be a good teacher.[1] The teacher, while not a therapist, should provide a therapeutic classroom atmosphere.

The referral function of the teacher is also important. The teacher must be able to recognize those children who are disturbed or are having more than the usual or expected difficulty in learning in the classroom, and assist them in getting any necessary help from the pupil personnel specialists who are available.

In the conceptual model developed in this book, in which the goal of education is the development of self-actualizing persons, all staff members in the school focus upon and contribute to this

---

[1]C. H. Patterson, *An introduction to counseling in the school* (New York, Harper and Row, 1971), Chapter 4.

goal. While the primary function of the classroom teacher is to facilitate personal development in children through helping them in the area of subject matter achievement, children learn more than subject matter from their teachers. Whether they intend it or not, or are aware of it or not, teachers are teaching children attitudes, values and the nature of social and interpersonal relationships. It is the contention of those who are concerned with humanistic education, or affective education, that these things should be taught consciously as subject matter. In a later chapter we will consider this area of psychological education. Here, however, we are concerned with the influence of teacher attitudes and the teacher as a person on the academic learning in the classroom.[2]

THE NEED FOR LIMITS OR STRUCTURE

In a later chapter we consider the dynamics of the classroom as a group and their implications for what is commonly called "classroom management." The utilization of the principles of behavior modification in the influencing of pupil behavior is also dealt with.

Behavior modification is often regarded as a restrictive, controlling approach—and it can be that. But it need not be. Essentially, the application of contingencies, or rewards, for appropriate behavior, systematically, that is, on a consistent and persistent basis, provides a stable, consistent and dependable or trustworthy classroom environment.

The humanistic approach to education, as in the "open classroom" or the "free school," is often conceived of as a completely permissive situation, with no restrictions or limits, where "anything goes." This is a misconception, similar to the misconception of Dewey's approach of progressive education as completely permissive, or of client-centered therapy as completely permissive, or of Neill's Summerhill as completely permissive.

In all social situations there are, and must be, limits on behavior. In the classroom there must be limits. The problem of limits

---

[2]A more extensive treatment will be found in C. H. Patterson, *Humanistic education* (Englewood Cliffs, Prentice-Hall, 1973).

is essentially the problem of discipline, and is one of the most difficult problems a teacher faces. If limits are too restrictive and unreasonable, they generate tension and interfere with learning.

Limits are necessary in a negative sense, to protect individuals from unfair impositions of, and interference by, others. From a more positive view they provide structure for the development of relationships. In the absence of limits, or where the limits are unclear, undefined or vague, students seek to determine what the limits are. Such behavior is know as "testing the limits," and constitutes most of the disciplinary problems in the classroom.

The teacher must determine reasonable limits and then enforce them consistently. The fewer the restrictions, the fewer the disciplinary problems. One of the most frequent complaints about teachers concerns the inconsistency with which limits are enforced. An articulate eighth grade boy seen in counseling by one of the writer's students expressed it well:

> *Student:* "It just seems to me that since the teachers and the principals are the people who are in authority, well, they kind of have to take care of everybody else; it seems like they ought to be a little more careful about what they say and things like that."
>
> *Counselor:* "You feel that the teachers and principals are not very careful about the way they use their power?" (*Student:* "mmh mmh") "And that they seem to sort of ... "
>
> *Student:* "A lot of times they'll, well, just for a little thing—if they're in a bad mood they'll take and—well not many times—I know it has happened to some people—take and send somebody out into the hall, when they didn't do anything—and sometimes, you know, it's what they're leading up to—they maybe hadn't done anything all day, and then just for a little thing they'll fly off the handle and get real mad and—it just doesn't seem fair that they should take it out on this one person. They should call each person down as he does something instead of waiting until ... "
>
> *Counselor:* "uh uh."
>
> *Student:* " ... finally taking it out on one person."
>
> *Counselor:* "It's sort of cornering one person in the class ... "
>
> *Student:* "uh uh."
>
> *Counselor:* " ... that usually causes most of the problems."
>
> *Student:* "I think that the schools ought to give the kids so much leeway and then enforce it strictly instead of saying you don't have

any leeway and then when they go ahead and do something they don't enforce it very strictly and . . . sort of like you give them an inch and they'll take a mile. I think they ought to stop you as soon as you get as far as you should go and after a while the kids would learn, but the way it is they let them go on and on until they decide they don't like it, then they take it out on one person and . . . "

Counselor: "You feel then that the rules are not defined . . . Is this what you're saying, that if you go beyond a certain point . . . "

Student: "They should, well, say they give you so much room . . . things you can do in the room—each teacher usually sets that up herself—and I think as soon as you've gone that far . . . if you're doing anything you're not supposed to I think they should call you down for it . . . maybe give you a warning—you know—one time— and then the next time you do it they send you out in the hall or down to the principal's office if you do it again. But the way it is they just let certain people go on past that and then after a while somebody else saw them do it and they didn't get into any trouble so they do the same thing and they'll get called down for it. And I think they should call everybody down for the same things. Because quite often one person does—maybe the teacher likes this person just a little bit more than another person . . . and this other person does something and gets sent out in the hall but this person does it and she just says 'now don't do that' . . . "

Different teachers set different limits, and students test out a new teacher or a substitute. The opening pages of Herndon's and Kohl's books portray the difficulties a new teacher faces.[3] Kozol also describes his early days in two classrooms.[4] These are extreme examples because of the nature of the schools they worked in. But every teacher faces the problem of structuring limits with every class. To some extent limits are determined by what the teacher can be comfortable with. But if a teacher is comfortable only with narrow limits which are not conducive to learning or which are not reasonable to impose on active, living children, then the teacher will need, probably with help from a psychologist or counselor, to learn to become comfortable with more

[3]James Herndon, *The way it spozed to be* (New York, Simon & Schuster, 1965); Herbert Kohl, *36 children* (New York, American Library, 1967).

[4]Jonathan Kozol, *Death at an early age* (New York, Bantam Books, 1968), pp. 46-47, 161-162.

reasonable limits. Too often strict limits represent fear of loss of control.

As noted earlier, some limits are necessary. In addition, as Combs and Snygg point out, "Limits have important growth-producing values for people, and the lack of limits makes adjustment to new situations more difficult. A stable structure has important positive values in providing expectancies against which to judge one's behavior. Clear and reasonable limits provide important security values."[5]

It has long been maintained that the goal of discipline is the development of self-discipline in students. Seldom, however, has the system made it possible for self-discipline to develop. Fear and lack of trust have stood in the way. But where students have been involved in or permitted to determine limits as in Summerhill and some of the open or free schools, there have been few discipline problems. Where students are interested in learning as a group, they will set the limits which are necessary for learning to take place.

One of the major problems in moving to the open classroom has been the difficulty experienced by children who have lived in a highly restricted classroom environment in adapting to an environment with few restrictions or limits. The result of the sudden change is excessive noise, activity and confusion, or, as Goodman suggests, "a great outburst of dammed up hostility."[6] Herndon, Kohl, and Kozol experienced this in their open classroom approach to teaching. They went through a long, slow process before the children "settled down" within the broad limits. Administrators—and parents—must expect such a reaction to the open classroom among students who are not used to it. If this approach to education has not begun in the first grade—or continued in the first grade, since kindergarten is often similar to the open classroom—perhaps it should be introduced gradually with older children. However, some of the difficulty is the result of the in-

---

[5]Arthur W. Combs & Donald Snygg, *Individual behavior: a perceptual approach to behavior*, 2nd Ed. (New York, Harper & Row, 1959), p. 391.

[6]Paul Goodman, *Compulsory mis-education and the community of scholars* (New York, Vantage Books, 1962), p. 39.

experience and uncertainty of teachers. If the limits are determined in advance, and are clearly understood by the teacher and the students, and are systematically adhered to, preferably through the use of positive reinforcement, the transition to the open classroom should be possible with less time and confusion.

THE HUMANISTIC TEACHER

The conditions which facilitate personal development in general are also the basic conditions for learning, including classroom learning. This being the case, it is necessary that teachers understand and implement these conditions in the classroom situation. Rogers has pointed out that the facilitation of learning is not simply a matter of knowledge of subject matter, teaching methods or skills, curricular planning, use of audio-visual and other resources, but is a matter of "certain attitudinal qualities which exist in the personal relationship between the facilitator and the learner."[7]

In Chapter 3 we described the characteristics of self-actualizing persons and noted that these characteristics included the conditions for facilitating personal development. Therefore, it is apparent that if one wishes to facilitate the development of self-actualizing persons, whether in counseling, teaching, or any other relationship, one must be a self-actualizing person oneself. Teaching is a relationship, and if it is to be a helping or facilitative relationship, it must include the basic conditions of empathic understanding, warmth and respect, and genuineness. We shall therefore consider these as they relate to the teacher as a person.

Authenticity or Genuineness. One of the basic attitudinal qualities or characteristics of a facilitative teacher is genuineness or authenticity. Too many teachers play a role. This role originates in their preparation for teaching and in their early experiences in teaching. Unprepared for relating to students, they retreat behind a facade of their concept of the teacher role. They are confirmed in this role by other teachers, by their supervisors, and by the demands and expectations of administrators. The fear of having disciplinary problems, and of a noisy classroom, lead

---

[7]Carl R. Rogers, *Freedom to learn* (Columbus, Ohio, Merrill, 1969), pp. 105-106.

the teacher to develop a routine and a method of teaching whose purpose is to ensure control. To be themselves, or open and warm in their relations with their students is to risk being taken advantage of, and to lose control. Thus teachers develop into the stereotype of a teacher—authoritarian, immobile, unfeeling, cold, and impersonal—hardly a human being.

If teaching is to be a genuine human relationship, it is no place for role playing. The teacher is a human being, a real person, and should not try to be something other than she naturally is. The humanistic teacher is genuine and real, not presenting a facade or the stereotype of a teacher.

A teacher who tries to be something she is not is under constant tension and anxiety. Moreover, her phoniness will be detected by students, even though they may conceal this recognition, and the teaching relationship is affected. A teacher who pretends to be something she is not creates feelings of uneasiness and tension in students who see beneath her pretensions. They begin to "test" her to see where she really stands, so they can know where they stand. A teacher who is trying to play a role is unsure of herself, vacillating, hesitating, inconsistent, and thus invites "discipline problems."

It often happens, of course, that a teacher who assumes the role of a controlling, dominating autocrat of the classroom becomes such in reality. To some people, especially administrators, such a teacher is successful and is presented as a model to beginning teachers. The classroom is quiet, the students appear to be working and studying, and there seem to be no disciplinary problems. But such an authoritarian environment is not conducive to learning, to the self-initiated change which is real learning. An authoritarian environment is not an atmosphere for the development of self-actualizing persons. The autocrat, even though genuine, is not a good teacher. Thus, when we speak of genuineness, we need to think of it as facilitative, or therapeutic, genuineness.

The genuine teacher, then, is not preoccupied with techniques or methods, which distract from a good personal relationship. "Authenticity frees the helper to devote his full attention to the problems at hand. His behavior can be smoothly congruent and *en rapport* with students."[8] The behavior of the authentic teacher is not highly self-conscious, but spontaneous, intuitive—based on a feeling that it is the thing to do. The teacher trusts herself.

The authentic teacher is not always free from so-called negative feelings and behavior. She may become impatient, irritated, even angry. When she has these feelings—when they are strong or persistent, not simply momentary and fleeting—she doesn't attempt to hide or suppress them. She doesn't feel one thing and say something else. (It isn't likely that she would be successful in concealing her real feelings from students completely or consistently.) But she recognizes and accepts her feelings as her own, and accepts responsibility for her own behavior. She doesn't project her feelings on her students and blame them for her feelings and behavior. She may say "I'm irritated," "I'm angry," "I'm disturbed," not "You irritate me," "You make me angry," "You disturb me."

Moreover, she can express her negative feelings about a student's work without condemning the students. "[She] can dislike a student product without implying that it is objectively good or bad or that the student is good or bad. [She] is simply expressing a feeling for the product, a feeling which exists within [herself]. Thus [she] is a person to [her] students, not a faceless embodiment of a curricular requirement nor a sterile tube through which knowledge is passed from one generation to the next."[9]

In any expression of feeling the teacher accepts responsibility for it as *her* behavior. If a child's behavior irritates or angers her, she makes it clear that it is the behavior, not the child, which does so. This is not to encourage teachers to express every feeling of anger, nor to imply that a highly volatile and emotional teacher is a good teacher. The damaging effects of anger directed at children are clear.[10] Children may disobey, fight with each other,

---

[8] A. W. Combs, D. L. Avila, and W. W. Purkey, *Helping relationships: Basic concepts for the helping professions* (Boston, Allyn & Bacon, 1971), p. 292.

[9] Carl R. Rogers, *op. cit.*, p. 106.

[10] Herbert M. Greenberg, *Teaching with feeling* (Toronto, Macmillan, 1969).

and do less studying. Realness or genuineness is important, but it is not an excuse for cruelty, nor should it be an excuse for continuing to employ a cruel or sadistic, or disturbed, teacher. The perceptive teacher, sensitive to her own feelings and the beginning of a situation leading up to an outburst of anger can often avoid this outcome by voicing her incipient anger: "All right, kids, cool it before I blow my stack."[11]

A student of the writer, recognizing the desirability of the teacher becoming aware of her feelings and doing something about them before they reach the explosive stage, reports her experience in student teaching:

> Last semester I went through a traumatic and distressing time, in connection with my student teaching. I had been given advice by teachers in how to conduct a good classroom; I was told not to smile too much, to establish my authority at the outset; and never to show my emotions, because the students would then know they could 'get my goat.' For six weeks I labored to follow this advice, because it came from supposed experts. One day I became so angry at the noise in the classroom that I burst out in an emotional attack upon the students, screaming at them for their terrible behavior. The students were startled, they felt that I had been unfair. If I had been more real in this situation I would have been able to tell the students that I got annoyed at this noise much earlier, and we could have worked out some sort of compromise on the noise level. This realness could have avoided my personal attack on them as bad persons. It could also have helped me to avoid my tremendous feelings of guilt for, even though my cooperating teacher felt that the students got what they deserved, I knew that I had been most unfair. In the future, when in the teaching situation, I will try my personal best to be real, to express my feelings as they occur truly in my awareness.
>
> If I am real, my students will be able to relate to me as I am— a human being with feelings and ideas, not an authority figure who issues mandates from above. They will realize that I am being my whole 'self,' and that I can and do make mistakes; furthermore, when I make mistakes, I will be able to admit them. It is only human to make mistakes, but very few teachers are accustomed to letting their students know that they are less than infallible. In my opinion, students would feel more at ease with a teacher who is able to admit errors, and who relinquishes his role of all-knowing author-

---

[11]*Ibid.*, p. 65.

ity. The teacher would also become a learner in the eyes of the student if he were able to admit that his ideas are not always absolutely correct.

A. S. Neill has said: "It doesn't matter what you do to a child if your attitude toward that child is right."[12] This of course does not mean that the teacher should take out all his negative feelings on children. Clearly, we are talking about feelings which are a result of the behavior of the children themselves, and not feelings originating from a disturbed personality. There is no place, as noted above, for the emotionally disturbed teacher in the classroom.

Being real is a difficult thing for many if not most people in our society, which is so impersonal, competitive, and evaluative. Teachers particularly find difficulty because of the fears engendered by the expectations represented in the myths of the good teacher. As a student put it, "I cannot become real just by verbalizing this wish; it is not an easy thing to become, because so much of my experience has conditioned me to put up appropriate fronts for the different roles I should play in society, according to normative standards." Rogers notes that:

> Only slowly can we learn to be truly real. For, first of all, one must be close to one's feelings, capable of being aware of them. Then, one must be willing to take the risk of sharing them as they are, inside, not disguising them as judgments, or attributing them to other people.[13]

The attitude of the teacher toward children is basic. This attitude is the second major condition for learning and self-actualization in students.

Respect for the Child as a Person. The humanistic teacher respects each child as a person of worth in his own right, as a unique human being. She accepts each child as he is, for what he is. This attitude makes no demand that the child be different to be accepted—it is unconditional. It is not an impersonal respect, but a real liking, and what Rogers has called a "prizing"

---

[12]A. S. Neill, *Summerhill* (New York, Hart), p. 144.
[13]Carl R. Rogers, *op. cit.*, p. 114.

of another—of his feelings, his opinions, his person.[14] It involves a caring for another, a feeling of warmth toward him. But it is a non-possessive caring and warmth, which recognizes his integrity as an individual. Such an attitude is inconsistent with controlling, directing, or guiding another in the way you think he should go, or manipulating him by subtle means.

Acceptance of another does not require that the other be perfect, that he always agree with us, or that all his behavior be acceptable or good or right. There is acceptance of mistakes, and errors, imperfections, changes in mood and motivation, etc. These are aspects of being human. But there is also a confidence in the basic goodness of each person, of his capacity to grow and to develop, and to actualize his potentials when given the opportunity in a facilitating environment.

Acceptance of a child as he is does not mean that one is satisfied in letting the child remain as he is. It is not inconsistent with having expectations for change and development. If one likes and cares for another one wants that other to be what he is capable of being, to be his best self. But one does not withhold one's caring or liking to control the behavior of another. That is, acceptance, respect and liking are not conditional on the other person meeting our specific expectations.

It appears that one cannot help another, through teaching or in any other personal relationship, unless one likes the other. Yet there are children whom a teacher just cannot like. If a teacher cannot develop a minimal liking for a particular child, it would be desirable that such a child be placed with another teacher who could feel some liking for him.

Respect for one's students engenders self-respect in the students. Such self-respect leads to a feeling of self-confidence and competence which is reflected in their performance.

Empathic Understanding. The third condition for real learning, and the third characteristic of the effective teacher, is empathic understanding. As indicated in the chapter on individual counseling (Chapter 4), this is a special kind of understanding. It is not the knowledge that may be obtained from the student's file

---

[14]*Ibid.*, p. 109.

or cumulative record. It is not the information passed on from one teacher to the next. It is not the understanding obtained from reports of psychologists, social workers or psychiatrists. Nor is it the understanding obtained from the usual case study of a child.

Empathic understanding requires that the teacher put herself in the place of the student, and become tuned-in to his perceptions and feelings about what is happening. "It is the completely unbiased attitude of seeing what an experience means to the child, not how it fits into or relates to other experiences, not what causes it, why it exists, or for what purpose. It is an attempt to know attitudes and concepts, beliefs and values of the child as they are perceived by him alone."[15]

Information and "facts" obtained from sources such as those listed above interfere with empathic understanding because they present an external point of view and prevent the teacher from taking the internal frame of reference of the student. Such comments and observations of others are not "facts," but represent their own perceptions, and are usually evaluative and judgmental.

Empathic understanding is rare in our society, with its evaluative orientation. It is rare in teachers, who are evaluators. Rogers writes that it is "almost unheard of in the classroom. One could listen to thousands of ordinary classroom interactions without coming across one instance of clearly communicated, sensitively accurate, empathic understanding." He continues: "If any teacher set himself the task of endeavoring to make one non-evaluative, acceptant, empathic response per day to a student's demonstrated or verbalized feeling, I believe he would discover the potency of this currently almost non-existent kind of understanding."[16]

These three basic conditions are the essence of love. They are nonthreatening. Self-initiated learning, which involves exploration, not simply memorization, can occur only in a nonthreatening environment.

---

[15]Clark Moustakas, *The authentic teacher: sensitivity and awareness in the classroom* (Cambridge, Howard A. Doyle, 1966), p. 30.

[16]*Op. cit.*, p. 112.

It is clear that the teacher, while an imperfect human being, must be a self-actualizing person. Only self-actualizing persons can foster self-actualization in others.

Teaching is a demanding occupation. It is in one respect more difficult than psychotherapy. It demands the same characteristics in its practitioners. But it is more difficult to provide the conditions for personal growth and development to thirty unique and often disturbed children for five or six hours a day than to provide the conditions to four or five clients or patients in individual interviews. The teacher, however, is not a therapist in the conventional sense of the term, but the humanistic teacher is therapeutic. Indeed, if the children were exposed to humanistic teachers (and, prior to entering school, to humanistic parents), few children would need formal counseling or psychotherapy.

IMPLEMENTING THE CONDITIONS IN THE CLASSROOM

It is not enough to tell teachers to be more genuine, more respecting and warm, more empathic. They ask: "But how do I act, just what do I do?" It may seem peculiar that we must consider how one functions as a human being, but in our society it appears to be necessary. And while it is not sufficient that teachers simply behave in certain ways, it is helpful for teachers to know some of the ways in which they can implement or practice the conditions for facilitating learning and personal development.

Listening. As listening is the first requirement of a counselor, it is also the first requirement of a humanistic teacher. One of the frequent complaints of students is that teachers don't listen to them. Studies have found that classroom teachers talk approximately 75 per cent of the time. When one is talking one is unable to listen.

Real learning is personal and is often accompanied by feelings and emotions, since it represents change in the student. If the child is to express his real feelings, he must feel that he is free to do so, that he won't be evaluated, criticized, or condemned for having negative feelings. If he is to express any ideas or thoughts, he must feel that they will be accepted as worthwhile. The teacher must therefore convey genuine interest, concern, and respect for the child by his willingness to listen, and his ability to listen empathically. The teacher expresses respect by listening. But the teacher who says to a student, "Never mind what you think about that, Jimmy, what does the book say?"[17] is not willing to listen or to respect the student.

Responding. Listening alone is helpful and can give another the feeling of being respected and understood. But it is often desirable and necessary that the listener communicate his understanding. If the listener is to effectively communicate empathic understanding his responses must remain in the internal frame of reference, and not be evaluative or judgmental.

There are a variety of understanding responses. Some are nonverbal, such as a nod of the head. There are simple verbal responses, such as "yes," "I see," "I understand," "Mm Hmmm." A simple restatement indicates that one has heard and understands. No one can completely understand another, and complete understanding is not necessary. Often it is enough that one is trying to understand, and pretending to understand when one does not is of course not useful or helpful. Questions help one understand more clearly what another is trying to say.

Responses beyond the initial response indicating understanding do not of course need to indicate agreement. Disagreements, or confrontations, can be fruitful. But each must first understand the other before disagreements can be explored fruitfully.

THE POWER OF EXPECTATIONS

The importance of expectations in behavior has long been recognized in the saying "Give a dog a bad name and he will live up to it." This is the theme of Shaw's *Pygmalion,* in which the flower girl becomes a lady when she is expected to be a lady and is treated like one. The influence of expectations has been referred to as the self-fulfilling prophecy since Robert Merton used this term.[18]

Teachers have beliefs and attitudes about individual children

---

[17]Arthur W. Combs, D. L. Avila, & W. W. Purkey, *op. cit.,* p. 95.

[18]Robert K. Merton, "The self-fulfilling prophecy." *The Antioch Review,* (summer 1948), reprinted in Robert K Merton, *Social theory and social structure.* Rev. Ed. (New York, Macmillan-Free Press, 1957).

and groups of children. These beliefs and attitudes create expectations which influence the behavior of the children. Teachers' expectations are a powerful factor in the actual performance of children in school.

Robert Rosenthal and Lenore Jacobson conducted a study of the expectations of classroom teachers. They administered a test of general ability to all the students in grades K through six of a school in the spring. The teachers were told that the test was able to predict which of the children would be expected to show a spurt in academic achievement, and the following September each teacher was given a list purporting to contain the names of these children. In fact, the names on the list were selected at random. The children were retested the next January and again in May. The authors concluded that those children whose names appeared on the lists gained more, on the average, than the other children.[19]

Unfortunately, the results of the study are poorly reported and have been questioned statistically. However, there has been a mass of literature supporting the effects of expectations, including research with animals. In one study two groups of psychology students were given rats to be tested for performance in running mazes. One group was told that their rats were maze-bright, while the other was told that theirs were maze-dull. In fact the rats were from the same litters. The results reported by the students, however, were in the expected direction—the students who thought that their rats were brighter reported better performance.

The way in which expectations alter behavior is not clear. A student of the writer's, in one of the most detailed studies of expectations, was able to identify few observable behaviors related to the expectancy effect. It appears that the behaviors may vary with the sex of the experimenter and of the subject, and are very complex. Awareness of the phenomenon of the expectancy effect may lead to an attempt to counteract an unfavorable

---

[19]Robert Rosenthal & Lenore Jacobson, *Pygmalion in the classroom* (New York, Holt, Rinehart & Winston, 1968).

effect, resulting in a "reverse effect."[20] The modes of influence are subtle yet effective, particularly over a period of time.

It is well known that expectations are transferred from teacher to teacher by the communication of stereotypes. A seventh grade boy who was a client of a counseling student of one of the writers expressed it as follows:

> *Student:* "It wouldn't have been so bad if it was like in the lower grades, you know, primary grades, where we had only one teacher. Now you've got four teachers, and Mrs. Johnson, she just about can't stand me, and then they go down and sit together at the lunch table and she tells all about the things I do, and I have a funny feeling she exaggerates just a little bit. And then the other teachers hear about it and they're on edge and every time I breathe too deeply they get down on me too and it's like having the whole school down on you."
>
> *Counselor:* "Things you do aren't quite as bad as what the teachers seem to . . ."
>
> *Student:* "uh uh."

Teachers pass on expectations from year to year. The student above went on later to say:

> *Student:* "You walk into a new class, you know, the teacher has never had you and she doesn't know all your names yet. You look up and she's all big smiles and everything. You know, and goes down the line asking everybody their names, and you say Ronald James—and she falls through the floor or something."
>
> *Counselor:* "It gets that bad."

Silberman states it clearly and simply: "The teacher who assumes that her students cannot learn is likely to discover that she has a class of children who are indeed unable to learn; yet another teacher, working with the same class but without the same expectation, may discover that she has a class of interested learners. The same obtains with respect to behavior: the teacher who assumes that her students will be disruptive is likely to have a disruptive class on her hands."[21]

---

[20]Nitza Yarom, Temporal localization and communication of experimenter expectancy effect with 10-11 year old children. Unpublished doctoral dissertation, University of Illinois, Urbana-Champaign, 1971.

[21]Charles E. Silberman, *Crisis in the classroom* (New York, Random House, 1970), p. 83.

Perhaps one of the major problems in the education of the "disadvantaged"—poor whites, blacks, Puerto Ricans, Chicanos, American Indians—lies in this matter of expectations. Teachers expect little, demand or require little, and get little. An unusual aspect of this problem is referred to by Silberman. He says that expectations can be lowered by empathy. That is, the efforts to help teachers of the disadvantaged by impressing on them that these children fail through no fault of their own leads teachers to accept—and expect failure.[22] It could be questioned, of course, whether this is really empathy. Yet the fact remains that whole classes of children are condemned to a poor education because it is assumed that they are not capable of learning. This is a basic theme of Kozol's book depicting the education of blacks in the Boston schools, of Herndon's book about the education of blacks in California, and of Kohl's book.[23] In these schools the communication of negative attitudes and expectations becomes clear and obvious. *The concepts which the teacher has of the children become the concepts which the children come to have of themselves.*

Silberman reports an example of negative attitudes:

> A fourth-grade math teacher writes a half-dozen problems on the board for the class to do. "I think I can pick at least four children who can't do them," she tells the class, and proceeds to demonstrate, for all to see, how correct the teacher's judgment is. Needless to say, the children fulfill the prophecy.[24]

That this situation can be changed, or reversed, has been shown in a number of experimental and demonstration projects. The essential element in these projects has been an attitude and expectation that the children could and would learn, and it is this factor, rather than the special methods or techniques, to which the success of these projects can be attributed, even though some would emphasize the methods and techniques.

The teacher who respects each student as a unique human being, who believes that each one has more potential than may

---

[22]*Ibid.*, p. 86.
[23]Jonathan Kozol, *op. cit.*; James Herndon, *op. cit.*; Herbert Kohl, *op. cit.*
[24]*Op. cit.*, p. 139.

be evident, conveys this in her treatment of the student. High expectations can be expressed in the maintainance of high standards. However, one must be careful that the standards are not too high or unrealistic, and standards must be adapted to the individual student.

Although it is not possible to identify just how expectations are communicated (except in extreme situations), it is possible for the teacher to become aware of her expectations and thus to anticipate the direction of her influence on students.

The teacher who is concerned about her students, who respects them, who recognizes the great unused potentials which they possess, expects much—even "demands" much. Love expects the best. The expectations others have of us act as a challenge to us to do our best, to be our best. The fact is that one cannot care deeply for another without expecting, or even demanding, that he do and be the best of which he is capable.

THE SELF AS INSTRUMENT

Interpersonal relations are not a matter of techniques. Good or facilitative teaching, therefore cannot be reduced to a bag of tricks or techniques. This is the error of those writers whose educational backgrounds have imprinted on them the importance of methods. In the effort to be objective, concrete, specific, and practical they have focused on developing lists of activities, procedures, projects, devices, etc. for the teachers to use. These are often not much more than tricks or gimmicks to initiate and give content to an interaction. To some extent, perhaps, this is necessary for teachers who have been so content oriented, so lesson-plan dependent, that they are unable to enter a relationship spontaneously, without an agenda. But to the extent that they are, and continue to be, dependent on such crutches they will be prevented from becoming free to enter and establish a spontaneous relationship.

It is true that some writers (e.g. Brown[25]) present evidence to support the effectiveness of such an approach. But they fail

---

[25]George T. Brown, *Human teaching for human learning: an introduction to confluent education* (New York, Viking Press, 1971).

to realize that the success was probably more dependent upon the effectiveness of the teachers as persons—their interest, concern, enthusiasm—than upon the methods or techniques *per se*.

One cannot really tell another how to express his caring or his love. Each of us must find his own way of doing it—his own style of implementing his attitudes and beliefs, his own way of giving himself. In a basic sense one's self is the instrument of teaching, as of all human relationships, and one must learn to use one's self as an instrument for facilitating the development of others. The teacher can be assisted in doing this but he must do it himself.

RECEPTIVENESS OF THE STUDENT

There is an important aspect of any human relationship that must be noted. Failure to recognize and be aware of this has caused many teachers to suffer feelings of guilt and inadequacy, or to feel that they have failed a student.

In addition to the offering of understanding, respect or warmth, and genuineness by the teacher, these must be received—or perceived and accepted—by the student. Young children are usually open and receptive. But some young children, and perhaps many older children, are not. Their experiences have closed them up, sometimes so tight that they are unaware of, or are insensitive to, warmth and genuineness. In other cases, their experiences have led to distrust and suspicion. In still others, resentment and resistance prevent them from recognizing or accepting the genuine interest and concern of the teacher. These children have been mistreated—deceived, mistrusted, let down, treated as inadequate, etc.

The teacher can only offer herself, and try repeatedly to break through walls of suspicion, distrust, resistance, hostility and insensitivity. The theme of many of the books concerned with humanistic teaching—Dennison, Herndon, Kohl and Kozol—is the attempt to break through to such students. When the attempt is successful the results sometimes appear as miraculous. But sometimes—too often—the attempt is not successful. When it is not, it is not always the fault of the teacher. It takes two to establish a good relationship, and mutual trust is necessary.

The books by Dennison, Herndon, Kohl and Kozol contain illustrations of students who were difficult, and sometimes impossible, to reach. Borton presents an instance from his experience:

> Bob—a senior in my slow section. On my first day of teaching he took the seat directly in front of my desk and interrupted my introductory remarks by asking 'you new?' When I nodded my head, he grinned, 'we got your number.' From then on he made my life miserable, always quitting just before I got to the breaking point. A month later he was suspended by some other teacher, a month after that he was jailed. At about the same time I learned that he had started out as a freshman in the best academic class, and had been moved down one track each year as various teachers retaliated for his wisecracks.[26]

Such children might have been reached by good teaching in the early grades. Later may be too late. Often psychotherapy is recommended and even attempted. These students usually do not accept therapy, however, and if it is attempted it is not often successful.

SUMMARY

This chapter has been concerned with the facilitation of personal development in the classroom. Such development, as well as more traditional subject matter learning, can occur only, or best, in a teaching relationship which is characterized by certain attitudes on the part of the teacher.

Before considering the specific attitudes, the necessity of limits on behavior in social situations, including the classroom, was discussed. The importance of limits for so-called disciplinary problems was pointed out.

The basic conditions of a good teaching relationship are the same conditions required for any other good human relationship, including counseling or psychotherapy. They are genuineness or authenticity, respect and warmth, and empathic understanding. The nature of these characteristics as related to teaching was described, and their expression or implementation in the classroom was discussed.

---

[26]Terry Borton, *Reach, touch, and teach* (New York, McGraw-Hill, 1970), p. 153.

An important element in student responsiveness to teaching are the expectations which teachers have of individual students or a group of students. While the means by which such expectations influence student behavior and performance are not clear, their power has been clearly demonstrated.

Throughout it was emphasized that teaching is essentially a relationship, rather than a matter of methods or techniques to be applied automatically. A total relationship is a unique, individual thing, and each teacher has, or develops, her own style of teaching or of relating to her students. Nevertheless, the basic conditions of a good human relationship must be present.

SUGGESTED READING

Combs, A. W., Avila, D. L., & Purkey, A. W.: *Helping relationships: basic concepts for the helping professions.* Boston, Allyn & Bacon, 1971.

Greenberg, H. M.: *Teaching with feeling.* Toronto, Macmillan, 1969.

Moustakas, C.: *The authentic teacher: sensitivity and awareness in the classroom.* Cambridge, Mass.: Howard A. Doyle, 1966.

Patterson, C. H.: *Humanistic education.* Englewood Cliffs, Prentice-Hall, 1973.

Rogers, C. R.: *Freedom to learn.* Columbus, Merrill, 1969.

Chapter 5

PUPIL PERSONNEL WORK: THE INTEGRATION OF THE FUNCTIONS OF SPECIALISTS

A LTHOUGH THE ROLE OF THE COUNSELOR has been stressed to this point, the entire school staff is involved in helping pupils in their quest for self-actualization. Traditionally, the school social worker and the school psychologist have worked with children who have problems. The work of these and other specialists has been incorporated into programs of pupil personnel services. In this chapter we shall consider how a program of pupil personnel activities can be integrated into a helping process whose goal is to help pupils in their development as self-actualized persons.

THE NATURE AND GOALS OF PUPIL PERSONNEL PROGRAMS

The counselor is a member of a pupil personnel unit whose function is to consider the needs of children in relation to their self-actualization, the ultimate goal of education. "The primary purpose of a program of pupil personnel services is to facilitate the maximum development of each individual through education."[1] If pupil personnel services are considered as one of the essential components of an educational program, then an organized program should be provided within each school district.

---

[1]*Responsibilities of state departments of education for pupil personnel* (Washington, Council of Chief State School Officers, 1960), p. 2.

Such a program provides assistance to pupils, teachers, administrators, parents, and community agencies. Because of the complexity of most pupil personnel functions, a balanced and coordinated program must be developed in order to insure that pupils receive comprehensive rather than fragmentized help. "While a coordinated program can contribute in a significant and effective way, a distorted and unbalanced program cannot be *effective* and may ultimately be rejected by education."[2]

ADMINISTRATIVE ORIENTATIONS

Two major administrative orientations can be used to organize pupil personnel programs. The first administrative orientation views pupil personnel functions as an adjunct to the instructional process. As a consequence, its help to pupils and staff is indirect and is in the form of technically oriented professional activities. Its focus is on children with whom the school is having problems. The chief functions of the specialists are to diagnose problems and to prescribe treatments. With the exception of some types of learning disabilities and physical handicaps, the specialists do not engage in treating the child. Because the help given to a pupil is serialized and segmented, coordination is required to insure that the treatment process is carried out.

The second administrative orientation views pupil personnel work as individualized assistance to pupils. It provides direct help to pupils so that their needs can be met. The focus is on all children rather than those who have problems or who are problems to the school. Although the staff is comprised of specialists (e.g., counselor, social worker, school psychologist, etc.), they function in total as a generalist because the work effort is integrated. This approach uses many alternative ways of helping pupils rather than relying on a single professional orientation.

It is rather difficult to achieve a balanced pupil personnel program because of the divergent opinions held by teachers, administrators, and pupil personnel workers regarding the ways in which

---

[2]Dean L. Hummel and S. J. Bonham, Jr., *Pupil personnel services in schools* (Chicago, Rand McNally, 1968), p. 39.

administrative concerns and pupil needs can best be met. Leadership is required to put the divergent views into proper perspective. Leadership helps "to utilize the skills of a person professionally trained in the behavioral sciences who can alleviate a mounting array of administrative problems, and problems of children and youth so as to strengthen the effectiveness of the educative process."[3]

The process of leadership is confounded by the interaction among the needs and demands of a given community, philosophies and objectives of a school district, state school codes of the state office of the superintendent of public instruction, and statements of professional organizations. The net effect of these interactions is that the local school administrator tends to evolve a "wait and see" policy regarding changing existing programs. Basically the delay results because the state and national leaders fail to agree as to the appropriateness of a given course of action. Local school administrators require definite guidelines for operation. They have learned from experience that the impressive listings of competencies and expectations by professional organizations tend to be unrealistic. The typical personnel specialist cannot do all that is demanded of him. As a consequence, most local school districts tend to reserve judgment regarding the validity of a new idea. The public judges the school more by its failures than by its successes.

The characteristics of a balanced pupil personnel program vary with the unit of administration (e.g., building, district, state). The role that each unit plays in the larger educative process, as recognized by other units in that process, varies. What is a balanced program to a building principal may be seen as "chaos" by the state office of the superintendent of public instruction. The integration of the helping process of pupil personnel workers with the larger process of education requires a great deal of accommodation by those who have a role to play in education. They should realize that "our traditional organizational structures require behaviors that tend to frustrate, place in conflict, and create

---

[3]*Ibid.*, p. 37.

failure for psychologically healthy individuals."[4] Although the difficulties pupils have in school are chiefly seen as "local problems," some of these difficulties are created by factors outside the school. The demands placed on schools by state offices of public instruction, the United States Office of Education, and national professional organizations may structure many activities within the school. Under these circumstances the principal functions more as a monitor than a leader.

The influence of state and federal legislation on education is well known. The impact of professional associations on the goals and functions of the school is little known. Professional organizations define the work of the professional domain in an organization and the skills and competencies required to function in the work domain. The organization, in this case the local school district, must accommodate to prescriptions stipulated by the professional associations. Levine and White suggest that in the health field the work domain is defined in terms of (1) disease covered, (2) population served, (3) services rendered.[5] This classification system can be used to differentiate the work domain of pupil personnel specialists; e.g. a school psychologist restricts his activities to appraising elementary school children who are suspected of being mentally retarded. Levine and White state that "the goals of the organization constitute in effect the organization's claim to future functions and to the elements requisite to these functions, whereas the present or actual functions carried out by the organization constitute de facto claims to these elements."[6] Since future functions are predicated on current functions, there is a reluctance to restructure the work domain by professional pupil personnel workers. They know that if their current work activities are deemed to meet certain school goals and that if certain standards of performance are met, then a legitimate

[4]Frank X. Steggert, "Organization theory: Bureaucratic influences and the social welfare task." In Ella W. Reed, ed. *Common elements in administration* (Columbus, National Conference on Social Welfare, 1965), p. 52.

[5]Sol Levine and Paul E. White, "Exchange as a conceptual framework for the study of inter-organizational relationships," *Administrative Science Quarterly*, Vol. 5, (1961), 584-601.

[6]*Ibid.*, p. 593.

claim can be made to any additional tasks. The delineation of the work domain is necessary for the survival of professional associations. In practice, it may impose unnecessary hardships upon pupils and school personnel.

The formal delineation of the work domain is usually done by means of legislation. The state school code may specify the certification requirements for the various pupil personnel workers, the tasks they may do, and the outcomes that should be obtained. In addition, the state school code may specify the types of personnel a school district may be required to employ. The shortcoming of most legislation regarding school personnel is that it emphasizes specialization and reflects competence in specific methodology. As a consequence, an integrated effort in helping children is precluded because only specialists can provide the necessary services. It is rather difficult to develop a balanced pupil personnel program when legislation and professional association prescriptions structure the program. Under these circumstances "balance" usually means that the school district has achieved the appropriate ratio between students and personnel workers as required by external agencies such as the school code and professional association. Meeting the ratio requirements does not guarantee the quality of the helping process being offered the children.

The current state of pupil personnel services reflects the antecedent conditions that brought them about. Generally speaking, compulsory education laws reflect the philosophy that all children are not only entitled to an education but can also profit from it. As a consequence, the instructional programs require a variety of assistance in helping to educate all children. The assistance to schools in many instances was originally provided by outside private or community organizations. As the demands on the schools increased, the need for professionally trained personnel to perform certain functions in the school became apparent. Since the demands on the schools arose in a piecemeal fashion, the pupil personnel program evolved in a similar fashion. An historical review of the development of pupil personnel services will be undertaken because it will help to understand the problems that arise when attempts are made to revise current pupil personnel programs.

THE SCHOOL SOCIAL WORKER[7]

School social work, like other pupil personnel functions, was initiated by sources outside the school, in 1906. Civic and private organizations became aware that compulsory school attendance laws placed a burden on schools and parents. Visiting teacher programs were developed in Boston and in New York in order to help schools and parents have a better understanding of one another so that by working cooperatively they could help the child have a meaningful educational experience. The establishment of home-school-community liaison became the chief function of school social work. The visiting teacher's task was to interpret to the school the child's environment and to interpret to the parents the demands of the school. When the visiting teacher concept was incorporated into school systems, work with truants and delinquents was included among the functions of the visiting teacher. Although ideas from the mental hygiene movement and from differential psychology had some impact on the work of the school social worker, the principal focus through the 1920's was on factors outside the school setting that affected the pupil.

The work of the school social worker was modified by the depression of the 1930's. Caring for the physical needs of the children became the chief task. This restructuring of the work of the school social worker gave impetus to casework service. Casework soon became more clinically oriented and focused on the emotionally maladjusted child. Although the school social worker continued to work with others in behalf of the child, work with parents became emphasized. Teachers were consulted for two reasons: (1) to interpret the child's problem to them; (2) to assist the teacher in recognition of emotional difficulties. Collaboration with other pupil personnel workers was usually restricted to developing treatment procedures. In some school systems social workers were consulted on administrative policy matters.

[7]This section represents a synthesis of the historical development of social work found in the writings of Lela B. Costin. *An analysis of the tasks of school social work as a basis for improved use of staff: A final report.* (Washington, U. S. Department of Health, Education, and Welfare, 1968); Vern Faust. *The counselor-consultant in the elementary school.* (Boston, Houghton-Mifflin Co., 1968), and Dean L. Hummel and S. J. Bonham, Jr., *Pupil personnel services in schools.* (Chicago, Rand McNally, 1968).

The social concerns of the 1960's affected the work of the school social worker. The restructuring focused on the premise that the school was a social system and that different subgroups within the system did not have equal educational opportunities. School social workers attempted to modify conditions and policies that blocked these subgroups from having a meaningful educational experience. The various activities undertaken by school social workers were highly reminiscent of earlier attempts to serve as a school-community agent. In general, the school social worker attempted to prevent, treat, and control problems that arose as a result of the interaction between the child's functioning in a school setting and social forces. The main difference in the helping process was a greater reliance on group work rather than on casework. When working with others in behalf of the child, the school social worker continued to utilize diagnosis and interpretation.

The school social worker continues to have a greater awareness of the influence of the external environment on the school setting than do other pupil personnel workers. He (or she) views the pupil's behavior in school not simply as an interaction between the child and his teacher but as a reflection of social forces operating upon both the child and the teacher. Consequently, by working with community organizations he can help modify the school setting so that children can obtain maximum benefit from their educational experience. The gain is not only to be in terms of learnings but also in terms of socialization. Priority is given to pupils who have problems in the school setting. It is assumed that conditions within the school precipitated the maladjustment rather than conditions within the individuals.

THE SCHOOL PSYCHOLOGIST[8]

The Bureau of Child Study, initiated by the Chicago Public Schools in 1899, was the first psychological services department in the United States. Its task was to study the physical and mental

---

[8] This section represents a synthesis of the historical development of school psychology found in James F. Magary (Ed.) *School psychological services* (Englewood Cliffs, Prentice-Hall, 1967); Robert E. Valett, *The practice of school psychology: Professional problems* (New York, Wiley, 1963); Verne Faust, *op. cit.*; Hummel and Bonham, *op. cit.*

development of children. Based on data of pupil characteristics and needs, the Bureau of Child Study established, first, classes for the mentally handicapped, and later, a variety of types of special instruction classes for exceptional children. The identification of exceptional children and their placement in special instruction classes has characterized the work of psychological services departments in most school districts. However, over the years many other services have been undertaken. Among them are remedial reading, district-wide testing programs, record keeping, work with juvenile delinquents, and work with emotionally disturbed children. In recent years responsibility for the instruction of exceptional children in many school districts has been transferred from psychological services departments to departments of instruction.

The school psychologist is seen by other staff members as a diagnostician. His task is to test pupils who have been referred to him and to recommend their placement for some type of specialized school experience. Placement in classes for gifted pupils or retarded pupils can be made by certified school psychologists in some states. Because of the larger number of pupils who require testing, most school psychologists have little time for working directly with pupils who require remediation or rehabilitation. Among some school psychologists there is some interest in moving away from diagnosis and a crisis orientation to working on prevention programs and learning disabilities.

There are a number of divergent views regarding the future role and function of the school psychologist. The proposed roles include moving from the traditional role of educational diagnostician to that of arbitrator of psychological services. In reviewing the literature on the future role and function of the school psychologist Magary[9] identified the following types of roles: Data oriented problem solver; consultant to teachers; educational programmer; facilitator of adjustment; facilitator of learning; coordinator of prescriptive teaching; specialist in preventive mental health; and master teacher. Some of these roles see the school psychologist as a "clinical psychologist functioning in the schools while others see

---

[9]Magary, *op. cit.*, pp. 686-705.

him as a general educational psychologist in the schools."[10] It is apparent that some of these roles overlap those of the professionally trained school counselor.

Although there is some confusion as to the future role and function of the school psychologist, there is no doubt that the current and traditional role of the school psychologist will be restructured. The movement will probably be away from a gross classification of children (e.g., as gifted and retarded) to that of identifying specific variables in the learning process. The prescribed treatment will be coordinated among the various pupil personnel service workers and will take place in the context of the regular class rather than in specialized instructional classes. The school psychologist will be directly rather than indirectly involved in the treatment process.

OTHER PUPIL PERSONNEL WORKERS

The counselor, school psychologist, and the school social worker are seen as key personnel in pupil personnel programs. Additional personnel are needed if the program is to be balanced and be most useful to staff and pupils. Usually included in a balanced program are the child accountant and attendence worker, school nurse, physician, dental hygienist, psychiatrist, speech therapist, hearing therapist, and personnel associated with pupil appraisal services, remedial services, and special education services. In large metropolitan school districts special education may be part of a regular instruction department or may have its own department. These other pupil personnel workers provide highly specialized services that are ancillary to the instruction phase and require special competencies and skills. For example, the attendance worker not only needs knowledge about compulsory attendance laws but also have an understanding about federal legislation and its impact on minority groups. Usually he determines eligibility for a variety of federally funded programs. Medical personnel may be actively engaged in treatment and prevention. In many school districts they have become teachers in sex education and drug abuse programs.

---

[10]*Ibid.,* p. 686.

DEVELOPMENT OF A
BALANCED PUPIL PERSONNEL PROGRAM

The leadership needed for the development of a balanced pupil personnel program must come from the superintendent of the school district. His view of the function of pupil personnel specialists in education structures the inter-relationships among the school staff. The pupil personnel program reflects how the school district accommodates "to the expectations of society while assisting the individual pupil to optimum development."[11] The inter-relationships among the various specialists are delineated by means of tasks and job functions. The process of pupil personnel work is formalized by means of rules and regulations that stipulate "who is to be seen by whom." It is assumed that rules and regulations lead to uniformity of operations and coordination of effort.

Rules and regulations, although helpful in administrative decision making, tend to generate discord between administrators and pupil personnel workers. For the most part, rules and regulations reflect bureaucratic expectations.[12] These expectations include standardization of work, division of labor, efficiency of technique, task orientation, uniformity of clients' problems, and loyalty to the school. In many instances administrative expectations are in direct contrast to professional expectations. The latter include uniqueness of clients' problems, alternative approaches to work, collaboration with other professionals, and loyalty to professional associations. Because of the differences in expectations, a balanced pupil personnel program is difficult to develop.

Differences in expectations among the professional pupil personnel workers also hinder the development of a balanced pupil personnel program. At times it is difficult for the social worker, school psychologist, and counselor to find agreement as to the manner in which the work in the pupil personnel program should be undertaken. The social worker tends to emphasize the need to understand the community and family, the school psychologist the need

---

[11]Hummel and Bonham, *op. cit.*, p. 64.

[12]Ronald Corwin, "Professional persons in public organizations," *Educational Administrative Quarterly*, Vol. 1, (1965), pp. 1-22.

for diagnosis and treatment, and the counselor the need for adjustment and self-actualization. These foci are reflected in the type of activities undertaken. For example, goals may be stated in terms of society or individual, data obtained on pupils may be idiographic or nomothetic, and the clients may be pupils or families. An additional obstacle to a balanced program in an elementary school is the counselor himself. He represents a threat to the school social worker and school psychologist in that he is a relatively recent addition to the pupil personnel program. Where does he fit in? Since the work requires an interdependency among the professional pupil personnel workers, the inclusion of the counselor affects the perception the staff has of the social worker and school psychologist. What is the counselor's status? This question must be resolved in order for the relationships among the professional pupil personnel workers to be amicable.

The status a person has is a function of the role he has in the organization. Although the term "role" has been defined in many different ways, inherent in most conceptualizations is that individuals "(1) in social settings (2) behave (3) with reference to expectations."[13] The expectations of the community, school administrators, and teachers have an impact on the work of pupil personnel workers especially if one considers "behavior as a function of action and reaction of others and influenced by normative and evaluative factors."[14] However, before expectations can be assigned to an individual, it is necessary "to specify an individual's location in social relationship systems or his 'relational identities.'"[15] In many instances it is difficult to assign a definite set of expectations to counselors, school social workers, and school psychologists because of the divergence of opinions as to their functions. The influence of divergent expectations on the behavior of individuals has been studied by social psychologists. In general, studies have shown that in most organizations members tend to hold incongruent expectations regarding most positions.

---

[13]Neal Gross, Ward S. Mason, and Alexander W. McEachern, *Explorations in role analysis* (New York, Wiley, 1966), p. 17.

[14]*Ibid.*, p. 18.

[15] *Ibid.*, p. 18.

Only in stable organizations is there consensus regarding role behaviors. As a consequence of these investigations, the staff of a school district should assume that there is *a range* of appropriate behaviors for pupil personnel service workers rather than a definite set of tasks that each should perform. There should be some agreement as to the probable range of appropriate behavior in order to help teachers to cognitively structure the situation. This would facilitate referrals and consultation.

The team approach to pupil personnel services has been proposed as a method for reducing the dissonance surrounding the role and function of its workers. Implied in the team approach is the idea that if the whole child is to be helped the entire school staff must be involved in the guidance function.[16] A pupil personnel services team assumes that it has a greater latitude in helping a child than any one member. In addition, when new demands are placed on the school, the team would have greater flexibility in adjusting to them. The basic weakness in most team approaches is that the question of responsibility has not been adequately answered. Who is responsible for the team's action? Since most school administrators are task oriented and are concerned with efficiency and effectiveness, assigning responsibility for the team's action is important to them.

In most descriptions of a pupil personnel team it is difficult to discern how the team functions. In some programs, the function of the team is to develop goals and policies for the pupil personnel program. This primarily consists of developing expectancies and setting boundaries for individual professional workers. The interrelationships among the professional workers are predicated on the skills and competencies. Some team approaches are based on the coordination of specialized activities. This differs from the first approach in that the diagnosis, treatment, and control of problems have been systematized. Case conferences and staff meetings are used to coordinate the help given to children. This concept of the team approach assumes that since each pupil personnel worker has a right to contribute to each case he should be consulted on

---

[16]Herman J. Peters and Michael J. Bathory (eds.), *School counseling: Perspectives and procedures* (Itasca, F. E. Peacock, 1968), p. 316.

all cases. As a consequence, a large backlog of cases can develop.

Most team approaches are based on coordination rather than collaboration. Coordination implies that a child's concern can be resolved by means of a systematic application of specialist skills. It requires that the child's concern be categorized so that the appropriate ordering of treatment can be developed. This view has several weaknesses: (1) serialization of treatment negates the "whole" child concept; (2) treatment tends to be impersonal; (3) responsibility for management is difficult to locate. When a team approach is predicated on collaboration, the child's concern becomes the concern of the entire team. Attention is given to the whole child rather than some part of him. Skills and competencies are used spontaneously rather than in some predetermined order. This approach requires the members to accept the goals of the program without any mental reservations. It further postulates that the specialists are concerned with children rather than with tenets of professional associations.

It should be noted that a "team approach" can function in a pupil personnel program without formally being labeled as such. The term "team" connotes the idea that a set of relationships, either formal or informal, exists among the specialists. The relationship among the specialists reduces the amount of overlap in the services provided, thereby increasing the efficiency of the program. The term "team" further suggests that there is an interdisciplinary approach to problems encountered by the specialists. Consequently, different alternatives to the resolution of the problem from the different disciplines can be considered simultaneously. The process by which a team resolves a problem depends on whether the emphasis is on collaboration or coordination. If the focus is on the skills and competencies of the specialists, then coordination is required. If the focus is on goals, then collaboration is required. There is a lack of evidence to support the idea that the "team approach" increases the effectiveness of the program. It does create a greater awareness among the specialists as to the type of function each undertakes. This may contribute to the development of a balanced pupil personnel program.

The key to the development of a balanced pupil personnel program is to set into proper perspective the relationship between the goals of education and the goals of the pupil personnel services. Just as schools do not focus solely on the 3 R's, the pupil personnel program cannot be just problem oriented. The functions of the program must be stated in proactive rather than reactive terms. To help students to develop into self-actualizing persons, the school staff requires a wide range of competencies, knowledges, and skills. No single specialist can be utilized to help the pupil in his quest for self-actualization. Nor can the "team approach" be employed without restructuring the attitudes and skills of its members. What is needed is for the pupil personnel program to redefine its boundary lines of operation. Instead of restricting itself to the pupil, his teacher, and the classroom, the program must encompass the child's total environment. The program should be balanced not in terms of specialists but in terms of needs of children.

SUMMARY

The counselor as a member of the pupil personnel program provides assistance in helping the school and pupils meet their needs. The school administrator provides leadership in developing a balanced pupil personnel program so that all facets of help are provided rather than a select few. The structure of the program is affected by state and federal legislation and by prescriptions of professional associations. The social worker and the school psychologist help the staff and the parents understand the environment and personal dynamics of the students. In addition, they provide consultation and treatment for those who require it. Other pupil personnel workers such as attendance workers, school nurses, and speech therapists provide highly specialized services that are auxiliary to the instructional process. The interactions among the staff are facilitated if there is consensus regarding the role behaviors of the personnel specialists. This consensus helps set into proper perspective the relationship between goals of education and the goals of pupil personnel work. The counselor in conjunction with the other specialists helps pupils in their development as self-actualized persons.

SUGGESTED READINGS

Peters, H. J., & Shertzer, B.: *Guidance: program development and management*. Columbus, Ohio, Merrill, 1969.

Zudik, L. *Implementing guidance in the elementary school*. Itasca, Ill.: Peacock, 1971.

PART II

THE COUNSELOR AND
THE CHILD

Chapter 6

INDIVIDUAL COUNSELING
AND
PLAY THERAPY

C OUNSELING, AS A CLOSE INDIVIDUAL RELATIONSHIP, is one of the most effective ways of helping another person, particularly a troubled or disturbed person, become more self-actualizing. There are many different theories and approaches to counseling or psychotherapy.[1] Rather than attempt to review these, or the major ones, leaving the student confused by the apparent differences, we shall consider here some of the basic common elements which are included in all approaches.

Counseling is often distinguished from psychotherpy. However, no one has convincingly demonstrated any essential differences. The basic general goal is the same, the process is the same, and the methods and techniques are the same. Perhaps the major difference is the setting in which the individual works. If it is a medical setting, what he does is called psychotherapy; in a non-medical setting the word counseling is usually used. A second difference emphasized by some is the severity of disturbance of the person who is being helped. Counseling, it is said, deals with the "essentially normal" individual, or "client," while psychotherapy is for the severely disturbed person, or "patient." Yet it is not possible to draw a sharp line between the abnormal and the normal. And in practice, those called psychotherapists do

---

[1] C. H. Patterson, *Theories of counseling and psychotherapy,* Sec. Ed. (New York, Harper & Row) 1973.

not work with a patient until he reaches "normality" and then turn him over to a counselor for help with his "normal" problems.

Here, we are not concerned with attempting to make an artificial distinction; our concern is with the nature of the helping relationship, whatever it is called.

THE NATURE OF COUNSELING

Counseling or psychotherpy is a relationship, as indicated above. It is a relationship between a person, the client, who has a psychological problem of some kind, and another person, the counselor, who is trained to provide the kind of relationship which helps the client.

The Goals of Counseling. Relatively little has been written concerning the goals of counseling or psychotherapy. The most comprehensive treatment of this topic is in the book edited by Mahrer.[2] On first impression, it appears that there are as many goals of counseling or psychotherapy as there are writers; at least each theory or approach seems to have different goals. Goals listed include such things as effective biological and social functioning, optimal functioning, personality reorganization, unlearning unadaptive and learning adaptive habits, reduction of anxiety, relief of suffering, maturity combined with adjustment, and facilitation of growth. When one looks closely at the various goals, it becomes clear that they range from highly specific (reduction of anxiety, for example), to very general (facilitation of growth), or from very immediate to ultimate goals. Thus, the concept of levels of goals, introduced in the discussion of the goals of education in Chapter 3, is applicable here.

Parloff, in Mahrer, notes that while the more specific goals appear to differ, differences in the ultimate goal appear to be small. Mahrer summarized the goals of the various contributors to his book as "achieving optimal functioning and reducing psychological pain." It would appear that the latter would occur if the former is achieved. Stated in other terms, the ultimate goal of

---

[2]A. R. Mahrer (ed.) *The goals of psychotherapy* (New York, Appleton-Century-Crofts, 1967).

counseling or psychotherapy is self-actualization. That is, the ultimate goal is the same as that of education.

Mediate goals of counseling or psychotherapy are the more specific or more short-term goals. They include most of the things which school counselors refer to as goals, such things as achieving up to one's ability academically, getting along with other students, and adapting to the classroom situation. The question should be, though it seldom is, raised regarding the criterion by which mediate goals are determined to be desirable. Counselors usually have no other criterion than that of adjustment to the requirements and demands of the school and of society in general. This is essentially a criterion of conformity, and can be detrimental to the development of the individual. The recognition of the ultimate goal of the development of self-actualizing persons provides the criterion for more specific or mediate goals. The counselor must ask the same question which administrators and curriculum specialists should ask in regard to academic requirements—do the specific goals contribute to the development of self-actualizing persons?

If there are ultimate and mediate goals of counseling or psychotherapy, what is the immediate goal? The immediate goal is to begin and continue the process which leads to the mediate and ultimate goals. There are many descriptions of the counseling or psychotherapy process, couched in varied terminology, depending upon the theory or point of view. One common aspect of the process emerges from theory and research. This is client self-exploration, or intrapersonal exploration. Truax and Carkhuff define self-exploration as client activity in "attempting to understand and define his own beliefs, values, motives, and actions," and developed a Scale of Depth of Self-Exploration which defines varying degrees of the process so that interview materials can be rated.[3]

Self-exploration perhaps consists of several aspects or stages. Before an individual can engage in intrapersonal exploration he must be able to reveal, expose, and express himself. Thus the

---

[3]C. B. Truax and R. R. Carkhuff, *Toward effective psychotherapy* (Chicago, Aldins, 1967) pp. 189, 195-208.

first step is self-disclosure. Self-exploration, including perhaps first the exploration of the negative aspects of the self, followed by exploration of the more positive aspects, follows. The later stages lead to increasing self-awareness, and perception of discrepancies between what one is and what one can be, or between the self and the ideal or desirable self. This forms the basis for action toward change in the self.

The Essential Conditions for Counseling or Psychotherapy. What are the conditions which set in motion, and continue, the process of self-exploration? They are the same conditions which facilitate self-actualization, since self-exploration is a means toward self-actualization. These are the conditions described in Chapter 3. They will be considered here again specifically as they apply to the counseling process. But first a word about the general assumptions and atmosphere of the counseling relationship. The counseling relationship is one in which an atmosphere is created in which the individual is able to take responsibility for himself, to begin developing, or restoring, the self-esteem which is necessary for his functioning as a healthy, responsible, independent human being, able to make adequate decisions and resolve problems.

This therapeutic atmosphere is created when the counselor offers or provides certain conditions to the client. These conditions are more dependent on the attitudes and feelings of the counselor than upon any techniques which he uses. They are expressions of the basic philosophy of the counselor toward other people. There are three basic beliefs, assumptions, or attitudes:

1.   Each individual is a person of worth in himself.

2.   Each individual is capable of assuming responsibility for himself, and can, and will under appropriate conditions, become a responsible, independent, self-actualizing person.

3.   Each individual has the right to self-direction, to make his own decisions, to choose or select his own methods or means of achieving self-actualization.

There are at least three basic conditions which are necessary if an atmosphere is to be created in which the individual can take responsibility for himself and his development into a self-actualizing person:

1. *Respect or nonpossessive warmth.* This is similar to Rogers' unconditional positive regard: "To the extent that the therapist finds himself experiencing a warm acceptance of each aspect of the client's experience as being a part of the client, he is experiencing unconditional positive regard."[4] Warmth includes acceptance, interest, concern, prizing, respect, liking. It is nonjudgmental, a valuing without conditions. It is not necessarily acceptance of, or being nonjudgmental with regard to, behavior, but refers to the client as a person. Truax and Carkhuff in defining their Tentative Scale for the Measurement of Nonpossessive Warmth, say that "it involves a nonpossessive caring for him (the client) as a separate person, and thus, a willingness to share equally his joys and aspirations or his depressions and failures. It involves valuing the patient as a person, separate from any evaluation of his behavior or his thoughts."[5]

2. *Empathy or empathic understanding.* A second major characteristic of the atmosphere or conditions for client progress is understanding on the part of the counselor, and the communication of this understanding to the client. It is important to recognize just what is meant by understanding. The kind of understanding which appears to be most effective in counseling is not knowledge of or about the client. It does not consist of the results of a battery of tests, nor of the data in the client's record, nor of extensive case studies, no matter how voluminous or complete. The understanding which appears to be most effective is an empathic understanding. It is understanding which has no trace of evaluation or judging, nor categorizing or labeling in terms of some problem areas or complex, or presumed etiological or causal conditions. An empathic understanding is a "feeling with" another, the entering into his frame of reference—the internal rather than the external frame of reference—so that one sees the world and the other person, insofar as possible, through the eyes of the other. The counselor places himself, or attempts to place himself, in the client's place. He realizes that in order

---

[4] C. R. Rogers, "The necessary and sufficent conditions of therapeutic personality change", *Journal of Consulting Psychology*, Vol. 21 (1957), pp. 95-103.
[5] C. B. Truax and R. R. Carkhuff, *op. cit.*, p. 58.

to really understand another's feelings, attitudes, and behavior, he must see things as the other sees them. For one does not behave in response to the world as it exists—or is assumed to exist —in "reality," but in response to the world as one perceives it.

3. *Therapeutic genuineness.* The third major condition of a good counseling relationship is genuineness. The counselor must be real, honest, freely and deeply himself. He is not playing a role—there is no such thing as a counselor role, which a counselor assumes when he enters the counseling office, or when the client enters his office. He has no facade which he places between himself and the client. In addition, there is no conflict between what he thinks and feels and what he says. This does not mean that the counselor must blurt out all his negative feelings or hostility, since this would be unlikely to be helpful to the client, but that he does not present a false friendship or liking.

Genuineness appears to be misinterpreted by some to mean an "anything-goes" policy. "Genuineness must not be confused, as is so often done, with free license for the therapist to do what he will in therapy, especially to express hostility."[6] There is a difference, as Carkhuff and Berenson point out, between a construct of genuineness and the construct of facilitative or therapeutic genuineness, since, as they note, a genuine person can be destructive. It is unlikely, for example, that a highly authoritarian person, no matter how genuine he is, would be therapeutic.

Nor does genuineness mean that the therapist discloses himself extensively or completely to the client. Truax and Carkhuff, in their definition of the Tentative Scale for the Measurement of Therapist Genuineness or Self-Congruence, note that "being himself... does not mean that the therapist must disclose his total self, but only that whatever he does show is a real aspect of himself, not a response growing out of defensiveness or a merely 'professional' response that has been learned and repeated."[7] Complete self-disclosure is the client's function in self-exploration, and, while the therapist often gains from the therapeutic encoun-

[6] R. R. Carkhuff and B. G. Berenson, *Beyond counseling and therapy* (New York, Holt, Rinehart & Winston, 1967), p. 29.

[7] *Op. cit.,* p. 69.

ter, therapy is for the client, not the therapist. "While it appears of critical importance to avoid the conscious or unconscious facade of 'playing the therapeutic role,' the necessity for the therapist's expressing himself fully at all times is not supported.... However, there exists some tentative evidence indicating the effectiveness in some situations of therapist self-disclosure ... in which the therapist (with discriminations concerning the client's interests and concerns) freely volunteers his personal ideas, attitudes, and experiences which reveal him, to a client, as a unique individual."[8]

These three conditions (or the "central therapeutic ingredients"[9]) appear to be well-established, both theoretically and experimentally. All have been demonstrated to be related both to client self-exploration and to various outcome criteria in counseling.

In addition to these three conditions, there are no doubt other conditions which contribute to a facilitative counseling relationship. Carkhuff and Berenson mention therapist spontaneity, confidence, openness, flexibility, and commitment, and the intensity of the therapeutic contact.[10] Truax and Carkhuff view intensity and intimacy of the therapeutic contact as theoretically a separate aspect of the process.[11] A tentative scale to measure this aspect yielded significant relationships with client self-disclosure and outcome. The scale, however, is significantly related to the three core conditions.

There is one condition, which is probably not closely related to the three core conditions and which, therefore, probably constitutes a fourth condition. This is concreteness or specificity. Concreteness means that the therapist and the client deal with specific feelings, experiences and behavior. It is the opposite of generality and abstraction, or vagueness and ambiguity. Carkhuff and Berenson suggest that concreteness serves at least three important functions: it keeps the therapist's response close to the

---

[8]R. R. Carkhuff and B. G. Berenson, *op. cit.*, pp. 29, 30.

[9]C. B. Truax and R. R. Carkhuff, *op. cit.*

[10]*Op. cit.*, pp. 4, 30.

[11]*Op. cit.*, pp. 289-290.

client's feelings and experiences; it fosters accurateness of understanding by the therapist, allowing for early client corrections of misunderstanding; and it encourages the client to attend to specific problem areas.[12]

Concreteness and specificity would appear to be the opposite of much that is included under interpretation. Many interpretations are generalizations, abstractions, higher level labeling or including a specific experience under a higher level category or classification. Such activity is often not useful. In addition to the threatening nature of many interpretations, which would tend to cut-off self-exploration on the part of the client. Interpretations which are abstractions or generalizations or simply labeling would appear to have the same effect. To take a simple or extreme example, suppose after a client has explored his relationship with his parents, the therapist should suggest that he has an Oedipus complex. The client might well feel that his problem has been solved, or he has insight. But there would probably be little if any change in his behavior. He would also no doubt feel that there was no point in discussing the matter further, or of engaging in further self-exploration.

Ratings on a tentative scale to measure concreteness have been found to be related to client self-exploration and outcomes.[13]

The presence of these conditions provides an atmosphere and a relationship characterized by lack of threat in which the client can engage in self-exploration. As Truax and Carkhuff express it, the conditions operate through four channels, which constitute a hierarchy of immediate goals in counseling or psychotherapy. The first in priority is the reinforcement of approach responses to human relating, which leads to self-disclosure. The second is reinforcement of self-exploration, which includes the identification of sources of anxiety. Third is the elimination of specific anxieties or fears; and fourth is the reinforcement of positive self-concepts and self-evaluations.[14]

---

[12]*Op. cit.*, p. 30.

[13]C. B. Truax and R. R. Carkhuff, "Concreteness: A neglected variable in research in psychotherapy", *Journal of Clinical Psychology*, Vol. 20 (1964) , pp. 264-267.

[14]*Op. cit.*, pp. 151-152.

It is worth noting that there is a reciprocal relationship between the conditions of a good human relationship and the resulting effects on the recipient of the conditions (what Truax and Carkhuff call the principle of reciprocal affect[15]). The recipient of the conditions begins to manifest the conditions in his own behavior. *The conditions are aspects of self-actualization.* Self-actualizing people facilitate self-actualization in others. The facilitative conditions are also the goal of the process—*the conditions of counseling are also the criterion.* Furthermore, the client, in becoming a self-actualizing person, becomes therapeutic for others by providing the conditions for their self-actualization.

The core conditions as they are now known are general and, no doubt, complex. It is possible that they might be broken down into more specific conditions, much as a general factor may be broken up into group and specific factors. It is also possible that there are other core conditions, which are present in successful therapy, which will become apparent as the present conditions are better isolated, defined, and measured.

A central element of the counseling relationship characterized by these conditions is the absence of threat. Although it may appear to be a negative way of looking at counseling and mental health, the concept of threat appears to be extremely important. Threat to the self and the self-concept seems to be the basis for personality disturbances, or poor mental health. The basic need of the individual is the preservation and enhancement of the self; all other needs or drives may be subsumed under this. Frustration of, or threat to, the satisfaction of this basic need results in a lowered evaluation of the self; a loss of self-esteem is the core of personality disturbance.

The influence of threat upon behavior has been demonstrated in many areas. Perception is narrowed, so that the individual literally does not see many aspects of the situation. Under threat the individual may withdraw, even to the point of freezing under extreme threat, being literally paralyzed with fear. On the other hand, under less extreme threat, the individual may become defensive, or aggressive. It may be that what has often been con-

---

[15]*Op. cit.,* p. 151.

sidered instinctive or natural aggressiveness is always a reaction
to a threat, a reaction which is universal because threat, in some
form or other, is universal. That is, while threat, or frustration,
may lead to other reactions besides aggressiveness, aggresiveness
is always a result of threat or frustration. Another method of defense against threat which may occur, in addition to not recognizing or seeing it, and withdrawal and aggression, is self-deception,
which serves as a method of avoiding loss of self-esteem, or of
restoring it.

In everyday life we are aware of the results of pressure or
threat. The individual is unable to perform effectively or efficiently. He is unable to learn easily; he persists in ineffective
attempts at problem-solving rather than in fruitful exploration.
We know that we create resistance when we attempt to change
people by pressure or threat, from the child who becomes more
insistent on doing what he wants to do, to the girl who insists on
marrying the clearly unsuitable boy to whom her parents object.

Changes in attitudes and behavior, self-actualization, the development of independence and responsibility—in short, mental
health or adequate personality development—occur only under
conditions of absence of serious threat to the self and the self-
concept. Since the goal of counseling is the preservation, or
restoration, of good mental health, or of self-esteem, and the
fostering of self-actualization, then it follows that the counseling
situation must be characterized by an absence of threat. Respect
for the client, interest in and acceptance of him as a person,
absence of evaluative attitudes, and understanding of him by
seeing his point of view—all contribute to an atmosphere devoid
of threat.

IMPLEMENTING THE CONDITIONS IN COUNSELING

Formal characteristics of counseling. One may ask if counseling is nothing more than the practicing of good human relationships, why it is so difficult to become a counselor—why shouldn't
everyone be a counselor? To some extent, everyone who practices good human relationships is a counselor, at times, with some
people. But there are certain characteristics of counseling which
set it aside as a specific kind of relationship.

In the first place, the principles of good human relationships, though many of them are known, are not obvious, nor necessarily natural, nor easily practiced. If they were, we should be much more advanced as a society, much happier, with less mental disorder or disturbance, than is the case at present. The understanding of the nature of good human relationships is something that must be learned.

Second, the practice of these principles requires training and experience. The ability to apply the principles is related to the psychological characteristics, or mental health, of the individual applying them. It is not a matter of information or knowledge; it is a matter of attitudes.

Third, the implementation of these principles in a counseling relationship differs somewhat from their practice in everyday relationships. This is because the counseling relationship is a special kind of relationship. It is a formal relationship between two persons who may, and perhaps preferably, have no other relationship. The counseling relationship is for the sole purpose of improving or restoring the mental health, adjustment, or functioning of one of the participants. The counselor consciously and purposefully practices, or applies, the principles of good human relations for the benefit of the counselee.

Fourth, the relationship is usually established between a trained individual and another individual who is in need of help or assistance by reason of being disturbed, unhappy, or in conflict because of an unresolved problem or another condition resulting in dissatisfaction with himself, or lack of self-respect or self-esteem. Whereas the application of the principles of good human relationships in general is for the purpose of maintaining good mental health among normal, or average, individuals, their application in counseling is to restore or improve the mental health of disturbed persons.

Fifth, the relationship is established at the request or desire of the disturbed individual, is continued at his wish, and is characterized by certain conditions: privacy, confidentiality, set time limits, and regularity, on an appointment basis.

Sixth, the counseling relationship, even though it is a formal relationship and may be limited in terms of time relative to the life of the individual (seldom more than an hour a day, more often an hour a week), is a closer, more intense, and deeper relationship than any ordinary social relationship. This is due to its purpose, and to the application of the principles of good human relations in their purest form, divested of the formalities of the usual social relationships.

Counselor activities. Our emphasis has been upon the attitudes of the counselor, as forming an atmosphere in which the client can achieve a feeling of security and self-esteem. But what does the counselor do; how does he act; what does he say? How does he express these attitudes; how does he understand the client and convey this understanding to him? While the attitudes of the counselor are of first importance, their implementation must also be considered. Their expression in a therapeutic manner is not usually natural or automatic. And while it is true that their expression must become natural, so that the counselor may be himself, genuine and not playing a role, it is also true that he must be his counseling and therapeutic self, not his social, or even teaching self.

The objectives of the counselor are to show his genuine interest in the client, to show that he accepts the client as someone worthy of respect and esteem, and to understand the client and communicate this understanding to him. How can the counselor do this, while at the same time allowing the client to be responsible for himself, for his behavior and his decisions, including his communications to the counselor, from the beginning of the counseling process?

The methods, or techniques, by which this can be accomplished, appear to be simple, and yet they are often difficult to practice. The first, and basic, activity of the counselor is listening. To listen is often a difficult thing for a counselor to learn. It is difficult to listen to another because one is thinking about what one wants to say. This kind of listening in order to have one's say in turn is not what is meant by listening in counseling. Listening is not, on the other hand, a passive thing, but an active following of what the client is saying or trying to say. It is listening without interference by one's own personal reactions or associations. The counselor's attention and interest are concentrated upon the client's communication. The listening is complete, in that the client is given freedom to express himself as he desires, to tell his story in his own way, without interruption, without questioning, without probing, without judgments. Remember that the counselor is not a Sergeant Friday trying to get "the facts," but is trying to see things as the client sees them. He is not concerned with obtaining an ordered, complete life history, to be recorded and filed away, but in helping the client express his attitudes, feelings, concerns, and perceptions of himself and the world.

Listening in this manner to what another has to say is a simple but basic manifestation of interest and respect; the client is worth listening to, and what he has to say is important. It is the first step in the client's taking responsibility for himself. The client who begins by asking the counselor what the latter wants to know, what the counselor wants him to talk about, or who suggests that the counselor ask him some questions, is expressing his dependency, his lack of responsibility and self-esteem. The counselor responds by pointing out that the client may decide what he wants to talk about, that the counselor is interested in whatever he has to say, and that the counseling time is his to use to discuss his concerns.

Listening of this kind is the basis for empathic understanding. It is the way by which the counselor is able to learn how the client sees things, and thus is able to perceive from the point of view of the client. Listening and understanding are the basis of, or perhaps constitute, empathy. Empathy is the ability to place oneself in the place of another, to take his role as it were, and to think and feel as he does.

While listening is perhaps the most important way of showing interest in and respect for the client there are other ways of expressing interest and respect. Simple acceptance responses, such as "Yes," "I see," "Uh huh," or "Mm ... Mmmm," are useful. These responses also may represent the second major class of techniques or responses used by the counselor. They indicate to the client that he is understood by the counselor. Simple acceptance responses, of which the above are illustrations, indicate that the counselor is following the client. The simple statement, "I understand," may be all that is necessary at times. To some extent simple restatement of the client's statements, usually called reflection of content, indicates to the client that the counselor understands.

But perhaps the most appropriate way of communicating understanding is by what is known as reflection and clarification of the client's feelings and attitudes. Reflection is the attempt to understand from the client's point of view and to communicate that understanding. The ability to reflect and clarify the feelings and attitudes of the client requires genuine understanding, based upon empathy. It requires skill in focusing upon attitudes and feelings expressed by the client, rather than attention to the content or the objective facts being expressed by the client. In counseling, the significant facts are the attitudes and feelings. This skill must be acquired through training and experience, including supervised practice in counseling.

It is important that the counselor not pretend that he understands when in fact he does not. If the counselor is not able to follow the client, which may happen when the client is confused himself, then he should say so. He may say, "I don't follow you," "I don't understand," or "I'm not sure I know what you're saying." Or if the counselor has some idea, but is not sure, of what the client is expressing he may say, "Is this what you are saying ... ?" or "Let me see if I follow you. Are you saying ... ?" etc. It is not necessary, indeed it is impossible, for the counselor to understand completely all that the client says or feels. He may misunderstand, and show this in his reflections. But the client will correct him, if a non-threatening atmosphere is maintained. As long as the client feels that the counselor is trying to understand him, and shows some evidence of doing so, it appears that progress can occur.

The application of the simple methods described above, at least by a skilled and understanding counselor, appears to be effective in helping clients. These seem to constitute the necessary and sufficient conditions for therapeutic personality change. It does not appear to be necessary for the counselor to question, probe, interpret, give advice, etc. Such techniques are inconsistent with the assumptions and goals of counseling. Interpretation, questioning, and probing may be threatening to the client. Support, persuasion, and advice may prevent the client from assuming responsibility for himself and for the solution of his problems.

It will be noted that no techniques for achieving rapport have been prescribed, because such techniques are neither necessary nor desirable. They are usually the result of insecurity on the part of the counselor rather than the need of the client. Counseling is not a social relationship, nor a social conversation, and should not be begun as such. If the client has come to the counselor voluntarily, he has not come to discuss the weather or the pending football or basketball game. And if he is referred and comes involuntarily, he knows he was not sent to discuss such topics. The counseling interview should be started simply and directly, recognizing what the client comes for. "What's on your mind?" "What would like to talk about?" or "Where would you like to start?" are usually all that is necessary to begin the counseling session.

Rapport is not something to be achieved by artificial techniques or social devices. It is something that develops and exists where the counselor is genuinely interested in the client and his problems. The expression of the attitudes described above are sufficient for the establishment of rapport.

It must be emphasized again that counseling is not a matter of techniques, even the techniques suggested above. Counseling is a relationship in which the attitudes of the counselor are expressed. This expression must be genuine and spontaneous, not labored, or self-conscious. It would perhaps be better if we abandoned the word technique, since it has connotations of being a deliberate, conscious, artful device for achieving a goal, even of manipulating a situation. The expression of the attitudes of the counselor in the counseling situation is not a matter of techniques in this sense. It is a matter of making known to the client his respect, his interest, his understanding, in simple, genuine, spontaneous natural ways.

The Client's Activity. We have discussed the conditions of counseling which must be provided by the counselor, and have indicated that these conditions, when presented and communicated to (or perceived by) the client, lead to such outcomes in the client as appropriate (for him) decisions or choices, increased independence and responsibility, increased self-esteem, or more self-actualizing behavior. But what is the client's contribution to the process? What does he do in the counseling relationship?

These conditions, which minimize threat, permit the client, as we have noted, to engage in the process of self-exploration. It becomes possible for the client to examine himself and his situation, and to see or recognize aspects of which he was unaware or not clearly aware.

Self-exploration is a complex process. It begins with self-disclosure. In the safety of the counseling relationship, where the client realizes he is not being judged or evaluated, he is able to disclose, or expose, his innermost, and often most negative, self, perhaps for the first time in any relationship. He is thus able to recognize, and if not accept, include in his self-concept aspects which he had been unable to recognize. He thus develops a more complete or realistic picture of himself. With this disclosure of himself, he is then able to explore himself, and in relation to others and to his situation. His thinking is more complete and more accurate because it includes elements and aspects which were not present before. In addition to negative and undesirable aspects of himself, he comes to recognize positive and desirable aspects. As a result of his self-exploration, he develops more self-awareness. He becomes more open to himself and to his experiences. He becomes aware of his potentialities and possibilities, of the self that he could be.

COUNSELING AND TEACHING

The fact that the ultimate goal of education and of counseling or psychotherapy is the same, and the basic conditions for achieving this goal are the same, raises the question as to whether teaching and counseling actually differ. The goal and conditions also apply to parent-child and family relationships, and the same question can be raised here also.

There are some differences; those specific to counseling and teaching will be considered here. All helping relationships may be considered as falling on a continuum, with perhaps simple information giving being at one end, and counseling or psychotherapy at the other, with teaching falling somewhere in between. In differentiating between these helping relationships, it is helpful to consider some of the variables underlying the continuum. One of these variables is represented by the cognitive-affective continuum. Thus counseling is highly affective, or concerned with affect, while teaching is more cognitively oriented. Another variable is specificity-generality. Teaching is more specific, while counseling, though dealing with specifics, is more general in that it potentially covers or is concerned with the client's whole life. Again, and probably related to this variable, teaching is more subject oriented, while counseling is less concerned with subject matter conceived as something external to the client. The subject or content of counseling is the client himself. This, again, is probably related to another variable, or a continuum running from relatively impersonal to highly personal. Teaching is less personal than counseling. Finally, while the interpersonal relationship is important, even necessary, in teaching, it is the medium for achieving subject matter learning. In counseling the relationship is the essence.

Thus, while in some instances giving information or suggestions may occur in counseling, the providing of information is not counseling. Giving advice, moralizing, or lecturing are not counseling. There is no sharp dividing line in terms of the cognition-affect continuum, and this contributes one of the greatest sources of confusion between teaching and counseling. Yet it is possible to recognize the difference. An illustration may help clarify this difference:

> *Student:* I've got to decide what I'm going to do this summer—whether to go to summer school and get a couple of courses out of the way so I can graduate early, or to get a job to earn money so I can get a cycle, or to take a good vacation so I will be able to really go at my studies next year. I've been going round and round in my mind, but I just can't decide what to do. My parents say it is up to me, but I need some help.
>
> *Counselor:* I see. You don't know how to go about making a decision. Maybe we should consider how to go about making a decision. Now, there are some good materials available on the decision making process that I can give you, and then we can discuss the procedure you can use in making a decision . . .

This is clearly quite cognitively oriented, and is essentially teaching (though it represents much of what is often called counseling). Another counselor might respond to the student as follows:

> *Counselor:* I see. You're having a tough time making up your mind. Perhaps it would help if we could talk over your feelings about the various possibilities . . . . .

This is clearly less cognitive, more personal, and more affective in nature, and should lead to a relationship more characterized by these latter variables.

PLAY THERAPY

Just as writers on school counseling avoid the term psychotherapy, so do they avoid the term play therapy. The term play counseling, however, is awkward and is not used. Instead, circumlocutions occur, and writers speak of the use of play techniques or play media.

Verbalization is the normal major means of communication among adults and older children. Young children also normally express themselves through play, and at the preschool level they often express themselves more easily through play than through verbalization. Older children are not as restricted in verbal expression; even preschool children often if not usually accompany their play with overt or covert verbalization. But some children have difficulty in verbal expression, particularly of feelings. As Nelson nicely puts it, "in contrast to his older sibling who can and does *verbalize* frustrations, love, anger, and acceptance, the younger child *acts* these feelings. He crashes cars together, he hugs his mom, he shoots his enemy, and he hands another child a toy. He tends to talk less about his feelings than to live them; he is an activist."[16] Nelson quotes Ginott's statement that "the child's play is his talk, and the toys are his words."[17]

The difficulty may be more a matter of not having been taught

---

[16]Richard C. Nelson, "Elementary school counseling with unstructured play media," *Personnel and Guidance Journal*, Vol. 45 (1966), pp. 24-27.

[17]Haim G. Ginott, *Group psychotherapy with children: the theory and practice of play therapy* (New York, McGraw-Hill, 1961), p. 51.

or allowed to express feelings, or having been taught *not* to express feelings, particularly to adults, rather than of inability to do so, however. Nevertheless, it is sometimes difficult to engage a child in a verbal counseling relationship.

When this is the case, play therapy is available, and some counselors use play therapy as the method of choice with young children. Every elementary school counselor thus should be prepared to engage in play therapy.

Facilities and Equipment. Play therapy requires special facilities and equipment. Ideally, a specially furnished room should be available, with a sink and running water, waterproof floors, and screens to protect the windows. The list of suggested materials and toys could be almost endless. A sandbox, clay and finger paints, with a table or easel, are often considered basic. Dolls, a doll family, and a doll house with furniture are felt to be necessary by most therapists. Cars, trains, trucks, airplanes, and toy soldiers and guns are usually included. Mechanical toys are not recommended. Games are best left out. In the writer's experience checkers, dominoes, Chinese checkers and cards can allow the therapist to be trapped in interminable games. Simple, large and sturdy toys are best. Large toys such as the doll house or playhouse materials, may be grouped in sections or corners of the room; smaller toys may be kept on low shelves.

A fully-equipped, special playroom is unlikely to be found in even the most modern elementary school. Most elementary schools do not even have a room suitable for private counseling interviews. Practicum students of the writer have counseled in supply rooms, closets, the nurse's office, or a screened-off corner in a hall. The lack of counseling facilities, particularly for play therapy, was one of the major concerns in conducting the NDEA Institutes for elementary school counselors. Such facilities were available for regular students in the program, who served their practicum in a counseling center operated by the staff of the program.[18] However, experience taught us that counselors can function, and engage in play therapy, in less than optimum facil-

[18]C. H. Patterson, "An off-campus counseling practicum", *Counselor Education and Supervision,* Vol. 5 (1966), pp. 166-168.

ities. Counselors can operate play therapy from a suitcase,[19] or even a briefcase, if necessary. Minimum equipment appeared to be paper and crayons and pencils, clay, and perhaps hand puppets. The only piece of large equipment which was sometimes available was a large, inflated plastic Bozo clown with a weighted bottom which rises back up after being hit. It is the relationship, not the toys, as Alexander notes, that is the key to growth.[20] Toys and equipment should be viewed as facilitators of the relationship, not as significant in themselves. While play in which the child engages by himself may be therapeutic, play in the presence of a therapist who provides a relationship is more effective.

The Process of Play Therapy. As in the case of interview counseling or psychotherapy, there are differences in the way in which play therapy is conducted. Some therapists prefer a structured approach, in which the child is presented with specific toys in a specific situation, often a doll family and doll house with furniture. Often such a structured situation is used in diagnosis and evaluation of severely disturbed children. Other therapists provide an unstructured, open situation for the child. Some limits are set, however. Time is limited, and the session ends when the time is up, as in interview therapy. While aggression may be expressed through the use of toys and equipment, such as dolls, guns, hammers, etc., the child is not permitted to smash windows or attack the therapist.

The basic processes in play therapy are the same as those in interview therapy. The child is free to express his feelings, emotions, confusion, ideas, in play and/or verbally. The therapist responds with interest and understanding through responses which reflect the feelings or thoughts of the child as they are being expressed in the play. Where there is no verbalization by the child, it is often difficult to discern the meaning of the child's activities. Thus, responses may be more a statement of what the child is doing, to indicate that it is acceptable and to allow him

---

[19]E. D. Alexander, "School centered play-therapy program." *Personnel and Guidance Journal,* Vol. 43 (1964), pp. 256-261.
[20]*Ibid.*

to continue, or they may take the form of questioning, indicating uncertainty and a desire to understand.

"The presence of an accepting, understanding, friendly therapist in the playroom gives [the child] a sense of security. The limitations, few as they are, add to this feeling of security and reality. The participation of the therapist during the therapy contact also reinforces the child's feeling of security. The therapist is sensitive to what the child is feeling and expressing through his play and verbalization. She reflects these expressed, emotionalized attitudes back to him in such a way as to help him understand himself a little better."[21]

The play therapist, then, offers the child in play therapy the same conditions which the therapist offers clients in the counseling or therapy interview process. These conditions lead to self-exploration on the part of the child. "In the security of this room where the *child* is the most important person, where he is in command of the situation and of himself, where no one tells him what to do, no one criticizes what he does, no one nags, or suggests, or goads him on, or pries into his private world, he suddenly feels that *here* he can unfold his wings; he can look squarely at himself, for he is accepted completely; he can test out his ideas, he can express himself fully; for this is his world . . . ."[22] He can become a more self-actualizing person.

SOME QUESTIONS AND PROBLEMS IN COUNSELING CHILDREN

An objection raised against counseling in elementary school was mentioned in Chapter 2. This is that most elementary school children are not able to verbalize or to conceptualize their problems. As indicated there, children vary in this ability. Also it was pointed out that the schools discourage and inhibit free verbalization; children are to be seen and not heard—they are not to speak unless they are spoken to and specifically permitted to speak. Thus, children who are capable of verbalizing are often inhibited and afraid to do so in the presence of adults.

---

[21]Virginia M. Axline, *Play therapy* (Boston, Houghton-Mifflin, 1947), pp. 18-19.
[22]*Ibid.*, p. 16.

Play therapy provides an opportunity for the nonverbal child to express himself, and as indicated earlier, is often the preferred approach to helping such children. However, play therapy may be routinely used by counselors when the child is able to verbalize. While it is true that behavior changes may result from play therapy in which the child never verbalizes, it would appear that the ability to verbalize feelings, attitudes, problems, conflicts and solutions would facilitate progress in therapy and allow for transfer and generalization outside the therapy situation. We live in a highly verbal and symbolic society, and the ability to verbalize is itself important in living in that society.

In many if not most play therapy situations the child verbalizes as he plays, and the verbal responses of the therapist encourage verbalization on the part of the child. Sometimes, therapy may be facilitated if play is abandoned and the child is seen in a counseling interview situation. That is, the child may engage in "only play," or relatively nonproductive play when he is always taken to the play room and expected to play. In some situations of this kind in the counseling practicum, where the child appears to be capable of engaging in purely verbal counseling, the author has suggested to the student counselor that, on the next appointment, the child be greeted by saying something like "Why don't we just go in my office today and talk." The point is that not every child should be routinely placed in play therapy, and that play therapy is not always the best approach to all children. As Faust notes, "many more young children are capable of establishing workable relationships at simply a verbal level (without play) than some counselors realize. In fact, in the case of some children, play appears to get in the way of moving the relationship with the counselor along at an effective pace."[23]

A second objection raised about counseling children is that such counseling is bound to be ineffective since almost all the problems of children are of external rather than internal origin, stemming from bad home and family, or sometimes bad classroom, situations. The child, it is claimed, is unable to influence or

---

[23]Verne Faust, *The counselor-consultant in the elementary school* (Boston, Houghton-Mifflin, 1968), p. 155.

change these external conditions. He is helpless in the face of his environment. Therefore, treatment should take the form of environmental intervention, such as working with the parents.

Now certainly efforts should be made to change a bad environment—in extreme cases a child may be removed from a bad home. And certainly, where it appears desirable, the counselor should work with parents and teachers to help the child. But it is not always necessary to work with the parents and sometimes it is not possible, even when it is desirable.

In such situations the counselor should not refuse to work with the child. In the first place, the child is not as helpless as he may seem to be. Children *can* influence their environments. In many if not most family situations the parents and child are caught in a vicious circle of interaction. While ideally, or in seriously disturbed family situations, the entire family should be treated, it is often effective, particularly in less serious situations, to work with the child alone. When the child's behavior changes, his stimulus value to his parents changes, resulting in changes in their behavior. Particularly where the child's behavior has become very irritating to the parents, resulting in behavior on their part which is damaging to the child, a change in such irritating behavior, if persistent, can lead to change in the way the parents treat the child. The vicious circle can be broken. Even in cases of a severely disturbed family situation, treatment of the child can lead to changes in the family environment. The case of Dibs is an excellent illustration.[24]

Secondly, even if, as in some cases, environmental conditions cannot be changed, or immediately corrected, the child can be helped through counseling to face the situation, develop an understanding of the circumstances and why they can't be changed, and obtain some relief from being able to talk with an understanding person about an impossible situation. In some cases, involving parents who will not or even cannot change, even a child can develop an understanding of their behavior, and change his perception of the situation so that it is not as damaging to him as a person.

---

[24]Virginia M. Axline, *Dibs: in search of self: Personality development in play therapy* (Boston, Houghton-Mifflin, 1964).

Axline states the situation clearly: "While the parent or parent-substitute often is an aggravating factor in the case of a maladjusted child, and while therapy might move ahead faster if the adults were also receiving therapy or counseling, it is not necessary for the adults to be helped in order to insure successful play-therapy results. . . . It seems as though the insight and self-understanding gained by these children brought about more adequate ways of coping with their situations, and, since the tensions ceased, this in turn brought about a certain change in the adults."[25]

Finally, some object that children will not come to a counselor voluntarily, in part because they are often not aware that they have a problem or that it is a problem which can be helped by counseling. Of course, the elementary school counselor who has a good relationship with teachers who understand his function is not dependent upon clients volunteering for counseling. No doubt young children do not have the awareness of their need for counseling that older children have. Thus, it becomes very important that the teacher recognize and refer those who might benefit from counseling. However, children will volunteer or ask for counseling if they are aware of the opportunity and have some familiarity with the counselor. It is important that counselors in the elementary school be visible to children, be available to children, and be familiar to the children. Visits to the classroom are helpful. The writer's students have found that children will ask or volunteer to see the counselor when he invites them to come in to talk with or see him.

SUMMARY

Counseling and play therapy are major means by which the counselor can work with individual students whose development as self-actualizing persons is inhibited or blocked by problems, particularly those related to lack of acceptance, understanding, respect or love in their lives. The counselor offers these conditions to children, in the counseling interview or in play therapy,

---

[25]Virginia M. Axline, *Play therapy, op. cit.,* p. 68.

who respond by developing self-understanding, a more adequate self-concept, and behavior which contributes to or represents the self-actualizing process.

SUGGESTED READINGS

Axline, Virginia M.: *Play therapy: the inner dynamics of childhood.* Boston, Houghton-Mifflin, 1947. This classic is still the most useful reference for counselors concerned with play therapy.

Axline, Virginia M.: *Dibs: in search of self. Personality development in play therapy.* Every counselor, and every teacher, should read this fascinating account of the discovery of self in a small boy who, it was speculated, was either mentally retarded, psychotic, or brain-damaged.

Ginott, H. G.: *Group psychotherapy with children: the theory and practice of play therapy.* New York, McGraw-Hill, 1961.

Moustakas, C. E.: *Psychotherapy with children: the living relationship.* New York, Harper & Row, 1959.

Patterson, C. H.: *Relationship counseling and psychotherapy.* New York: Harper & Row, 1974.

Schiffer, M.: *The therapeutic play group.* New York: Grune & Stratton, 1969.

Chapter 7

GROUPS IN
THE ELEMENTARY
SCHOOL

M AN, AS ARISTOTLE NOTED, is a political or social animal. Men have always lived in groups. Because of the prolonged period of helplessness of the human infant, the minimum family group of mother (or mother substitute) and child has been universal for countless ages. Membership in a group is necessary for human survival. Moreover, the individual becomes a person and develops a self only in a group. Children who grow up with little close human contact, such as those who are institutionalized at a very early age in a situation where only minimal physical care is provided, suffer psychological damage.

In the past, and until relatively recently, society provided an adequate number and kinds of small social groups (primary or face-to-face groups as sociologists have designated them) to meet the needs of the developing individual. But this is changing. The family has become smaller; neighborhood groups hardly exist any longer; the small, close church groups have given way to large, formal congregations in which the members hardly know each other.

With the decline of the family, the neighborhood and the church, the school has been given more and more responsibility for the child and his development. One of the functions which the school has not yet adequately assumed is the provision of a continuing group experience for children. With the decline of the family, it is important, and necessary, that some agency or institution of society provide the opportunity for children to learn to live with others in groups. At the adult level, we are already seeing the demands of parents that the school become a center for the community, thus in effect, to some extent, replacing the informal neighborhood gathering places.

SOME DEFINITIONS OF TERMS

Cattell has defined a *group* as "a collection of organisms in which the existence of all (in their given relationships) is necessary to the satisfaction of certain individual needs."[1] Homans defines a group as "a number of persons who communicate with one another over a span of time and who are few enough so that each person is able to communicate with all others, not second hand, through other people, but face to face."[2] Warters (1960) extends the definition of a group "to common purposes, satisfaction of individual needs, interaction, and interdependence of members."[3] Muro and Freeman define a group "as a collection of individuals who have a common goal, interact, are interdependent, have similar or common needs and stay together for a period of time."[4]

Group dynamics has been defined in various ways. Basically it is concerned with the structure and function of groups. "Group dynamics is a term which refers to the interacting forces within the group as they organize and operate to achieve their objectives."[5] Cartwright and Zander summarize, "We have proposed that group dynamics should be defined as a field of inquiry dedicated to advancing knowledge about the nature of groups, the laws of their development, and their interrelations with individ-

[1] R. B. Cattell, "New concepts for measuring leadership in terms of group syntality," *Human Relations*, Vol. 4 (1951), pp. 161-184.

[2] G. C. Homans, *The human group* (New York, Harcourt, Brace & World, 1950).

[3] Jane Warters, *Group guidance: principles and practice* (New York, McGraw-Hill, 1960).

[4] J. J. Muro and S. L. Freeman (eds.), *Readings in group counseling* (Scranton, International, 1968).

[5] B. Shertzer and S. C. Stone, *Fundamentals of guidance* (Boston, Houghton-Mifflin, 1966).

uals, other groups, and larger institutions."[6] The essential focus
of group dynamics is on why: Why do groups form? Why do
changes take place in groups? Why are some groups more co-
hesive than others? Although knowledge of group dynamics is
essential for being a skilled group counselor, group counseling is
more than the application of principles of group dynamics.

Group guidance can be thought of as a vehicle for providing
information about the environment rather than providing opportunities for exploration of feelings and attitudes. Its focus is on
some guidance objective. Group guidance is task oriented. Its
purpose is the completion of some specified or stated goal of the
group or institution. This would include orientation programs,
group testing programs, dissemination of educational and occupational information, etc.

The many activities included under the term group guidance
are not counseling. Group guidance is closely related to teaching. It is focused on content or subject matter, and its orientation
is intellectual or cognitive in nature. It is relatively impersonal,
in part because of the nature of the content, which, even if it
deals with the opinions or perceptions of individuals, does not
focus on the person who is expressing them but upon the content. Thus, group guidance which is concerned with life problems,
life adjustment, mental hygiene, human relations, personality and
interpersonal relationships deals with these areas from a content
or informational point of view, rather than with their meaning or
implications for the individual. The object is to impart information rather than to change the person receiving the information
in some way.

The concern with subject matter leads to a certain structuring
of the process. It is essentially a discussion method of teaching.
But rather than a free discussion, it is guided, both in terms of a
sequence in which material is presented, or assigned for reading,
and in terms of the control of the discussion by the leader or instructor, who sets limits in terms of the topic to be discussed.

Group guidance usually involves large groups of students of

[6]D. Cartwright and A. Zander (eds.), *Group dynamics: research and theory*, Sec.
Ed. (New York, Harper & Row, 1960).

classroom size or even larger. This is possible because the focus, while concerned with reaching individuals with information, is not on the individual's use of the information, his reaction to it, or his problems in accepting and using it. While the group may be problem centered, it is the general problem of the group which is dealt with, rather than the individual problems of members of the group. The objective is to use the group to get information to individuals in a more economical way.

Even groups which are not strictly instructional are not usually counseling groups. Some groups are formed to attempt to solve problems or reach decisions. These are usually designated as *task-oriented groups*. Their purpose is to achieve a group objective; they are concerned with developing group concensus as a prelude to group action. They are not concerned with the problems or actions of individuals. While these groups involve psychological factors, usually contained under the rubric of group dynamics, and while they do involve feelings, attitudes and emotions, they are not concerned with the psychological development of the individual.

Group counseling is quite different from both these kinds of groups. It is not concerned with doing something to or for the members of the group—to educate, inform, or train them. Like individual counseling, it assumes that students in the group are not interested in or in need of counseling simply because they lack information. There is no common specific goal for all members of a counseling group. Group counseling has no content agenda, no planned sequence of topics to be covered. There is no limitation upon open expression, and no limitation upon content or subject matter.

Group counseling is usually differentiated from *group psychotherapy* in that the latter's focus is on severe emotional problems, and the reconstruction of personality, and is long-term in nature, while the former is concerned with normals, problem-solving, and reality situations. Attempts to differentiate between them are unsatisfactory and lead to artificial and often meaningless distinctions. Group therapy is practiced by psychiatrists and psychologists, in a medical setting. Group counseling is practiced

by counselors (and to some extent by others such as social workers and clergymen) in a nonmedical setting. The difference is in
the degree of disturbance of the clients. As Ohlsen notes, "psychotherapy differs from counseling primarily in terms of the persons treated rather than in the treatment process."[7] The process
of group counseling is essentially the same as the process of
group psychotherapy.

Group counseling—and group psychotherapy—may appear to
be like other groups which are rapidly springing up in our society
under such designations as *sensitivity groups, T groups* and *encounter groups*. There are some basic similarities, but there are
differences, which, however, are becoming blurred in practice.
Counseling and therapy groups are usually considered to be for
persons who have problems or are disturbed more than the average or "normal" individual. While this may be so, this is actually
not a significant difference. There is no sharp line between the
normal person and the disturbed person—we all have problems
and we all are disturbed at times. We all have feelings, attitudes
and emotions which are at some time to some degree disturbing
to us and constitute a problem. All—or almost all—can benefit
from improved interpersonal relationships, from developing close
and open relationships with others, of the kind experienced in
group counseling. These are the goals of counseling, or are included in the general goal of self-actualization or the search for
identity. Thus individuals at all levels of "adjustment" can become more self-actualizing. And the method or process for
achieving this is the same, regardless of the level at which the
individual is functioning. The method consists of the experiencing of a good (therapeutic) human relationship.

It is the recognition of this which has been part of the driving
force behind sensitivity and encounter groups. They are being
offered to "normal" individuals, who perhaps would not like to
become members of counseling or therapy groups. There would
appear to be no harm in using these terms, rather than group

---

[7]M. M. Ohlsen, *Group counseling* (New York, Holt, Rinehart & Winston, 1970),
p. 46.

counseling, for groups of people with no pressing or serious problems, including many students in the school.

There are, thus, various kinds of groups, differing in, among other things, size and purpose. They range in size from a classroom to the encounter or counseling group of five to ten. They range in purpose from simple dissemination of information, as in guidance groups, through rather specific group goals, as in task oriented groups, to the improvement of intrapersonal and interpersonal adjustment or functioning. We shall consider briefly several kinds of groups which should be part of elementary school education.

THE CLASSROOM AS A GROUP

The teacher who faces a class of from twenty-five to forty children in September does not face a group. And usually, unfortunately, the teacher leaving that same class in May or June does not leave a group. A class is usually an "aggregate," defined by Gorman as "a collection of human beings brought together to accomplish some task." He continues: "An *aggregate* differs from a group in that members of an aggregate maintain their individual defenses at all times, interact in a formal manner, refuse to deal with their feelings with each other, and remain fairly tentative, untrusting and suspicious of each other. The typical school classroom is a setting in which students do not know other students, and no one really knows the teacher as a person."[8]

A class may become a group. One of the requirements of a group is that there be interaction and communication among all its members. In the usual classroom, communication is almost entirely from the teacher to the students, with some, but usually little, communication from the student to the teacher. Even in active, informal, and effective classrooms there is usually little, if any, communication among the students; this is usually true of so-called discussion groups in the classroom.

This chapter is not concerned with the social psychology of the classroom, classroom dynamics, or classroom management,

---

[8]Alfred H. Gorman, *Teachers and learners: the interactive process* (Boston, Allyn & Bacon, 1969), p. 3n.

nor with teacher attitudes and behavior as related to the facilitation of the personal development or self-actualization of students. These topics are considered in other chapters. Here we are interested in the use of classroom size groups for providing a group experience, and experience in interpersonal relations for students.

While the classroom size group is too large for the intense, intimate experience possible in a small group, it is possible to provide a learning experience in interpersonal relations and psychological education in a classroom size group. Clark Moustakas at the Merrill Palmer School in Detroit began offering a two-semester Seminar in Interpersonal Relations for teachers, counselors and principals over twenty years ago. The purpose of the seminar was "to help the individual teacher express and explore the values, meanings, and dynamics of personal and professional experience, to achieve self-awareness, and to develop sensitive, understanding, responsive attitudes in relations with children and parents."[9] Teachers in the seminar worked with students in classroom groups on a regular basis of one or two periods a week, sometimes more. Although some teachers structured the meetings, and some introduced activities such as drawing, or writing of student journals, the meetings usually consisted of free discussions, particularly in the upper grades.

John Seeley conducted a project a number of years ago in which teachers were trained in human relations over a period of a year. Part of the training consisted of conducting "Human Relations Classes" in schools. These were designed "to afford 'normal' children in everyday classrooms a regular exposure to . . . 'free' discussion . . . to aid the child to understand himself, his peers, and the rest of the world in which he lived, at least in its most immediate bearing on his self-definition and his most general and profound feelings."[10] The classes were based on "the belief that people (in this case children) really free (externally)

[9]Clark E. Moustakas, "A human relations seminar at the Merrill Palmer School, *Personnel and Guidance Journal*," Vol. 37 (1959), pp. 342-349. Reprinted in C. H. Patterson (ed.), *The counselor in the school: selected readings* (New York: McGraw-Hill, 1967).

[10]John R. Seeley, "The Forest Hill Village," "Human Relations Classes." *Personnel and Guidance Journal*, Vol. 37 (1957), pp. 424-434.

to talk about anything will finally talk about everything, but also, in the curious circling way such communication has, will concentrate on those matters that have for them vital psychodynamic import." The sessions were conducted weekly in several classes from the fourth to the twelfth grades by a teacher (or a project staff member) from outside the school, unlike the Merrill Palmer seminar procedure, where the teachers worked with their own students.

The reactions of the students and teachers in these group meetings were interesting. Moustakas reports that the teachers had difficulty in convincing the students that what they talked about would be held in confidence. Seeley notes that the teachers in his project were surprised at the lack of problems of discipline or control, at the emotional involvement of the children, at their active participation, and at the content of their discussions. Some teachers were uncomfortable about the lack of logical problem-solving, the "waste of time" in coming to a point—taking hours for what a good teacher could tell them in ten minutes—the jumping about from topic to topic, and leaving things unfinished.

William Glasser emphasizes the use of groups to reduce failure in children in the school.[11] He recommends "classroom meetings," led by the teacher, beginning with the first grade. In the lower grades the meeting should last from ten to thirty minutes, and from thirty to forty-five minutes in the upper elementary grades (or through grade 8). He describes three types of meetings: (1) *educational-diagnostic* meetings, dealing with student understanding of the curriculum; (2) *open-ended* meetings, concerned with intellectually important subjects; and (3) *social-problem-solving* meetings, relating to the student's social behaviors that constitute problems in the school.

In all of the meetings the teacher leads a nonjudgmental discussion. It is the social-problem-solving type of meeting which is most closely related to the kind of groups discussed in this chapter. Here the students deal with any problem brought up by a student about himself or another student, by the teacher, or

---

[11]William Glasser, *Schools without failure* (New York, Harper & Row, 1969), Chapter 10.

by an administrator. The discussion is directed toward solving the problem, not to judge or punish the student or students involved. The class, though not the teacher, may make judgments which work toward positive solutions.

The class forms in a circle for these meetings, since they are not successful when the students are seated in the usual classroom arrangement. Glasser states that teachers often resist this requirement.

According to Glasser, in these meetings "each child learns that he is important to every other child, that what he says is heard by everyone, and that his ideas count . . . children learn that their peers care about them. They learn to solve the problems of their world."

The fact that in a group there must be communication—or the opportunity for communication—among all possible pairs of students places a limit on the extent to which a classroom can become an effective group. The larger the group, the less opportunity there is for each person to interact which each other person in the group. This becomes a limitation upon the group process and progress.

It is therefore necessary that smaller groups be made available for student learning of interpersonal relations.

TASK ORIENTED GROUPS

Although most groups in the school, and in society as a whole until very recently, have been task oriented groups, very little has been written about such groups, except for the particular kind of task oriented group known as the T (for training) group. Task oriented groups are groups which are formed to achieve a specific and restricted purpose which, though involving the group, is usually imposed from the outside. Thus, the T group has as its purpose the training of its members in the techniques and dynamics of interpersonal relations.

The classroom, as a group, is a task oriented group. Other groups which have externally imposed goals, representing the demands of society, are Four-H groups, Boy Scouts and Girl Scouts, Future Farmers of America, etc. Other groups in the school in addition to the classroom are remedial teaching groups, tutoring groups, study habit groups, extracurricular clubs and societies, etc.

Task oriented groups are characterized, then, by having a specific and limited goal. This goal determines the structure and function of the group. Such groups, then, are restricted in function, and highly structured. Much of the literature on groups and the group process is directed toward task oriented groups. Parsons and Shils view behavior in its most elementary form as including the following aspects:

1. Behavior is oriented toward attaining *ends* or goals.
2. It takes place in *situations.*
3. It is *normatively regulated.*
4. It involves an expenditure of *effort* or *"motivation."*[12]

All behavior is thus considered to be structured, so that actions are performed in a socially approved manner and are directed toward some end. The end is the answer to the question: What to do? And it leads to answers to the following questions: How to do it? When to do it? And, in the case of a group: Who is to do it?

Cowley suggests that groups and organizations in order to reach their goals should systematically develop structures and functions that help them achieve their objectives. Outlined below are the steps that Cowley believes are essential for group or organizational development:

1. General emphasis
   a. core functions (main activity)
   b. complementary functions (activities that are inherent in the total action)
   c. self-continuity functions (policy control, operational control, routines)
2. Purpose or intent
   a. aim, end goal
   b. value of purpose or intent

---

[12]Talcott Parsons and E. Shils (eds.), *Toward a general theory of action* (Cambridge, Harvard University Press, 1951).

3. Operations
   a. people (personnel, clientele, external to organization)
   b. resources (*tangible:* facilities, equipment, funds; *intangible:* spirit, public opinion, desire)
   c. structure of organization (formal and informal)
   d. plan of operation (process, routines, time requirements, assignments)
4. External controls and pressures
   a. Institutions (federal, state, local government, schools, home)
   b. Environment (parents, clientele)
   c. Historical antecedents
5. Outcomes
   a. Product (what is accomplished; criteria for evaluation of product)
   b. Professional accomplishment
   c. Organizational or group accomplishment[13]

The above outline is presented because an analysis of it suggests that most task oriented activities minimize individual development. The group activities focus on goals external to the individual and as a consequence, personal development is a by-product of the group process. This is in contrast to groups like those formed for counseling or therapeutic purposes whose objective is individual development. Task oriented groups demand that its members assume instrumental roles so that the goals of the group can be achieved. The roles are prescriptive and normative in nature. Personal development is enhanced when the individual has an opportunity to undertake expressive roles. These roles occur when the situation can generate self interest and self activity. In essence instrumental roles are *other* oriented while expressive roles are *self* oriented. Most of the functions in a task oriented group require instrumental roles rather than expressive roles. Consequently, the adult leader should provide some opportunity for expressive behavior.

---

[13]W. H. Cowley, "A tentative elastic taxonomy applied to education." In Esther Lloyd-Jones and Esther M. Westerveld (eds.), *Behavioral science and guidance* (New York, Teachers College Press, Columbia University, 1963).

The work of Parsons and Bales suggests that group activity goes through a set of phases.

> One can hypothesize that the necessity of adaptation to the outer situation leads to instrumentally oriented activity, which in turn tends to create strains in the existing integration of the group. When these strains grow acute enough, activity turns to the expression of social-emotional tensions and the reintegration of the group. While integration is being achieved, however, the demands of adaptation wait, and activity eventually turns again to the adaptive-instrumental task.[14]

The above hypothesis was reified into a model that was called AGIL (A=adoptation; G=goal attainment; I= integration; L= latent pattern maintenance). Parsons and Bales developed a series of 2 x 2 grids that depict how the AGIL model operates in task oriented situations. They suggest that "both therapy and socialization involve the same basic phases as task performance."[15] However, the socialization is the reverse of the task performance.

A composite of the various grids is shown in Figure 7-1.

Dorothy Stock and Herbert Thelen advance a theoretical formulation that in part complements that of Parsons and Bales. They suggest that the group's mood and members' individual affective reactions to their situation generate an emotional state that affects the goal-seeking aspects of the group. An individual's expressive behavior is influenced by the group mood and his own predispositions. The emotional tensions inherent in group work do not necessarily follow a predictable sequence. "Movement toward maturity involves an increased integration of emotionality with work such that the emotional needs of the group are progressively more stimulating to and supportive of the work needs."[16] Parsons and Bales suggest that "expressiveness" is characteristic in the integrative phase.

---

[14]Talcott Parsons and R. Bales, *Family: socialization and interaction process* (New York, Free Press, 1955).

[15]*Ibid.*

[16]Dorothy Stock and H. Thelen, *Emotional dynamics and group culture* (New York, New York University Press, 1958).

Figure 7-1.

AGIL MODEL (Adapted from *Family: Socialization and Interaction.* Parsons & Bales)

A

G

Adaptive Instrumental

Imposed goals and situational exigencies generate
Concerns for group
Action Reaction
Cognitive Differentiation
Conversion of old structures into motivation
Goal Striving
Reality Testing
Approval

Goal Attainment

Response to demands of situation
Purposive effort required
Commitment
Implementation
Expectancies based on degree of mastery & competence
Supportive Activity (by group and leader)
Creative Expression (Process and Product)
Reward of acceptable performance
Expression of Affect by individual
Appreciation

Latent Pattern Maintenance

Pattern maintenance roles (Ascribed, normative, achieved, and negative)
Accomplishment
Status Recognition
Esteem

Integration-Expressive

Value and Norm integration
Group Loyalty
Stability of behavior pattern
Development of interpersonal relationship
Group responsibility
Stability of process
Identification

L

I

An individual's expressive behavior can be enhanced if a group process based on TARGET is utilized. TARGET is an acronym for a group process model derived from the work of Stock and Thelen. (T=topic; A=affect; R=role; G=group; E=expressiveness; T=togetherness). A topic (project) selected by the leader is presented to a group but the specific means and aims for accomplishing or completing the task are defined by the group. The roles necessary for completing the task are achieved by individual group members rather than prescribed by the leader. Defining the means and aims and permitting members to achieve roles allows the group to be expressive and the resultant interaction generates normative behavior (togetherness). Although the boundary lines for interaction are set by the leader, the process leads to emotional satisfaction because it is predicated on allowing members to assume expressive roles. The concept of TARGET is very similar to the I (integrative) quadrant of AGIL.

A leader should be aware that the primary function of TARGET is to facilitate socialization (learning social control) rather than task performance. The task in TARGET is used as a vehicle through which an individual learns an instrumental role through expressive behavior. The TARGET concept permits an individual to differentiate between "self" and "others" while operating within prescribed social conditions. The task, because it presents only a limited threat, helps to generate a relationship that enhances objectivity and reality testing. In dealing with social reality (the task or project), the individual has an opportunity to evaluate his life style. In his appraisal of how he carries out instrumental roles (functions that facilitate reaching a goal) he can contrast this behavior with his expressive self. In contrasting the discrepancies between instrumental and expressive behavior an individual can arrive at an index of social maturity. The TARGET process provides an avenue through which an individual can acquire acceptable modes of self expression.

Effective group work requires a careful orchestration of principles of group dynamics and individual development. Stock and Thelen suggest that the individual's current maturity level be considered in the formation of groups. This proposition sug-

gests that youth leaders be familiar with the concepts of interpersonal orientation, and information processing. These two
factors, interpersonal orientation, and information processing, reflect the level of conceptual development. In part the quality of
interpersonal relations is determined by the degree of flexibility
inherent in the individual's cognitive make-up.

The child's skill in differentiating between people, things, and
situations and his flexibility in meeting the demands of people,
things, and situations affect the quality of interpersonal functioning. Hunt makes the following relationship between trainee
characteristics (group member) and objectives of training (task,
topic, or project):

TRAINEE CHARACTERISTICS	RELATED INTERVENTION CHARACTERISTICS
skill level	content of presentation
cognitive orientation	structure of presentation
value orientation	value content of presentation
motivational orientation	form of feedback and reward[17]

Task oriented groups following the AGIL or TARGET model
require the group members to have an adaptive orientation towards the demands placed on them. The group members must
be able to differentiate the task's component parts and be able
to order them into a sequence appropriate for accomplishment.
Becoming aware of the content enhances ego involvement and
personal commitment to the task. The skill with which one can
differentiate the demands affects the motivational level. Schroder,
Driver, and Streufert suggest that the skill with which an individual can process information can be classified into four levels. A
person at the lowest level of information processing is basically
a rule follower, has some awareness of the goal, and has minimal
differentiating ability. His behavior is externally controlled and
his thinking is categorical (i.e. an object is classified as belonging
either to one of two categories on the basis of a simple fixed rule).

A person who functions at the highest conceptual level is more

---

[17]D. E. Hunt, Differential training in teacher education and its implications for increasing flexibility in teaching. Quoted in B. R. Joyce, *New strategies in social
education* (Chicago, *Science Research Associates,* 1972), pp. 227-229.

than a rule follower. He makes inferences from rules, makes connections between rules, and feels free to combine rules from various rule following activities to meet the demands of the situation. The individual's behavior is internally controlled; that is, the individual perceives and acts selectively rather than impulsively. In part, his behavior is guided by future considerations. In Piaget's conception the person at a high level of conceptual development can deal effectively with abstractions while the one at the lowest level is essentially concerned with concrete matters.[18]

It can readily be inferred that the content, structure, process, and feedback are affected by the conceptual level of the group members. The practice of grouping children by age levels may not necessarily be appropriate. The nature of the task, skills required for its completion, and the type of reward system should be used to group children for project activity.

Hunt suggests that a child's interpersonal orientation progresses through a set of four stages. "Conceptual development is a continuous process which under optimal conditions, proceeds in a given order to the most abstract state." Hunt postulates the training or environments that facilitate the optimal development of each stage. Figure 7-2 gives a brief résumé of Hunt's sequence for conceptual development.[19]

The various theoretical formulations that have been reviewed do not by themselves provide the means for insuring instant success with task groups. Part of the difficulty with leading task oriented groups centers on the purpose for developing the groups. These groups tend to be "target groups," that is, individuals in these groups have been selected for change from a framework external to their life style. Most youth groups are formed to develop certain types of competencies, assist in value formation, or facilitate creative growth. Usually personal adjustment of the members receives very little consideration. It should be remem-

---

[18]H. M. Shroder, M. Driver, and S. Streufert, *Human information processing* (New York, Holt, Rinehart & Winston, 1967).

[19]D. E. Hunt, "A conceptual systems change model and its application to education". In O. J. Harvey (ed.), *Experience, structure and adaptibility* (New York, Springer, 1966).

Figure 7-2.

STAGE	SELF-OTHER ORIENTATION	STAGE CHARACTERISTICS	ENVIRONMENT	GROUP WORK	PRESCRIBED ENVIRONMENT
SUB I	(dashed circle)	Unorganized before assimilation of cultural standards	Clearly organized within normative structure. / Normatively unclear or inconsistent.	Egocentric, very concrete, impulsive, low frustration tolerance.	Highly structured consistent environment, providing many specific experiences.
OPEN I	other / self	Learning the "ground rules" for interpersonal relations	Emphasis on autonomy within normative structure	Concerned with rules, dependent on authority categorical thinking	Encourage autonomy within normative standards
OPEN II	self / other	Learning about oneself and how distinguished from general standards	Highly autonomous with low normative standards	Independent, inquiring, self-assertive, more alternatives available	Highly autonomous with opportunity for self-selected individual projects and activities.
OPEN III	self	Applying these self anchored dimensions to an emphatic understanding of other persons and the difference between them			
OPEN IV		Placing these dimensions applicable to self and others into meaningful integrated relations			

Figure 7-3.

GROUP	GOAL	LEADER	CHILD	MATERIALS
Unstructured materials approach	1. Recognition of self 2. Understanding that impulse can be controlled 3. Living within social boundaries	1. Cognitive stimulant 2. Rewards 3. Intrudes (approves, disapproves, etc.) 4. Provides materials but not goals	1. Forced to think 2. Free to use material	1. Conductive to creation, control, and change 2. No end product 3. Freedom of action
Unstructured material Structured approach	1. Improved Self-concept 2. Improved impulse control 3. Improved social interaction	1. Activity pre-selected 2. Acts as participant 3. Helps child manipulate things and people in acceptable manner	1. Forced to think about something 2. Reality testing 3. Basic interaction with others	1. Designed to place limits on action 2. Some skill developed 3. Process rather than product emphasis
Unstructured material Unstructured approach	1. Reduce egocentric behavior 2. Build relationship between things & people 3. Deal effectively with social realities 4. Evaluation of personal goals	1. Materials selected with child 2. Facilitates interpersonal relations 3. Active in skill presentation (minimal emphasis) 4. Identifying figure 5. Rewards behavior	1. To learn practical working relationships 2. Internalizes hostility 3. Respects property	1. May facilitate skill development 2. Used to develop relations and cooperation 3. No end product 4. Has an acceptable standard of performance
Structured material approach	1. Improved social reality 2. Development of acceptance 3. Reality relationships	1. Materials selected with child 2. Provides for success 3. Formal 4. Teach skill 5. Facilitator	1. Completes project 2. Tries to exhibit selective behavior 3. Independent	1. Conductive to generating a product 2. Cognitive or creative skill development 3. Enhances reality relations

Adapted from *Play Therapy with Mentally Subnormal Children*, Henry Leland and Daniel Smith, N.Y., Grune and Stratton, 1965.

bered that focusing on instrumental activity may minimize expressive behavior. Hunt postulates that a low level of interpersonal orientation may prevent or hinder meaningful group activity. To what degree should a youth leader provide assistance or activities that enhance conceptual development? Personal adjustment? Stock and Thelen are of the opinion that the emotional tone of the group and individual predispositions affect the work output.

What should a youth leader do if children in the group have an inadequate interpersonal orientation set? To a certain degree the answer to this question depends on the purposes of the organization. If this is within the general policy, a youth leader could provide the necessary environment (Hunt's idea) to promote conceptual development. The problem child or children would generally be in Hunt's sub I stage of development. Leland and Smith offer a series of suggestions that may be of use to youth leaders. (One should not minimize the value of their remarks because of the title of their book.) Figure 7-3 is a chart that summarizes their suggestions.[20]

The dilemma can be ameliorated but not necessarily resolved by using a theoretical formulation advanced by Argyris. He proposes that the concept of competence acquisition, a process for resolving interpersonal problems, can be learned through appropriate group work. The process is especially useful for those who are competence or growth oriented. Although Argyris focuses on expressive behavior, his observations can be extrapolated to instrumental behavior that is inherent in task performance.[21]

Argyris states that the quality of interpersonal relations is predicated, in part, on self-awareness, self-acceptance, and trust in others. These preconditions to interpersonal relations are dependent on the individual's level of conceptual development. Another factor that affects the quality of interpersonal relations is the manner in which an individual perceives the situation. If the individual perceives the situation as non-threatening, need

---

[20]H. Leland and D. Smith, *Play therapy with mentally subnormal children* (N. Y. Grune and Stratton, 1965).

[21]C. Argyris, "Conditions for competence acquisition and therapy," *Journal of Applied Behavioral Science*, Vol. 4 (1968), pp. 147-177.

satisfying, and is willing to become involved in it, he is said to be "open." If the individual perceives the situation as threatening, non-need satisfying, uses defense mechanisms to distort it, and is not willing to participate in it, then he is said to be "closed." A person's amount of "openness" or "closedness" varies with situations. The value of this observation for youth leaders lies in being able to vary tactics for encouraging participation in an activity. If the leader senses that the situation is "closed," then a different structure and content must be used from those situations that are classified as "open."

Argyris believes that an essential aspect of competence acquisition is the provision for psychological success. He uses the writings of Kurt Lewin as a source for developing the concept of psychological success. Argyris includes the following as being necessary for generating psychological success; (1) definition of their own learning goal; (2) development of their paths to the goal; (3) relating the goal and paths to control needs; (4) challenging them to achieve beyond their present level of abilities.

Psychological success can also be enhanced through appropriate feedback that provides information that is (1) minimally distorted; (2) directly verifiable; (3) minimally evaluative. This type of feedback is especially useful in competence oriented situations. In these types of situations the youth leader should help children differentiate between observable and inferred information. The leader should minimize feedback that is characterized by interpretation and psychological insight. The suggested feedback procedures work better in open rather than closed situations. Although in some task performance situations evaluation is necessary, the type of appraisal should be based on the conceptual development of the children. Figure 7-4 depicts a modified version of the Argyris concept of competence acquisition.

The central thesis inherent in Argyris is that the leader does not manipulate people but the environment. The leader provides conditions in which an individual can be both expressive and creative. Hunt complements this viewpoint by stating that "a major educational goal ... is to encourage greater adaptive capacity and flexibility." Hunt does suggest that conceptual de-

Figure 7-4.

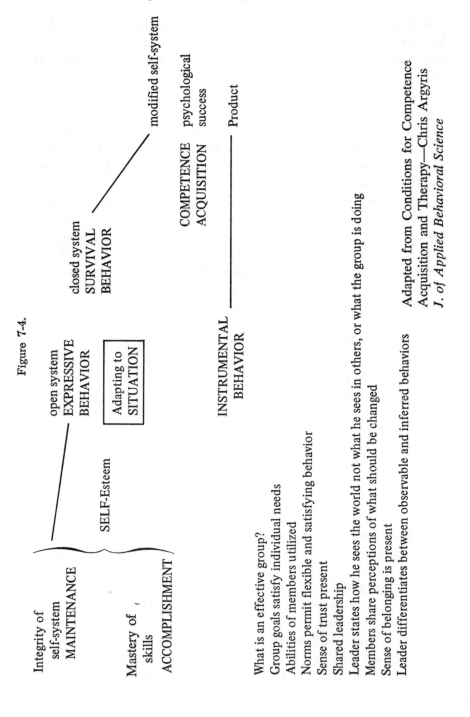

Integrity of
self-system
MAINTENANCE

open system
EXPRESSIVE
BEHAVIOR

closed system
SURVIVAL
BEHAVIOR

modified self-system

SELF-Esteem

Adapting to
SITUATION

Mastery of
skills
ACCOMPLISHMENT

INSTRUMENTAL
BEHAVIOR

COMPETENCE
ACQUISITION

psychological
success

Product

What is an effective group?
Group goals satisfy individual needs
Abilities of members utilized
Norms permit flexible and satisfying behavior
Sense of trust present
Shared leadership
Leader states how he sees the world not what he sees in others, or what the group is doing
Members share perceptions of what should be changed
Sense of belonging is present
Leader differentiates between observable and inferred behaviors

Adapted from Conditions for Competence
Acquisition and Therapy—Chris Argyris
J. of Applied Behavioral Science

velopment can be concomitant with skill acquisition. It can be inferred that youth group activities can be structured so that both skill acquisition and cognitive development can occur.

It is possible to extrapolate some of Argyris' statements to situations that would enhance competence acquisition while working on individual projects. The process is called "management by objectives." The youth leader and the child interact so that the latter develops his own plans, defines his objectives, sets up criteria evaluating the project, and decides the date when the project should be completed. It is important that specific items be agreed upon. Specificity generates commitment and a date precludes wishful thinking. This process of management by objectives permits evaluation of personal goals, reality testing, and creative expression.

The various concepts of interpersonal relations make similar observations. The quality of interpersonal relations is affected by the members' levels of conceptual development, degree of "openness" to the situation, need of the group, and flow of feedback. Successful group work does not occur because the leader has mastered a set of techniques. It occurs because the leader has orchestrated the situation so that the members have an opportunity to satisfy personal needs through the task. Group work is essentially an art form rather than a scientific exercise. When a youth leader accepts this premise, his groups will be successful.

ENCOUNTER GROUPS

In contrast to the highly structured task oriented group is the freedom and lack of structure of most encounter groups.[22]

The Purpose of Encounter Groups in the School. The purpose of the encounter group is broadly to contribute to affective education and to its goal of developing self-actualizing persons. Its particular contribution is that it provides experience in interpersonal relations. It thus involves learning by doing, or through experience. The learning of interpersonal relations would appear to be one place where cognitive instruction and computer assisted

---

[22]The following material is adapted from C. H. Patterson, *Humanistic education* (Englewood Cliffs, Prentice-Hall, 1973), chapter 11.

learning would be inappropriate, or at least relatively ineffective. You can't teach human relations by machines. Actual experience in groups seems so clearly superior to any other method of learning that it is amazing that it hasn't been widely utilized long before this. There is no substitute for learning human relations through interacting with others. Sitting in a classroom while actually being alone, not really knowing the other students, while listening to the teacher talk about "mental hygiene" or "human relations" is not sufficient. Nor is being in a classroom and going through a series of games and exercises which, while involving some realistic interpersonal reactions are not actually "for real."

In the encounter group students can learn through experience:
1. to listen to others
2. to accept and respect others
3. to understand others
4. to identify and become aware of feelings
5. to express one's own feelings
6. to become aware of the feelings of others
7. to experience being listened to by others
8. to experience being accepted and respected by others
9. to experience being understood by others
10. to recognize the basic commonalities of human experience
11. to explore oneself
12. to develop greater awareness of oneself
13. to be oneself
14. to change oneself in the direction of being more the self one wants to be

In groups learning occurs without the input of external content. This is in contrast to the approaches where content is used to teach human relations, or new content is created for this purpose. Such approaches require the use of techniques. Groups provide learning in human relations without the necessity for providing content or techniques. Content and techniques put distance between the learner and what he learns. Group encounters eliminate this distance.

The encounter group differs from T-groups in a significant respect, and should not be confused with T-groups when used in affective education. The T- or training group is concerned with consciously teaching so-called human relations skills (often reduced to "techniques of handling others"). T-groups are a mixture or alternation of spontaneous interaction and cognitive analysis of the interaction—the so-called dynamics operating in the group. The development of skills is primary; personal development in the broader sense is secondary or accidental.

In encounter groups there is no separate, cognitive analysis of "the process." The interaction is not stopped to study group dynamics. It is not a training group in group dynamics. It is not necessary that cognitive analysis or awareness—or "insight"—be present for learning to occur.

Encounter groups provide the most relevant and the most realistic education in human relations. It is learning through practice, or a practicum in interpersonal relations.

In addition to this direct contribution to the personal development of students in the school, encounter groups are extremely useful in areas where there are problems of interpersonal relationships. These include relations between administrators and teachers, teachers and parents, and administrators and parents. Certainly there is need for greater understanding among these groups, and the relationships among them influence the education of children.

But our concern here is with the students and their relationships with others. The teacher-student relationship could be improved if students and teachers could participate together in encounter groups. Students and administrators could also benefit. In the few instances where meetings between students and faculty and administrators do occur they are formal and stilted, or at times angry confrontations, with little if anything being accomplished. Teachers and administrators seem to resist open, free encounters with students; yet they complain about lack of understanding by students. Students and parents also should be brought together. The lack of understanding—the so-called generation gap—could be reduced by encounter groups. A few schools have used encounter groups to bring black and white students together with good results.

The only remedy for conflict and lack of understanding between groups is a group experience of the kind provided by an encounter group where understanding and acceptance is fostered.

The Encounter Group Process. In the encounter group where there is an atmosphere of safety, individuals are free to express their feelings toward themselves and each other. Mutual trust, liking, concern, and understanding develop. Each individual sees himself as he is and as he is capable of becoming. Not needing to be defensive, the individual is open to change in attitudes and behavior. He can learn from others, who are concerned about him, including learning how he affects others. He becomes freer to become his potentials, to become a more self-actualizing person—more understanding, warm and genuine.

Rogers has defined and described the stages in the process. The stages are not separate or discrete but constitute trends, sometimes overlapping and reversing, but roughly sequential. The following is an adaptation of Rogers.[23]

1. *Milling around.* When the group is initially given freedom, with little structure except that it is a place where individuals can relate to each other and get to know each other, there is a period of confusion, silence, frustration, small-talk, lack of continuity. There is often a demand for the leader to "do something." In one group conducted by the writer, after two hours of this, one member addressed me and said: "Why haven't you done something, why don't you do something?" Before I could respond she said: "Well, I'm going to do something," and then she launched into a very personal expression of her problems.

2. *Resistance to personal expression or exploration.* Although one member may reveal something personal, there may be a hesitancy, reluctance or refusal of others to respond on a personal level. There may be an embarrassment in others, who may even cover over the personal statement. People don't disclose themselves in ordinary social situations, and it takes time for them to feel comfortable in doing so even when they have been, in effect, given permission to do so. A trust in the group must develop first.

3. *Description of past feeling.* Expressions of feelings begin with telling about past feelings. They are experienced as in the

---

[23]Carl R. Rogers, *Carl Rogers on encounter groups* (New York, Harper & Row, 1970), pp. 15-37.

past, not in the present. They do not involve members of the group.

4. *Expression of negative feelings.* The first current feelings to be expressed about other members in the group are often negative. The feelings are often first directed at the leader or facilitator, as in the illustration above. Negative feelings are apt to be expressed first because of feelings of threat, anxiety, defensiveness, because we are not used to expressing positive feelings, and also perhaps as a testing of the freedom and safety of the group.

5. *Expression and exploration of personally meaningful material.* The voicing of negative feelings is followed by someone revealing himself to the group. Rogers says that "the reason for this no doubt is that the individual member has come to realize that this is in part *his* group. He can help to make of it what he wishes." This was beautifully illustrated by the woman in the writer's group referred to above, who took responsibility for her contribution to getting the group started. A climate of trust begins to develop. Members are willing to take the risk of disclosing themselves.

6. *The expression of immediate interpersonal feelings in the group.* Members became able to express their feelings and attitudes about each other, both positive and negative. The negative feelings are not critical, bitter attacks, but simple statements of feelings and reactions. The result is not conflict, but exploration in an atmosphere of trust.

7. *The development of a healing capacity in the group.* Members of the group begin to help each other. They begin to care for each other, to understand each other, to try to help, each in his own way.

8. *Self-acceptance and the beginning of change.* This is an awareness of what one is, an admission even, of what one really is behind the facade. This recognition of what one is, is necessary before one can begin to change. One can then explore what one is. A growing sense of realness, genuineness, or authenticity, develops. Members feel they can be *themselves,* both their strong and weak selves.

9. *The cracking of facades.* The growing recognition of oneself leads to the throwing off of defenses, the taking off of masks and

facades. Each group member, apparently realizing the possibility of a deep encounter when everyone is real and open and honest, demands or requires that other members be themselves.

10. *The individual receives feedback.* As the group members become open and honest with each other, the members learn how they seem to others, how they affect others. Again, this is positive and negative, and the negative takes place in a concerned and caring environment. Feedback can lead to greater self-understanding. Glasser reports on a group in which two class leaders were quite shocked to find that they were feared rather than respected, and that their behavior was considered irrelevant rather than funny. They recognized that their self-image differed considerably from the way they were perceived by their peers.[24] Feedback, lets us see ourselves as others see us.

11. *Confrontation.* When one member reacts to another very strongly, usually in a negative manner, confrontation seems to be a better term to use than feedback. Sometimes people do feel strongly against others and these feelings have to come out. But it is only when people have come to know each other well that these feelings can be meaningfully expressed with the possibility of constructive results.

12. *The helping relationship outside the group sessions.* Group members relate to each other outside the group in a more human way, and often are very helpful to another member of the group who is going through the painful process of self-awareness and change.

13. *The basic encounter.* Group members feel close to each other, are highly empathic with each other, feeling for each other. An extremely close personal relationship develops, a basic human encounter, an I-thou relationship.

14. *The expression of positive feelings and closeness.* The group becomes warm, trusting, with a sense of human togetherness and closeness.

15. *Behavior changes in the group.* Group members change and become different right before one's eyes. They become more empathic and understanding, they become more accepting, re-

---

[24]William Glasser, *op. cit.,* pp. 150-151.

specting and warm, they become more honest, real, and genuine —they act like self-actualizing persons! Interpersonal relationships change, personal problems are resolved. A member in one of the writer's groups, who had presented himself as needing to be strong and independent, to have people lean on him (at the age of 6 he had taken his younger brother on a train halfway across the country) began openly to ask for and accept help from others. A man who could not bear to be touched by a woman was unaware later when a woman touched him, and when he touched her. There is considerable evidence that people are different following even a brief but intensive group experience. Too often, in the reality of the world outside the group, changes fade away, however. It is difficult to be really human in a world where there are so few really human beings—or where so few human beings express their humanness.

This description of the process of the encounter group is not derived from therapy groups with disturbed people. It is based on experience with average, normal people, including adolescents. To be sure, the same process occurs in therapy groups. The only difference between encounter groups and therapy groups is the nature of the members—some have more problems or are more disturbed than others.

The development of a group to the point where its members can be open, honest, trusting and really themselves takes time. There is no such such thing as "instant" group, instant intimacy, or instant relationship. One of the problems in many groups is the desire of the inadequately trained facilitator to produce this, or to speed up the group process. This is a reason for the introduction of games, exercises and gimmicks. It seems to be a characteristic of our society that things must be done in a hurry, must be speeded up. But if a group is to be highly facilitative for its members it cannot be pushed, and the facilitator must be patient and allow the group to grow into relationships at its own pace. While a few couples may meet and marry after one date, most go through a process requiring time, called "courtship," in which a relationship leading to the intimacy of marriage develops. Groups must also have time to develop.

Facilitating a Group. The encounter group is not, or should not be, a place where the facilitator (or teacher) engages in a controlled, planned program of exercises, games, etc. As indicated above, there is no content introduced by the facilitator; the content arises from the participants, and consists of their feelings and relationships with each other. The major function of the facilitator, then, is to create, set up, or "permit" a situation where group members can express themselves, can start out on and continue along the pattern delineated in the last section. The facilitator is not a controller, with his hand on the throttle, pushing and pulling to speed up or slow down the process by manuipulating the behavior of group members, as if he were trying to reach a preconceived destination on a time schedule. The encounter group is a real life situation and should be allowed to develop naturally. The purpose of the facilitator should be to help provide an atmosphere in which the members can interact more naturally, more realistically, more honestly and more humanly than is possible in the so-called real, but actually artificial, social environment in which we live. How does the facilitator do this?

The facilitator is not a leader in the usual sense of the word. He is definitely not a teacher, in the usual sense of the word. But his role and function may be defined quite like that of a humanistic teacher who is attempting to make possible self-initiated learning, exploration, and the achievement of personal meaning. There is no specific goal for the group, or for individuals, as there is in lesson plans in teaching. The goal is simply to make possible personal interaction on a human level.

1. *Structuring.* The amount of structuring necessary or desirable depends on the group and the situation. If the group has no idea of what is expected of them, some structuring is necessary. If the group, or some of its members, have some misconceptions about the group and how they are to function, then structuring is necessary.

In general, structuring should be kept to a minimum. Because of the fact that in encounter groups people are expected to function differently than in "real life," some structuring seems to be necessary. Rogers, in starting the group depicted in the Academy Award winning film "Journey into Self," began as follows:

I'm glad we all had a chance to have dinner together because it gives a little chance to get acquainted, at least a few of us; but I feel as though really, we really are strangers to each other in spite of that—with lots of geographical distances and occupational distance, and everything. And, I feel like saying just one or two things to start with, from my point of view. One is that this is our group. We really can make of it anything we want to make of it, and, for myself, I don't have any prediction, except that by the time we end Sunday afternoon, we'll probably know each other a lot better than we do right now; but how we may want to go about it, or what we want to do, that's really up to us. And I think that it is an opportunity to *be* in the group as fully as we can; maybe in some respects to try ways of being or ways of relating to each other that we never quite have had nerve enough to try before, when in ordinary life situations it seems like it's too impossible. In a sense, it's an opportunity to try out new ways of behaving with other people; there's that in it too: things that we have sort of wished we might be or do with others and never have quite had the nerve—maybe we will have the nerve here. I don't know, but at any rate from here on in, as far as I'm concerned, it's up to us. . . . Oh, yes, one thing I did want to say. I feel a lot of anticipation about this group; I really look forward to getting to know you. And at the same time, I'm apprehensive; and I don't think it has much to do with the lights and the cameras. I think I'm always a little apprehensive in not knowing what a given group is going to be like. I don't know who we are, how we're going to get along, whether anything is going to come of this. Ah, so I feel a very double feeling: I feel excited and full of anticipation; I feel a little on the scared side, too.[25]

Structuring is designed to give participants some idea of what to expect, what is expected of them, thus reducing initial anxiety and threat. With students in a school setting, the structuring would be different, and perhaps briefer. It is perhaps necessary to indicate that the group is different from a class discussion, that there is no topic or problem, that the facilitator is not a teacher and will not "lead" the group. The purpose can be stated as a chance to get to know each other in a different situation and way than in the classroom or other social situations.

2. *Listening.* The facilitator listens carefully to *everything* everyone says, focusing upon the feelings being expressed. This

[25]Included in William Coulson, "Inside a basic encounter group," *The Counseling Psychologist,* Vol. 2(2) (1970), pp. 1-27.

is an intense, personal listening, to whatever the member of the group is expressing.

3. *Acceptance and Respect.* Each member is accepted and respected as he is, as a person. There is no pressure for change, no attempt to make the group "jell," "get down to business," begin expressing feelings, or to "speed up" the group process. There is no attempt to get each member involved, to force participation, to "psyche out" a silent member, or to delve beneath what persons say. Each person's contribution is taken at face value.

4. *Understanding.* The facilitator attempts to understand what each member is thinking, feeling and trying to express. He attempts to place himself in the shoes of each person, so he can understand the personal meaning of what he is saying and feeling.

5. *Responding.* The facilitator attempts to convey his understanding of what is said by his responses. It is not necessary, nor desirable, that the facilitator respond to every statement by a member of the group. To do so would tend to lead to the development of a two-way interaction. Group members respond to each other, and the facilitator must allow for this. But, as a trained and experienced person, the facilitator can often better understand what a member may be trying to say, and can often, in communicating his understanding, put it in a clearer form, reducing the incoherence or lengthy attempts at expression. By responding to feelings rather than intellectualizing, the facilitator can focus the group upon feelings. The facilitator can sharpen differences among participants by bringing them out clearly, thus helping participants see their differences more clearly and engage in a more meaningful interaction.

The reader will recognize these methods of facilitating a group as being familiar. They are the basic conditions of a learning or facilitative interpersonal relationship. The encounter group is no exception when it comes to these conditions. As a model for good, open, honest interpersonal relationships, these conditions must be present in the encounter group. While some groups might be able to function as an encounter group without the presence of a facilitator, since these characteristics are present, to a greater or lesser extent, in most individuals, their presence to a sufficient degree cannot be counted on. Groups without a facilitator would at best be less efficient—that is, move more slowly. The facilitator is thus necessary. Attempts to encourage "leaderless" groups through providing audiotapes are questionable.

The presence of the conditions provided by, and fostered by, the facilitator leads to a nonthreatening, safe atmosphere in which people can become less defensive, less inhibited, less constricted, and more open, free and honest. They can become more real, more human, and thus more the kind of person they are capable of being. And in doing so, in being so, they make it more possible for others to be so. *They become facilitators themselves for each other.*

For the person who has been used to directing, leading, guiding and controlling others, and who has been concerned about cognitive learning involving thinking and rational problem solving, facilitating an encounter group means a great change in approach. This is one reason why teachers have such difficulty, and why educators tend to highly structure and introduce techniques into affective education. This is also one reason why teachers need special preparation for facilitating groups—or for that matter, to engage in any aspect of affective education.

Part of the difficulty in maintaining a "hands off" approach is perhaps a lack of trust or confidence in the group to function without direction and guidance. Perhaps this is a common problem of teachers—as well as parents and other adults—with children and adolescents.

Some Questions and Problems. Encounter groups pose some questions or problems which need to be considered. One of the most serious of these will be considered first.

1. *Are encounter groups dangerous?* It is not possible to consider all the questions related to potential harmful effects of encounter groups. While there are some instances of people being hurt psychologically, they are very few in number. With the lack of controls over who leads groups, who participates in groups, and what is done in groups, the incidence of harm is amazingly small, giving testimony to the toughness of human beings. If groups are composed of "normal" individuals there is little danger. More important, in the writer's opinion, is the role of the facilitator. If the facilitator functions as indicated above, and

avoids stimulating or providing feelings, putting pressure on group members, and introducing bizarre gimmicks and techniques, the danger is slight.

There is another possible effect of groups on individuals which warrants mention. The danger of coercion in groups, not only in the pressure toward conformity behavior outside the group, but in the group itself, is inadequately recognized. Group pressure can lead to a member saying and doing things in the group which he may not wish to say or do, which may cause him pain or discomfort, and which may be damaging to him as a person. His freedom is imposed upon. He does things not because he believes they are good for him, but because he does not want to be different, because "everyone else is doing it." Group members put up with, or take abuse from the other members, and from the group leader, because they don't want to be seen as weak, lacking in courage, and won't "chicken out" by leaving the group when it is uncomfortable and even harmful for them to stay. Some group leaders promote and encourage members to attack and pressure each other, and even do it themselves. The competence of such leaders should be questioned.

2. *Provoking aggression.* One of the widespread misconceptions of encounter groups is that to be successful or effective the members must be at each other's throats, and the sooner this happens the better. This misconception is fostered by some leaders, who are, in the opinion of the writer, incompetent and dangerous. This misconception is so widespread that many persons who become members of groups believe that aggressive behavior is expected of them, and do their best to show it. Now it is true that while most persons (though not all) have suppressed or repressed aggressive feelings (aggression is not universal or innate, however), it is not desirable that such feelings be expressed immediately in the group and directed to other members of the group. There are good psychological reasons for this, which can't be gone into here. But one reason is that it can be harmful to the persons to whom aggression or anger are directed.

If aggression is not innate, an instinct, but a response to frustration and threat, then, in a group where threat is minimized, aggression should be reduced rather than stimulated. Aggressive feelings toward others outside the group may be present, of course. But why should members feel aggressive toward each other, unless aggression is deliberately stimulated and provoked? Some leaders do this, insisting that everyone, in effect, hates everyone else, including other members of the group, and that this must be expressed. Members are made to feel abnormal, uncooperative, resistant, unless they come up with their quota of anger and aggression. If they are provoked enough, they will. And they may suffer from guilt and remorse later, wondering where their anger came from, being convinced that it must have been in them all the time, when in fact it was provoked by the leader, and often by other members of the group.

This is a source of some of the damage an encounter group can cause, and leads to another problem which should be considered.

3. *The Responsibility of the Facilitator.* There are some who disclaim any responsibility of the facilitator for what happens (particularly of a negative nature) in the group. This is irresponsible behavior. The facilitator is in the group, and as presumably the most highly trained person, is responsible, not only for his own behavior, but for the behavior of others *at least insofar as he provokes it.* The facilitator is responsible for creating the atmosphere or the conditions under which the group functions. If he follows the procedures discussed above, there should be no problem regarding harmful aggressive behavior or vicious attacks by members of the group on each other. But if such attacks do occur, through misconceptions of a group member as to what is desirable or permissible, or because a group member is a seriously disturbed person, then it is the responsibility of the facilitator to protect the attacked group member from harm, both physical and psychological. In addition, no member of a group should be forced or coerced by the facilitator or any other group member, to do anything which he does not wish to do.

4. *Selection of Group Members.* Reference to who should participate in encounter groups, and to group members who are seriously disturbed leads to questions about the selection of group members. In the writer's opinion, selection of members for a group is undesirable, except to exclude individuals who are seri-

ously disturbed emotionally. In general, any student who is permitted to attend school should be permitted to be in an encounter group.

5. *Should All Students Be Required to Participate in Encounter Groups?* The quick answer to this question might be "no." But there are some considerations which lead to "yes." There is no more danger in an encounter group conducted as recommended in this chapter than in the usual classroom. In fact, it could be contended with considerable justification that there is *less* likelihood of psychological harm. Second, if the encounter group is, as the writer believes, the most effective method of affective education and of learning in the area of interpersonal relations, it is more justifiable to require this of students than it is to require any other course or experience.

6. *Is the Encounter Group Actually a Counseling Group?* The only difference between an encounter group and a counseling group is that in the latter case the members consist of persons who in their own eyes or the eyes of others, have "problems," at least to a greater extent or degree than other persons. The conditions of facilitative interpersonal relationships, which are the conditions of an encounter group, are also the conditions of counseling or psychotherapy, as has been pointed out in earlier chapters. The encounter group is therapeutic, while the counseling group is therapy. It is true, that the facilitator (or counselor) in a counseling group should have greater training and experience than the facilitator of an encounter group.

7. *The Facilitator as a Group Member.* We have emphasized the lack of control or direction of the facilitator. The facilitator becomes, as much as it is possible, another member of the group —more experienced in human relations, perhaps, but still a member. True, he cannot become just like any other member—because of his status, the group will usually be unable to allow him to become exactly like themselves. And he does have certain responsibilities, as indicated above, which distinguish him from the other members of the group, but if he remains outside the group, psychologically, he is not a facilitator, but a teacher, ob-

server, or commentator. This leads to his being evaluative rather than being understanding, being detached rather than being involved, inhuman rather than human—an unnatural appurtenance to the group. No natural social group has such a person in it—or rather outside of it—observing and evaluating.

8. *How, then, Does the Facilitator Affect the Group?* Part of the answer to this question has already been implicit in the discussion so far. The facilitator is (usually and at the beginning) the most experienced, knowledgeable, empathic and genuine person in the group, and his responses are thus more effective and facilitative. In addition, as such a person (and having some prestige and recognition) he is or becomes a *model* for the group.

Students thus learn the conditions through modeling and through practicing them with each other. One of the most difficult things to be learned is the ability to listen to and hear what another person is saying without analyzing, judging or evaluating. The evaluative attitude is the prevalent one in our society, and is the major deterrent to real empathic understanding. We don't hear what another person is really saying or feeling, and understand how he sees things, because we listen from our own frame of reference—the external rather than the internal frame of reference.

Rogers has suggested a way to facilitate listening and understanding which can be used in any group, whether an encounter group or a discussion group. This method can often get a group to the point of listening to each other quickly, and may be used as a rule when a group is getting started. The rule is simply that before a member of the group can respond to something another member has said, he must restate what the other person has said in a way that the other person agrees reflects what he was saying or feeling. This is, in effect, a technique, and should not be used routinely or as a technique. It is not necessary in many groups. But in a group where it is apparent that members are not listening to each other, it can be helpful if the facilitator suggests that, for a brief period, this rule be followed, as a way to help the members to really listen to each other.

GROUP COUNSELING[26]

Group counseling differs from task oriented or problem solving groups. As indicated earlier, it is not concerned with doing something to or for the members of the group—to inform, educate or train them. Students who are in need of group counseling are not simply lacking in information. There is no common specific goal or externally imposed task in a counseling group.

Group counseling is individually centered. The focus in the group is upon the individual members as persons—persons with feelings, attitudes and emotions which concern or disturb them, either because of their nature or strength or because they are reactions to behaviors. Group counseling is thus not cognitively oriented—it is not a discussion *of* feelings, but a place where feelings are expressed and responded to by the counselor and other group members. Its focus and orientation is related to the expression of feelings and attitudes in a group setting. Membership in a counseling group is always voluntary, which is not always the case in guidance groups. Counseling groups are smaller than guidance groups, which allows for greater interaction among members.

It is apparent that group counseling is very similar to encounter groups. The difference reduces to the difference between group counseling and group psychotherapy referred to earlier. Students in group counseling are presumably students with "problems," while encounter groups are for all students, or "normal" students. But as noted earlier, there is no sharp line between the normal person and the disturbed person.

Group Counseling and Individual Counseling. There are many basic similarities between individual and group counseling. The goal is the same—the development of self-actualizing behavior. The essential conditions are the same, with the counselor providing empathic understanding, respect and warmth, and genuineness. The counselor functions in much the same way—un-

---

[26]The following is adapted from C. H. Patterson, "The group relationship in the elementary school," in M. M. Ohlsen (ed.), *Counseling children in groups* (New York, Holt, Rinehart & Winston, 1972).

derstanding the communications of individuals and facilitating communication. In the group the counselor must be alert to the interrelationships among group members as well as the relationships between himself and the individual members.

The interrelationships among the group members constitute perhaps the major difference between individual and group counseling. For the counselor, this is more a quantitative than a qualitative difference. For the participants, however, it introduces a number of elements not present in individual counseling.

The presence of other individuals in the counseling relationship makes it possible for each client to have experiences which are not possible in individual counseling. In individual counseling, there is usually concern with the interpersonal relationships of the client. He discusses these relationships with the counselor, and he may engage in efforts to change his interpersonal behavior, and report these experiences to the counselor. The counselor also can develop some understanding of the client's ways of relating to others by the way the client relates to him. This, however, may not be typical of his relationships with other persons in his environment. The counselor is a special person, with special training and experience, leading the client to view him as an authority, at least a professional authority. In the case of school counseling, the counselor is older, and is identified often with the authority aspects of the teaching situation and administration. The client may relate quite differently to his peers, and to his subordinates or to younger people.

In the group situation the client demonstrates the nature of his relationships with others, and this becomes one of the major concerns of the group. The client can thus develop a direct understanding of his effects on others, and of their perceptions of him, on the basis of immediate feedback from them. Moreover, he can experiment in changing his interpersonal behavior and obtain immediate knowledge of the results.

Moreover, in the group the client, in addition to learning about his impact on others, can experience the impact of others on him in a situation where he can become more aware of this and can communicate it to others. This two-way communication of perceptions and experiences provides practice in human interpersonal relationships in a situation which is optimal for learning. Individual counseling does not provide this direct learning experience in interpersonal relationships.

This experience involves learning to listen to, accept, and understand others—in effect learning the principles of good human relationships. It amounts to training in human relationships through experience rather than instruction. This is the basis for the description of T groups as laboratory groups in human relations. Thus participants in group counseling gain experience in helping others, with its resulting satisfactions.

Group counseling, finally, may have the advantage over individual counseling that some individuals may find it easier to express and discuss their problems in a group than with the counselor alone. The example of other clients, the recognition that others have similar, or equally or more serious problems, may make it easier for a particular group member to bring out his problem. The acceptance and support of the group is also a facilitating factor. On the other hand, some clients may find it easier to talk to an individual counselor, even though he (the client) may be considered to be potentially able to benefit, perhaps later, from group counseling.

This discussion of the differences between group and individual counseling indicates that they are sufficiently different that they are not necessarily a substitute for each other. Groups are not necessarily a more economical method of helping students than individual counseling, since experience has indicated that they often lead to requests by the participants for individual counseling in addition to group counseling. On the other hand, for many clients, group counseling may be the preferred method, without the need for individual counseling in addition.

There are some aspects of group counseling which are not necessarily beneficial, but can be harmful. To the writer's knowledge, these have not been discussed in this way in considerations of group counseling. Group dynamics are powerful, and thus have the potential for harm as well as good. The characteristics of group cohesion and group identification are significant in this regard. Most group leaders desire, and thus foster, group cohesion and the identification of individuals with the group. The

productivity of the group may be increased as these characteristics develop. This may be a desirable outcome for a task-
oriented group. But in a counseling group too great a level of
group cohesion and group identification may not be desirable.
Two dangers arise. First, the individuals may become so closely
identified with the group that their relationships outside the
group can suffer. They may become overdependent on the group.
The counseling group may become an in-group, leading to conflict with out-groups. A second danger lies in the power of the
group to lead to conforming behavior. Acceptance in the group
requires a certain amount of conformity. Overemphasis on group
cohesion may result in excessive demands for conformity. There
is some evidence that counselors in the schools view group counseling as a means to "shape up" or bring into line nonconforming
students. Group pressures are powerful, and the use of group
pressure to manipulate the behavior of students is unprofessional
if not unethical.

Group Composition. Group Size. There seems to be general
agreement on group size for counseling: The group should be
small. The exact number varies, however. Ohlsen, citing Loeser,
gives four to eight as the ideal size.[27] Mahler states that the group
should not consist of less than seven nor more than ten, and feels
that "the optimum number in group counseling, in terms of full
participation and communication among members seems to be
about ten."[28] Many would set the optimum lower. Mahler does
suggest smaller groups for elementary school children. The larger
the group, the less time there is for each member, and the less
interaction each member has with all the other members. In fact
interaction is reduced by the tendency for members in a large
group to direct communication to a few others, or to the counselor. This is one reason why guidance groups are not counseling
groups. In large groups in which counseling is attempted, and
which do not become leader centered, subgroups or cliques may
develop.

[27]M. M. Ohlsen, *Group counseling* (New York, Holt, Rinehart & Winston, 1970),
p. 58.
[28]C. A. Mahler, *Group counseling in the schools* (Boston, Houghton-Mifflin, 1969),
pp. 54-55.

Frequency and Duration of Sessions. Counseling groups follow the same frequency pattern as do individual counseling sessions. Most of them meet once a week. Two or three times a week may be desirable when the total time period in which the group can continue is short, and when a more or less specific and urgent problem is the focus on the group. Daily groups are sometimes scheduled in institutions. Mahler suggests that, with a limited number of counselors and large numbers of students, if, as would appear desirable, every student is to be given an opportunity for a group experience, groups might be organized to meet on a monthly basis.[29] While such groups might be of value, skepticism might exist that they could achieve some of the desirable goals of an intensive group experience. It is likely that they would become discussion groups, with most students quickly losing interest in them.

Like individual counseling sessions, most group counseling sessions are scheduled for an hour, or a class period. However, many counselors find that groups of more than four or five often find an hour insufficient for everyone to have his say. An hour and a half is not too long for adolescents and adults. Elementary school groups, however, probably should last no longer than an hour. The so-called marathon group, lasting from several hours to twenty-four hours, has not yet been introduced in schools, as far as the writer knows. They undoubtedly will be, however. These groups sometimes pose special problems with adults, and it might be anticipated that even more or greater problems might arise with students. Nevertheless, with a skilled counselor, and acceptance by the staff and parents, such a group might be beneficial for some students.

Selection of Members. No student should be forced or compelled to join a group. On the other hand, no one should be permitted to join a counseling group without being aware of the nature of the group, its purpose, and what is expected of him. Particularly in the case of counseling groups, members should be screened in terms of their need for and adaptability to group counseling, and for the particular group being formed. This can

---

[29]*Ibid.,* pp. 57-58.

be accomplished by an interview. Seriously disturbed, extremely aggressive or dominating, or extremely shy or nonverbal students probably should not be placed in a group of average students, since they may impede the progress of the group. Some writers advocate that relatives or close friends should not be included in the same group on the basis that such persons may be inhibited in expressing personal concerns and problems in each others presence. This might be questioned, however, particularly since it may be just these relationships which are a problem, and it is in such relationships that openness and understanding are most important. Current developments in group therapy include working with family groups.

Ohlsen emphasizes the importance of assessing the applicant's readiness for and commitment to group counseling, stating that "the prospective client must convince not only the counselor but also himself that he is ready for counseling."[30] While rigorous selection increases the likelihood of success in group counseling, and may be justified if only a limited number can be accepted, some would question the desirability of a highly restrictive admission policy. As is the case in highly selective procedures for individual counseling, the results are that those who are accepted are those who are less in need of help. In the case of group counseling, the factors used in selection, such as ability to verbalize one's problems, and to listen to and accept others, are actually characteristics which the group is expected to develop, and should not to be used too restrictively to reject applicants. It would appear that the selection process might best focus upon rejecting the few applicants who could not benefit from the group or who might prevent others from benefitting.

Heterogeneity versus Homogeneity. Most writers emphasize the importance of homogeneity in a counseling group, though recognizing the desirability of some heterogeneity. The emphasis upon homogeneity may be overdone, however. It could be argued that it is enough that all group members have in common the fact that as human beings they share some basic characteristics and common problems to be considered. But is is not necessary,

---

[30]*Op. cit.,* pp. 103-104.

and perhaps not desirable, to limit the group to the consideration of specific problems, such as underachievement, for example. Where homogeneous groups are involved, it seldom happens that they limit themselves to the specific problem they were formed to consider. Moreover, it is not necessarily the case—at least this has not been demonstrated by research—that a homogeneous group of underachievers is better than a heterogeneous group with underachievers. It is, perhaps, more convenient to deal with a number of underachievers in one group, particularly if the school and counselor are problem oriented and concerned specifically with underachievement, and do not have resources to offer help to many students with a variety of problems. Homogeneous groups appear to be more appropriate for guidance or content-oriented groups of a problem-solving or instructional nature.

The problem of communication may suggest the desirability of some homogeneity. Persons of widely different ages may have difficulty in communicating with and understanding and accepting one another. The purpose of the group enters here, however; it may be a purpose to foster such communication and understanding.

In the writer's opinion, too much concern has been given to achieving homogeneity in groups. It has been found that heterogeneity among students in a school and within a classroom has certain advantages. We do not segregate the sexes in classrooms. One of the problems in our society is the barriers between groups of different educational, socioeconomic, and cultural backgrounds. It is desirable that our young people learn to understand and communicate with others from all kinds of backgrounds.

The Life Span of the Group. There is no fixed number of sessions appropriate for all groups. The life of the group sometimes depends upon external circumstances, such as the end of a semester or a school year. Where there are no such restrictions, it would seem to be appropriate to make the duration of the group a matter of group decision, providing the counselor is available and willing to continue with the group. Mahler (1969, p. 57) suggests that about ten sessions should be a minimum. This appears to be reasonable, provided that no one is compelled to remain in the group who wishes to leave before ten sessions are completed.[31] A less acceptable recommendation made by Mahler (p. 61) is that ordinarily the number of sessions be determined by the counselor before the group begins, on the basis of the purpose of the group. This may be possible for groups with a limited, problem-centered focus. Also, time-limited groups may have certain accelerating effects. However, it is probably not possible to predict in advance the optimum ending date for most groups. It would seem desirable to allow the group to determine its own termination.

The Group Counseling Relationship. Some writers, under the influence of behavioral approaches to counseling, feel that counseling groups should have highly specific goals, represented by observable behavior changes in the members of the group— changes that might be different for different members, however. Ohlsen, for example, states that "specific goals are necessary for effective counseling." Yet he recognizes that such goals cannot be completely set prior to counseling, since "additional goals also are defined during counseling. Sometimes the needs for new goals are disclosed and defined within the group."[32]

The matter of goals and outcomes. There is a place in the school for groups which are concerned with specific problems, which thus have as a goal a rather specific outcome. Groups may be concerned with underachievement, boy-girl problems or relationships, study methods, etc. These groups are more appropriate for secondary school students, however. Such problem-oriented groups, composed of students who are homogeneous in terms of the nature of the problem, may be called counseling groups. They are more likely to be discussion groups, or even instructional groups, however. Groups which have a relatively specific purpose which is the same for all members of the group are closer to teaching than to counseling.

In the kind of groups discussed here, which are not always counseling groups in the sense that all the members have "problems" or need counseling or therapy because they are disturbed or abnormal in some respect, no specific goals are necessary. The

---

[31]*Ibid.*, p. 57.
[32]*Op. cit.*, pp. 41-44.

purpose of the group may be defined very simply, to students or parents, as an opportunity for the members to get to know each other better, to understand each other better, to be able to have a continuing relationship with a group of other students.

In a broader sense there is a common goal for all groups, which is the same as the goal for all facilitative human relationships. This common goal is referred to by several terms: self-realization, self-enhancement, the fully functioning person, or self-actualization.

The development of self-actualizing persons is, as has been indicated, a goal for all groups, whether counseling or encounter groups. It is also the goal toward which family relationships, education, and other institutions of society should be directed. When it is asked where this goal comes from, and whether it is a limited, culturally determined goal which should not be imposed on people, it may be answered that this goal is a given, being the inherent goal of human life, or, in other terms, the single, basic motivating force of life itself.

The counseling process. There has been much discussion of the nature of the counseling process, and of the stages through which groups progress in their development. Concepts of stages such as the involvement stage[33] or the establishment stage,[34] the transition stage, the working stage, and the ending stage may be useful. These concepts, while involving individuals, are focused upon the group. Groups are composed of individuals, and the effects of groups are upon individuals, not upon some mystical group. It is therefore desirable to look upon the process from the standpoint of individual group members. Here it is suggested that the essence of the counseling process for the individual is the process of self-exploration, including self-disclosure, specific self-exploration, and the development of self-awareness.

The counselor's contribution. The counselor's function or his contribution to the group counseling process is identical to the function or contribution of the counselor in individual counseling

---

[34]W. C. Bonney and W. J. Foley, "The transition stage in group counseling in terms of congruence theory," *Journal of Counseling Psychology,* Vol. 10, (1963), pp. 136-138.

[33]Mahler, *op. cit.*

or the facilitator of an encounter group. It is the providing of the conditions for self-exploration and of self-actualizing behavior. These include empathic understanding, respect or warmth, and facilitative or therapeutic genuineness, the conditions described in Chapter 3, and in the discussion of encounter groups earlier in this chapter.

In the discussion of encounter groups the matter of aggression and its promotion was considered. The comments apply to counseling groups as well. It should be apparent that such a situation would be threatening, and impede the process of self-disclosure and self-exploration. Unbridled attack on others can also hurt others. While a trained and experienced therapist may be able to repair, in time, the damage (if the person who is hurt is able to remain in the group), the danger of harm from groups conducted by relatively untrained and inexperienced therapists is real. One might also question why a trained and experienced therapist would allow or encourage such an antitherapeutic process. One of the functions of the group counselor, in the opinion of the writer, is to maintain a nonthreatening climate, and to protect himself, as well as other group members, from damaging psychological attack as well as physical attack. The former may be more harmful than the latter.

Relevant here is what Truax and Carkhuff refer to as the principle of reciprocal affect, or like begets like.[35] Hostile behavior on the part of one participant evokes hostile behavior in the one to whom it is directed. On the other hand expression of the core facilitative conditions by the counselor elicits them in the clients or group members. Thus, the members of the group become therapeutic, or facilitative, for each other. In this respect, it should also be noted that the core conditions are aspects of self-actualization: The characteristics of a self-actualizing person are the characteristics of a good interpersonal relationship. Therefore it follows that a counselor must be a self-actualizing person.

As Mahler notes, "There seems to be no one best way to start

[35]C. B. Truax and R. R. Carkhuff, *Toward effective counseling and psychotherapy* (Chicago, Aldine, 1967), p. 151.

a group or to get people to share."[36] The counselor must depend
on his training and especially his experience in helping the members to establish themselves as a group. Each group is unique.
Each progresses at its own pace. Some need little time for discussing or clarifying the group purpose, and may actually not be
concerned about developing any expressed purpose but just
plunge into their concerns. Other groups spend much time on
hammering out a purpose. To some extent, how much time is
spent on this phase of the process depends on how strongly the
counselor feels about the need for an explicit purpose. The group,
especially at the beginning, is feeling the counselor out, and may
seek to find out what he thinks or wants and follow his lead.

The process of getting acquainted also varies in length. Some
groups already know each other to a greater or less extent at the
beginning. The time required for the development of trust in the
counselor and each other varies. Group members may have many
doubts, even fears, about exposing themselves to the group. Much
of ordinary social interaction is at a formal and very superficial
level, and it takes time to get down to basic feelings and genuine
expression of them to others. The development of trust cannot be
forced or accelerated by the leader, but must come at its own
pace.

The forming of good interpersonal relationships requires time.
Impatience seems to be a characteristic of many group leaders
or facilitators, leading them to resort to gimmicks to attempt to
speed up the process. But, as noted earlier, there is no such thing
as an instant group. Adults often find it difficult to enter an
open, close personal relationship, which no doubt is the reason
for the gimmick approach to groups. Such an approach is less
defensible with children, who have not developed the inhibitions
and reserve against self-disclosure, but are more open and spontaneous.

SUMMARY

Groups are an important aspect or element in our society. The
increasing interest of adults in a group experience is more than
a passing fad. It represents a basic need of individuals to relate

---

[36]*Op. cit.,* p. 108.

to others in close interpersonal relationships, a need which is not being adequately met by our existing social institutions.

One of the problems involved in this movement is the great difficulty many adults have in relating to others on a close, personal basis. Social relationships have become formalized, on an increasingly impersonal basis. People increasingly are not open, spontaneous, honest, or genuine in interpersonal relationships. They have developed facades to cover up the real self, and are self-conscious in social relationships. This is a barrier to the development of the kind of relationship which is the object of encounter groups. People want this kind of relationship, but are inhibited in developing it. This difficulty or obstacle is the basis for the gimmicks and "techniques" which are developing in the encounter group movement. Group leaders or facilitators are impatient, and are attempting to find ways of speeding up the group process, or the development of personal closeness or intimacy.

It is important that the schools prepare people for the group living which is a basic part of life. Some have questioned the readiness of children for group experiences.

But children, in contrast to adults, are characterized by openness, spontaneity, honesty and genuineness in their social relationships. Often these characteristics are embarrassing to adults. The group relationship among children is much more easily developed than among adults, or adolescents. Rogers, who has worked with a wide variety of persons in groups, makes the following ranking of difficulty, from greatest to least, in initiating "encounter groups." Administrators, college faculty, high school faculty, elementary teachers, college students, high school students, elementary school students. While admitting that he and his associates have had relatively little experience with elementary school children, he reports that what experience they have had has been exciting.[37] Thus, children are more ready for a personal group experience than are most adults. And furthermore, if they are not to become like these adults, they should have the

---

[37] C. R. Rogers, *Freedom to learn* (Columbus, Merrill, 1969), p. 338.

opportunity for continuing group experiences of the kind represented by the counseling group or the encounter group.

The reaction against groups, and the feelings by some, influenced by sensational publicity, that the movement is simply a fad, has led to some reluctance and even strong opposition to the use of groups in schools. It would be unfortunate if encounter groups were denied a place in education because of this.

Students as well as adults are interested in and need groups. The usual clubs and other student activities are not sufficient. These are exclusive, in the sense that a certain interest, skill or ability is required for membership. They are relatively formal, with a limited purpose—they are what is called task-oriented groups. They are academically oriented. The less academically oriented students are thus excluded—and as a result are more apt to belong to nonschool connected groups, such as gangs. The less socially oriented or socially adept students are often not drawn to or accepted in student activities groups, and even less so in the informal, spontaneous student groups. Adolescent groups, particularly, even though their members may be sensitive to their own needs for acceptance and group membership, are often insensitive to others and cruel in their rejection.

This chapter has considered the major kinds of groups which are appropriate in the elementary school. The classroom size group was dealt with only briefly, since its usefulness is limited, because of its size, and the dynamics of the classroom as a group is considered in another chapter. Considerable attention was given to the task-oriented group because, even though this is, or has been, the most common kind of group in the school as well as in society in general, there is almost no attention given to it in textbooks in counseling and student personnel work. The other two groups considered were the encounter group and the counseling group. There are other groups which may have a place in the elementary school which could not be considered in this chapter, which is no more than an introduction. These other groups include group play therapy, psychodrama and sociodrama.

SUGGESTED READINGS

Mahler, C. A.: *Group counseling in the schools.* Boston, Houghton-Mifflin, 1969.

Ohlsen, M. M.: *Group counseling.* New York, Holt, Rinehart & Winston, 1970.

Ohlsen, M. M. (ed.): *Counseling children in groups.* New York, Holt, Rinehart & Winston, 1972.

Rogers, C. R.: *Carl Rogers on encounter groups.* New York, Harper & Row, 1970.

Chapter 8

THE CHILD
WITH A
LEARNING DISABILITY

INTRODUCTION

O NE OF THE BASIC PROBLEMS confronting the school concerns children who have behavior patterns that disrupt many activities in the classroom. These children are problems because most instructional procedures assume that children have a behavior repertoire which is conducive to learning. In order to induce a satisfactory learning climate, many primary grade teachers spend time reducing the behavioral divergencies among their pupils, for they are of the opinion that extreme or hyperactive behavior is disruptive to instruction. If, after a reasonable time, a pupil fails to show improvement in his behavior, the teacher turns to the professional pupil services staff for a validation of her observations and in some cases, for assistance in managing the problem.

The consultation with the counselor or school psychologist generates some concern in the teacher because her perspective of the situation usually differs from that of the pupil services staff member. Although the focus of the consultation is the child's low achievement and, at times, his disruptive classroom behavior, the teacher tends to feel uncomfortable because she is forced to admit to another person that she is unable to help the child to achieve. The failure of a teacher to reach the professional goal of helping pupils to achieve is threatening to many teachers, since most communities expect their schools to foster the acquisition of basic skills and knowledges in their pupils.

> The evaluation of academic achievement is usually in the hands of the teacher, who is thus not only the individual charged with helping the child learn, but also the judge of what the child has learned. This dual role may confound the evaluation, for the teacher is thus asked to judge not only the child but himself.[1]

In some consultations the focus may not only be on learning difficulties but may also include the topic of retention of the child. Teachers tend to be ambivalent about retaining a child because they know that factors other than the inability to learn enter into the decision. These factors may include motivation, classroom behavior, physical appearance, social maturity, and ability to profit from retention. Teachers tend to be reluctant to discuss these matters with the consultant for they fear that they may reveal some of the biases they have towards the child.

The general expectation that the teacher has from a consultative conference on a child's low achievement is a confirmation of her observations and some suggestions as to the manner in which she can help the child. The teacher believes she should be provided " . . . with some operational tools and underlying concepts that will assist him in analyzing and diagnosing where children are in respect to their development and intelligence, so that the new concepts of the child may become functional in the classroom." [2]

The counselor and the school psychologist view the child's inability to learn from a different perspective than does the teacher. Essentially they see the problem as originating in the child rather than as a consequence of the interaction between the child and his teacher. Thus, their first step in helping the child is to attach a diagnostic label to the child so that appropriate treatment may be prescribed. However, the classification of the child's

---

[1]Alan O. Ross, "Learning difficulties of children: Dysfunctional, disorders, disabilities," *Journal of School Psychology*, Vol. 5, (1967), pp. 82-92. Reprinted in N. J. Long, W. C. Morse, and R. G. Newman (eds.), *Conflict in the classroom: The education of children with problems* (Belmont, Wadsworth, 1971), p. 168.
[2]Ira. J. Gordon, *Studying the child in the school* (New York, Wiley, 1966), p. 5.

problem into one of many learning problem categories is difficult because most experts disagree as to the exact nature of these categories. Such terms as "perceptually handicapped," "brain injured," and "exogenous" may be useful in grouping children who exhibit certain behavioral patterns but this procedure does not automatically lead to the prescription of appropriate treatment. In addition, the use of these terms interferes with the communication during the consultation since most teachers do not understand them.

It is the purpose of this chapter to review some of the concepts of learning disabilities, their causes, how they can be evaluated, what can be done about them, and what is the nature of administrative functions in overcoming them. The variety and complexity of learning disabilities are such that we can only provide an introduction or orientation to the problems. School psychologists and counselors should have extended preparation to qualify for dealing with learning disability problems.

CONCEPTS OF LEARNING DISABILITY

One of the basic problems in developing a program for the remediation of learning difficulties is to define the nature of the learning difficulty. In recent years such terms as "educationally handicapped," "minimal brain dysfunction" or "minimal brain syndrome," "psycholinguistic disability," "perceptual disability," "reading disability," and "slow learner" have been used to refer to learning disabilities. Typically, a child is assumed to have a learning difficulty when his academic achievement falls below his intellectual potential, i.e., he is an "underachiever." The discrepancy between actual performance and expected performance is taken as an indication of the presence of a learning disability. This procedure presents the school staff with a series of complex problems to resolve. Chief among them is the establishment of criteria for the evaluation of academic performance and for the estimation of intellectual potential. Each conceptual approach to learning disability must take a position on these matters.

A definition of learning disability which is widely accepted is that given by Kirk and Bateman.

A learning disability refers to a retardation, disorder, or delayed development in one or more of the processes of speech, language, reading, writing, arithmetic, or other school subjects, resulting from a psychological handicap caused by a possible cerebral dysfunction and/or emotional or behavioral disturbances. It is not the result of mental retardation, sensory deprivation, or instructional factors.[3]

This is obviously a very broad and inclusive definition.

Several years later Bateman modified this definition, suggesting that children who have specific learning disabilities are those who

1. Manifest an educationally significant discrepancy between their estimated intellectual potential and actual performance ...
2. related to basic disorders in the learning process ...
3. which may or may not be accompanied by a demonstrable central nervous system dysfunction, and ...
4. which are not secondary to generalized mental retardation, educational or cultural deprivation, severe emotional disturbance, or sensory loss.[4]

The above definition differs from the earlier one in that it includes the notion of discrepancy between actual performance and estimated ability and rules out emotional disturbance as a causal factor.

Myers and Hammill suggest that specific learning disorders are associated with one or more of the following three impairments of prelinguistic and/or linguistic functions:

1. Loss of an established basic process.
2. Inhibition of the development of such a process.
3. Interference with the function of such a process.[5]

They suggest that these three impairments affect the child's perceptual, language, and motor performance by disrupting his de-

---

[3]Samuel A. Kirk and Barbara Bateman, "Diagnosis and remediation of learning disabilities," *Exceptional Children,* Vol. 29 (1962), p. 73.

[4]Barbara Bateman, "An educator's view of a diagnostic approach to learning disorder," in J. Helmuth (ed.), *Learning disorders* (Seattle, Special Child Publications, 1965). Quoted by P. I. Myers and D. D. Hammill, *Methods for learning disorders* (New York, Wiley, 1969), p. 2.

[5]*Op. cit.,* p. 6.

coding (receptive) pathways, his encoding pathways, or the association between encoding and decoding. For example, a child's reading difficulty may stem from a problem of visual decoding. Typically, the child who manifests a learning disability experiences more than one problem in varying degrees of severity.

Most definitions of learning disability exclude children who are mentally retarded, who have suffered cultural deprivation, who have a sensory defect, or who show signs of severe emotional disturbance. This exclusion of exceptional children reflects in part the procedures that are used to help them. Typically the exceptional child is placed in a special class for the entire day. Most programs designed to help children with learning disabilities emphasize tutoring by the regular classroom teacher or by an itinerant specialist for only part of the day. The reason for helping the child for only part of the school day reflects the assumption that the child is "normal" intellectually, emotionally, and sensorally, and therefore can profit from most of the activities of the typical classroom.

It is apparent that, even with these exclusions, learning disabilities constitute a broad and varied class of behaviors or problems.

Mention must be made of another term, related to learning disability—"the slow learner." Slow learning, like learning disability, is subject to many different interpretations. From an administrative point of view, slow learning may include the following types of students: underachiever, mentally retarded, sensorily impaired, emotionally disturbed, and culturally deprived. Younie describes the slow learner in the following manner:

> There is general agreement that the condition of slow learning exists but very little agreement as to just who the slow learner is. The term "slow learning" adequately describes a global concept but does not serve to define consistently the school functioning of the individual learners. The general concept of slow learning includes the implication that intellectual development has been somewhat retarded to the point that persons defined as slow learners cannot meet the standard learning expectations of the school.[6]

---

[6]William J. Younie, *Instructional approaches to slow learning* (New York, Teachers College Press, 1967), p. 5.

Younie lists the following characteristics of the slow learner:

1. Typically the slow learner's intelligence range is 75 to 90.
2. The slow learner is 1½ to 2 years behind in academic achievement.
3. The slow learner's emotional and social behavior is within the normal range accepted by the school.
4. The slow learner has exhibited this problem for a long period of time.[7]

He believes that the above characteristics are useful in developing screening procedures, in evolving instructional materials, and in developing administrative procedures for the slow learner program. The concept of the slow learner would appear to be outside the area of learning disabilities. It essentially refers to those students whose relatively low academic ability retard their learning or academic progress.

ETIOLOGY OF LEARNING DISABILITIES

The concept of learning disabilities assumes that there is a relationship between neurological functioning and learning. It is postulated that a learning disability exists when there is a deficiency in the ability of the brain to receive, categorize, and integrate information which affects the child's actual performance in the classroom. However, it is the child's behavioral manifestations in the classroom and home and not neurological evidence of the nature and extent of the brain involvement that determines the diagnosis of minimal cerebral dysfunction.

It is difficult to establish the role that brain damage plays in any learning disability. Although a child may be classified as having minimal cerebral dysfunction it has been demonstrated that neurological impairment does not follow any typical preconceived set of behaviors.

> While evidence suggests that such behavior seldom exists in the absence of brain damage, organicity appears to be the consequence of certain types of brain damage, and should in no sense be mistaken as a prototype of disturbances which may accompany all instances of injury to the brain. Thus, cerebral dysfunction is complex and

---

[7]*Ibid.*, p. 19.

individualistic; its manifestations may depend on the locus, extent, and character of the dysfunction as well as the developmental stage during which the dysfunction originated and the nature of the causal agent(s).[8]

Although in many cases of learning disabilities it is impossible to make a definitive identification of the brain injured area, it can be assumed from a clinical point of view that neurological damage did occur. McCarthy and McCarthy make the following observation on the causes of neurological impairment.

> Typically, cerebral dysfunction in children dates from events preceding or surrounding the birth process. Germ plasm defects, noxious influences and agents affecting the development of the embryo, fetus, or infant, and chemical or mechanical factors may damage, directly or indirectly, the delicate and irreplaceable neural tissue of the newborn. Traumatic, poisonous, or infectious factors may be responsible for postnatal insult. Verifiable neurological impairment, such as cerebral palsy, is known to be associated with a history of prematurity, anoxia, toxemia of pregnancy, Rh incompatibility, maternal rubella or unusual delivery.[9]

It should be pointed out that a complete neurological examination including an electroencephalographic test can fail to discover positive evidence of brain injury. Hallahan and Cruickshank make the following observation on this point:

> We feel strongly that functional causes may bring about the abnormal development of certain learning patterns in the child without necessarily causing cellular disturbance. For example, it may be that a child can learn to be hyperactive or may, through lack of experience, not learn or develop appropriate perceptual-motor behaviors. Educational programming for the learning disabled child with demonstrable neurological impairment and for the learning disabled child without brain injury, should virtually be the same, if the *behaviors* of the two are alike.[10]

They also believe that there are three aspects of human development which separately or in combination with one another may

---

[8]James J. McCarthy and Joan F. McCarthy, *Learning disabilities* (Boston, Allyn and Bacon), p. 11.

[9]*Ibid.*

[10]Daniel P. Hallahan and William M. Cruickshank, *Psychoeducational foundations of learning disabilities* (Englewood Cliffs, Prentice-Hall, 1973), p. 13.

be influential in inducing neurological impairment which results in a perceptual dysfunction that can be related to a specific learning disability. These factors are specific neurological insults, nutritional deprivation, and factors of environmental deprivation. Hallahan and Cruickshank suggest that neurological damage can be inferred from impairment of such factors as gross visual motor skills, tactual perception in relation to fine-motor movement, and the ability to accurately perceive material. However, they suggest that it is rather difficult to point out how nutritional and environmental deprivation can produce a cellular dysfunction which results in a specific perceptual disorder. Since most of the data on these two factors are obtained from studies of animals and uncontrolled studies of human beings, it is difficult to make a definitive statement as to their explicit role in learning disabilities.

CHARACTERISTICS OF A LEARNING DISABLED CHILD

Most instances of learning disability are discovered by teachers because the overt behaviors displayed by these children disrupt classroom procedures. The behaviors most frequently noted by teachers are hyperactivity, impulsiveness, and distractability. A more complete list of characteristics is presented by Capobianco. He suggests that a teacher will find no difficulty in recognizing that all is not well with a child who:

Follows no logical pattern in his behavior

Never sticks with anything over a long period of time

Wanders aimlessly about the room apparently concerned with everyone else's business.

Never sits still for a minute—always runs, never walks.

Acts before thinking, seldom considering the consequences of his behavior

Repeats, excessively, a task or movement

May be able to read but not comprehend the significance of what he reads

Experiences difficulties in arithmetic, performing at a level far below expectancy

Demonstrates visual-motor difficulties

Seems at times to be out of contact—does not hear you

Rapidly changes his mood or temperament

Performs inconsistently and with marked variability in the various school subjects.[11]

Many of the above characteristics have been derived from studies of children who have been classified as having a learning disability. It should be pointed out that not all of these characteristics need be present in any one child, nor should any single characteristic be used as an indicator of learning disability. If a teacher observes several of them in a child, she should ask for a consultation with a pupil services staff member so that additional steps can be taken to ascertain the presence and the degree of learning disability.

DIAGNOSIS OF LEARNING DISABILITIES

The diagnosis of a learning disability is a complex process because of the lack of definitive criteria for assessing the child and his behaviors. The problem is further complicated by the lack of a clear-cut approach to diagnosis of learning disabilities which in turn affects the role relationship problems of those who are responsible for carrying out the diagnostic process.

EVALUATION STRATEGY

Bateman suggests that the evaluation strategy is influenced by the *orientation* (i.e. medicine, psychology, education) of those who undertake the process, their *focus* (i.e. on etiology, diagnosis, or remediation) and what *problems* (i.e. visual-motor, communication disorders, reading) they believe are signs of learning disability.[12] She believes that no matter what approach is used in the evaluation, the process "must include assessment of both the level of performance and the manner of performance and that it must seek the precise formulation of a specific disability."[13] She suggests that a "standard battery" approach should be used for

---

[11]R. J. Capobianco, "Diagnostic methods used with learning disability cases," *Exceptional Children,* Vol. 31 (1964), p. 190.

[12]Barbara Bateman, "Learning disabilities—yesterday, today, and tomorrow," *Exceptional Children,* Vol. 31 (1964), pp. 167-177.

[13]*Ibid.,* p. 171.

initial screening while an "individually chosen" test approach should be used for the identification and defining of the specific learning disability.

The diagnostic-etiological approach attempts to establish the cause of the learning disability by using the services of such medical personnel as pediatricians, neurologists, ophthamologists, and otolaryngologists. A detailed developmental case history of the child is obtained as well as his current anatomical-physiological-cognitive functioning.

> Special emphasis is placed upon neurophysical and neuroanatomical disorders of which the following are most common: developmental defects (malformation of the spinal cord and brain), infections (e.g., poliomyelitis, encephalitis, syphilis), vascular lesions (circulatory changes or dysfunction), tumors, trauma (head or spinal injuries), metabolic diseases (endocrine gland and blood diseases) diseases caused by toxins (tetanus, lead, barbituates).[14]

Specific remedial procedures for the child are generated from the obtained medical and psychological data.

The diagnostic-remedial approach is designed to bridge the gap between the etiological oriented process and the remedial process. Its purpose is to discover what to teach the child as well as how to teach the child. "Once the child's pattern of perceptual, integrative, and expressive strengths and weaknesses has been reliably assessed and verified, a decision must be made as to whether he should be taught by methods which capitalize on his strengths or require exercise of his weaknesses."[15] Bateman suggests that an individualized remedial plan for the pupil be derived from the interaction between the child-study findings and the subject matter and methods used to teach it. However, it should be pointed out that in order for a meaningful remedial plan to be developed for a child the diagnostic findings must be specific rather than general. Most teachers would find it difficult to translate the diagnostic observation that a child has performed

---

[14]Thomas Oakland, "Diagnostic help 5¢: Examiner is in," *Psychology in the Schools,* Vol. 6 (1969), p. 360.

[15]Barbara Bateman, "Three approaches to diagnosis and educational planning for children with learning disabilities," *Academic Therapy,* Vol. 2 (1966), pp. 196, 217.

poorly on a test of perceptual motor ability into a specific remedial plan.

The task analysis approach focuses on what specific educational tasks the child needs to learn rather than on the general extrapolation of diagnostic observations. Bateman believes that the nature of the tasks a child should learn can be obtained by asking either the norm referenced question "When do other children ordinarily learn certain tasks?" or the criterion referenced question "What does the child need to be taught in order to accomplish a specific educational outcome?"[16] This procedure requires that there be specific objectives for all of the students, not only learning disabled, as well as the development of criterion-referenced tests, baseline observations of children, and the assessment of actual performance. The child's failure to learn the material is looked upon as an inadequacy in the instructional process rather than his inability to learn it.

Most educational programs designed to help the learning disabled child incorporate all three approaches, for not to do so would do a gross injustice to the child.

ROLE OF SCHOOL PERSONNEL

The teacher plays an instrumental role in identifying those children who are suspected of having learning disabilities. She does this primarily by systematically observing the behavior of all her pupils. Rating scales are useful for this purpose since most of them provide for an orderly procedure for observing and recording pupil behavior. They can help to identify those children who have short attention spans, erratic behavior, and who exhibit hyperactivity. In addition, the sociogram may be used to validate some of the teacher's observations for there is a tendency for pupils to reject the uninhibited child. Poor academic performance, unusual drawings, and lack of motor coordination may also be used as signs of learning disability.

It is not too realistic to ask the teacher to keep detailed records on all of the pupils in her class. It is for this reason that assistance in the form of in-service training in observation, availability

---

[16]*Ibid.,* p. 220.

of rating scales developed by learning disabilities specialists, and help in observing the child should be available to the teacher. The counselor as a coordinator of personnel services should see that this type of assistance is provided. In addition, he should arrange for consultation with the school psychologist and when necessary, set up the schedule for the psychological testing of the child.

The school psychologists play an instrumental role in the psychological assessment of the child. The evaluation may include the Illinois Test of Psycholinguistic Ability, the Frostig Test of Visual Perception, Wepman's Test of Auditory Discrimination, Purdue Perceptual Motor Survey, the Developmental Reading Tests, and Stanford Diagnostic Arithmetic Test. In addition an individual test of intelligence will usually be administered. This psychological assessment is used to corroborate and quantify information obtained in the medical case history.

It is difficult if not impossible for one person to integrate all of the information obtained about the child into a meaningful remedial program. It is for this reason that the counselor, school psychologist, social worker, teachers, and principal should be involved in developing the individualized remedial program for the child. Parents should also be involved in the process since many home activities could be used to supplement the work of the school. If the school district does not have a learning disabilities specialist, then either the counselor or school psychologist could serve as a coordinator of the effort used to help the learning disabled child.

THE REMEDIAL PROGRAM

One of the basic concerns of school administrators is to evolve a meaningful instructional program which provides for individual differences. Shane, et al. have observed that although numerous approaches have been made to resolve the problem of individual differences no basic solution has been derived.[17] They cite studies

---

[17]June Grant Shane, Harold G. Shane, Robert Gibson, and Paul F. Munger, *Guiding human development* (Worthington, Charles A. Jones Publishing Company, 1971), p. 50.

which show that the reduction of the ability range in a class-room does not automatically lead to increased academic achievement. They are of the opinion that the quest for a magical plan which significantly improves individualized instruction is futile. This conclusion supports the contention of the advocates of the diagnostic-remedial approach that children who have learning disabilities are best helped by custom-made programs rather than preconceived or standard remedial plans.

SPECIFIC ASPECTS OF PROGRAM DEVELOPMENT

Younie suggests that the following aspects must be considered when planning programs for children who have been classified as either slow learners or learning disabled:[18]

1. Grouping
2. Selection procedures
3. Class size
4. Integration
5. Communication
6. Remedial services
7. Guidance
8. Record keeping
9. Marking
10. Reporting
11. Promotion and graduation
12. Research
13. Teacher competencies

He believes that there is very little research evidence which can be used to develop a universal set of guidelines for any of the above areas. He suggests that decisions about these factors "must be made at the local level after weighing the type or types of slow learners enrolled, the level at which the slow learners are accepted by the school, the specific adaptability of the school itself, and the willingness of the school to expend the effort and money required by certain choices."[19]

TEACHER'S ROLE IN THE REMEDIAL PROGRAM

The teacher is the key person who translates the school's concern for the learning disabled child into action. She must be skilled in matching the needs, strengths, and limitations of the child to the available instructional resources. In addition she should be adaptive, creative, and have a positive outlook.

---

[18]Younie, *op. cit.*, p. 58.
[19]*Ibid.*

Patience is essential if the child is to have the time and opportunity to express himself; but the child must also have a measure of instructional challenge born of intellectual patience. The teacher should know how to minimize unnecessary failure.... The teacher should exercise his imagination concerning program goals but must always temper his dreams with the reality of the child's background and the attitudes of school and society.[20]

Since teacher attitude and competency play such an important role in helping the learning disabled child, the administrator should use the grouping procedure suggested by Thelen, who advocates an individuality-centered approach to elementary education.[21] Thelen suggests that grouping of students be based on answers to the following two questions: "What sort of student can a given teacher teach most effectively?" and "What sort of teacher can a given student learn from most effectively?"

The Thelen approach suggests that a learning disabled child should not be assigned to a classroom teacher without first assessing the degree of compatibility between the child and the teacher. The assessment provides a means for determining whether the classroom teacher can successfully carry out the remedial program prescribed for the child. Although a teacher may be successful in teaching normal children she may lack the personal qualities, such as great patience, which are necessary for helping the learning disabled child.

It is perhaps because of the unwillingness of school districts to evaluate the personal attributes of teachers that many of them have turned to a pre-planned approach of helping the learning disabled child.

CLASSROOM PROGRAMS[22]

The programs which are briefly described below refer to recent attempts to extend and extrapolate from programs designed for the normal child to methods for those children judged to have an established handicap. Since the learning disabled child's problem comes from dysfunctions in the perceptual or conceptual proc-

---

[20]*Ibid.*, p. 56.

[21]Herbert Thelen, *Classroom grouping for teachability* (New York, Wiley, 1967).

[22]This section is based on Chapter 5, McCarthy and McCarthy, *op. cit.*

esses, two major approaches are used to help him. The process orientation approach developed by special educators "attempts to identify the learning process responsible for the defective performance and apply remediation at this level hoping for the improvement in all tool subjects which rely on the adequate functioning of that learning process."[23] The tool subject approach developed by remedial specialists "attempts to develop techniques to teach a tool subject (e.g., reading or arithmetic to children who have failed to learn via methods employed in the regular classroom)."[24]

VISUAL-PERCEPTUAL-MOTOR APPROACH

This type of instructional program is based on the movigenic theory of Barsch which advocates that perceptual and motor skills must be established before academic learning can take place. Thus the program features such activities as walking rails, patterning exercises, rhythms, visual training, individual activities, and reading.

LINGUISTIC PROGRAM

Linguistic programs stress activities which stimulate the child's talking, listening, and reading. Toy phones, doll houses, and conversation pieces of all sorts are used to help the child verbalize. Conferences, group meetings, and school visits are used to help parents to understand the child's problem and show them how they can assist in the remediation process.

DIAGNOSTIC-REMEDIAL PROGRAMS

This program features remediation exercises which are used to enhance the child's academic functioning and which are based on patterns of disability discovered during the diagnostic process. Typically, the child receives remediation in the regular classroom or in the resource room, but may be placed in a special self-contained classroom for the entire day if the disability is severe. The

---

[23]*Ibid.*, p. 75.
[24]*Ibid.*

goal of the program is to utilize the child's strengths in remediating his weakness.

In general there is a need for greater integration of approaches. The ideal is to match the child to the program. Since this approach can only take place in large school districts, most districts feature only one or two basic tactics in helping the learning disabled children.

DRUG THERAPY

Drug therapy is sometimes used in conjunction with programs that feature remedial education and individualized task prescription. When drugs are used either to calm the overactive child or to energize the anxious or inhibited child, they tend to be used with treatment programs that feature conditioning or counterconditioning procedures. Werry believes that pharmacotherapy must take place within the context of a multi-lateral treatment program because drugs "will not of themselves do anything permanently to strengthen (or condition) the non-hyperactive behaviors or to weaken (or extinguish) the hyperactive behaviors though resultant changes in environmental responses to the child's drug-induced behavior or his discovery of successful learning may result ultimately in durable changes in behavior."[25] Keough, in her review of research on drug therapy, observed that improvement in learning was found to occur in only one-third of the studies while improvement in the child's behavior occurred in one-half of the studies.[26] This observation supports Werry's contention that drug therapy should be used as an adjunct rather than the main treatment procedure in helping children who have learning disabilities.

Stimulant drugs such as dextraamphetamine and methlyphenidate and depressants such as chlorpromozine and thioridazine are commonly prescribed for children who have a learning disorder. The specific manner in which these drugs influence the

[25]John S. Werry, "The diagnosis, etiology, and treatment of hyperactivity in children," in J. Hellmuth (ed.), *Learning disorders* (Seattle, Special Child Publications), Vol. 3 (1968), p. 179.

[26]Barbara Keough, "Hyperactivity and learning disorders: Review and speculation," *Exceptional Children*, Vol. 38 (1971), pp. 101-110.

learning process is not known. It has been noted that these drugs do have such side effects as gastrointestinal upset, insomnia, and alterations in pigment metabolism. Although drugs can be useful in making some children more tractable, they should be administered only after understanding how they influence the child's total personality and the world around him.

PSYCHOTHERAPY

Werry suggests that there is little research evidence to indicate that traditional psychotherapy can be useful in treating children with learning disabilities particularly if they manifest hyperactivity.[27] He recommends that a behavior modification program which uses a variety of reinforcement and punishment contingencies in conjunction with parental counseling and with appropriate instructional materials be used. He believes that this type of treatment program has greater utility than traditional psychotherapy.

Friedland and Shilkret suggest that group counseling may be appropriate "in those instances of hyperactive behavior which occur in an interpersonal context; that is, where the interaction with another person seems to result in an increment of hyperactive behavior." They are of the opinion that some children who are anxious about forming a relationship with adults use hyperactivity as a coping device.[28] Peer groups may be useful in helping the child improve his interpersonal skills so that he becomes more comfortable in relating with adults.

PROCEDURAL CONCERNS

Any treatment procedure should be seen as an active intervention into the life of the pupil and his family rather than as a resolution of a problem. The school staff should be sensitive to the impact that the diagnosis and prescriptions have on the child and should therefore structure the helping process about humanistic as well as utilitarian values. Wood suggests that the initial

---

[27]Werry, *op. cit.*

[28]S. J. Friedland and R. B. Shilkret, "Alternative explanations of learning disabilities: Defensive hyperactivity," *Exceptional Children,* Vol. 40 (1973), p. 214.

intervention plan be formulated by a special educator with assistance by the regular classroom teacher, school administrator, psychologists, and parents.[29] He further recommends that the intervention plan be negotiated and justified so that the rights of the child are protected. "A model who actively justifies and negotiates his interventions into the lives of others in terms of their needs as well as his own needs is preferable to one who appears to children to impose his objectives on them arbitrarily through his control of important environmental contingencies."[30] Essentially Wood is suggesting that the child and his parents be informed about what is going on, how they can help in the treatment process, and what outcomes should be expected. In many instances the interpersonal context of the intervention can be instrumental in helping the child overcome his learning disability.

SUMMARY

There are two basic problems in helping the learning disabled child. The first is that there is little agreement among authorities as to the nature and cause of the dysfunction. There are many different kinds and degrees of learning disabilities, singly and in combination. The lack of a clear-cut definition of learning disability gives rise to the second problem which is the scantiness of prescribed diagnostic procedures for use with children who are suspected of having a learning disability. In general the type of help that is given to a learning disabled child is an artifact of the interaction among the orientation of the helper (e.g., medical or psychological), the focus (e.g., etiological, remedial, task analysis), and the types of problems (e.g., reading, visual-motor) used as signs of dysfunction.

All school personnel are involved in helping the learning disabled child. The classroom teacher plays the key role in the helping process for she identifies the child who needs help, assists in the diagnostic process, prescribes some of the corrective exercises, and carries certain phases of the remedial program.

---

[29]T. H. Wood, "Negotiation and justification: An intervention model," *Exceptional Children*, Vol. 40 (1973), pp. 185-191.

[30]*Ibid.*, p. 190.

The school counselor plays only a minimal role in helping learning disabled children; he typically helps the teacher validate some of her observations, may act as a consultant for parents, and on occasion act as a coordinator of the program. The school psychologist and social worker play instrumental roles in that the latter helps with observing the child's behaviors and with working with parents while the former undertakes many of the psychologically oriented diagnostic activities.

Many different approaches are used to help the learning disabled child. In part the programs reflect the theoretical orientation of those who direct them. The multiplicity of programs points out that no single tactic can be used to help these children. Their problems are varied and complex and the help given them must by nature be flexible and interdisciplinary.

SUGGESTED READINGS

Frostig, Marianne and Maslow, Phyllis: *Learning problems in the classroom.* New York, Grune and Stratton, 1973.

Holt, Fred D. and Kicklighter, Richard H.: *Psychological services in the schools.* Dubuque, Wm. C. Brown Company, 1971.

McCarthy, James J. and McCarthy, Joan F.: *Learning disabilities.* Boston, Allyn and Bacon, 1969.

PART III

THE COUNSELOR AND THE SCHOOL AND COMMUNITY

Chapter 9

CONSULTING AND COUNSELING WITH TEACHERS AND ADMINISTRATORS

E LEMENTARY SCHOOL COUNSELING has incorporated consultation as one of its functions. Because consulting is in the
process of evolving, elementary school counselors are having
problems in relating different kinds of consultation with desired
ends. Since many other professional fields have used consultation
to intensify and enhance the services they provide their clients,
a review of what others have done may be helpful to counselors.
This chapter will critique the concepts, uses and outcomes of consultation in other fields. By comparing consulting activities of
elementary school counselors with those undertaken by other professional workers, a better understanding of the process may be
achieved.

SCOPE OF THE LITERATURE

Mental health consultation evolved out of the need for increased mental health services. In the early 1950's mental health
consultation was seen as a "vehicle for the systematic extension of
mental health principles and practices to other professionals and
community service workers."[1] Case collaboration and psychiatric

---

[1] C. H. Haylett and L. Rapoport, Mental Health Consultation. In *Handbook of
community psychiatry and community mental health*, L. Bellak (ed.), New
York, Grune and Stratton, 1964).

case consultation techniques were used to enhance the skills and understandings of workers who provided mental health services. By the end of the 1950's the term "mental health consultation" was extended to include assistance given to referred clients and to development and appraisal of mental health programs.

The term consultation is not indigenous to mental health services. Medicine, business, nursing, education, and engineering are among some of the fields that consider consultation as a professional activity. Mannino, conducting a systematic review of literature on consultation, identified 646 articles on the subject.[2] In his review he suggests that the articles reveal a lack of consensus regarding theory and practice of consultation.

Patouillet was among the first to state that consulting should be one of the professional activities of the elementary school counselor.[3] Believing that guidance is everybody's business, Patouillet suggested that the elementary school counselor should coordinate the program because of his skill in human relations. "The guidance worker, therefore, is essentially a consultant in human relations who involves, in a cooperative enterprise, all those who affect the development of the child."[4] In the 1960's the emphasis changed from coordination to direct consultation with teachers, parents, and administrators. Eckerson and Smith suggest that the elementary school counselor should work with teachers and parents to help all children maximize their abilities for their own development and for the good of society.[5] Identification of problem children and prevention of mental illness were principal goals of the consultation program.

Faust, who has been influential in shaping elementary school counseling, believes that the elementary school counselor should primarily serve as a consultant to teachers.[6] He sees in-service

[2]F. V. Mannino, *Consultation in mental health, and related fields: a reference guide* (Washington, Public Health Service Publication, 1969).

[3]R. Patouillet, "Organizing for guidance in the elementary school," *Teachers College Record*, Vol. 58 (1957), pp. 40-44.

[4]*Ibid.*, p. 40.

[5]L. O. Eckerson and H. M. Smith, "Elementary school guidance: The consultant," *School Life* (July, 1962).

[6]V. Faust. *The counselor-consultant in the elementary school.* (Boston, Houghton-Mifflin, 1968).

training and staffing of cases as the two chief means of assisting teachers. Kaczkowski recommends that the child, not the teacher or parent, be the focal point of consultation.[7] He believes that when the counselor acts as a consultant he should help the adult examine the relationship that the adult has with the child. The consultant plays the dual role of problem solver and human relations mediator.

DEFINITIONS OF CONSULTATION

Consultation is a comprehensive term that includes a diversity of meanings and activities. Because of a lack of uniform terminology, a definition acceptable to all professional fields cannot be made. Nomenclature developed by Caplan is usually used to describe the activities of a consultant.[8] Typically, the "consultant" is a specialist who works with another professional, a "consultee," who requires some type of assistance with a current work problem. The "client" is someone who is served by the "consultee."

Caplan defines mental health consultation "as an interaction process taking place between two professional workers, the consultant and the consultee. In the interaction the consultant attempts to help the consultee solve a mental health problem of his client or clients within the framework of his usual professional functioning." Although the consultant may offer "helpful clarifications, diagnostic interpretations, or advice on treatment, the professional responsibility remains with the consultee."[9]

Some definitions of mental health consultation are rather vague. For example, Rieman defined mental health consultation as a "helping process, an educational process, and a growth process achieved through interpersonal relationships."[10] Spielberg sees mental health consultation as "a mechanism whereby the mental

[7]H. Kaczkowski, "The elementary school counselor as a consultant," *Elementary School Guidance and Counseling*, Vol. 1 (1967), pp. 103-111.

[8]G. Caplan, *Concepts of mental health and consultation* (Washington, U. S. Department of Health, Education, and Welfare, 1959).

[9]*Ibid.*, p. 52.

[10]D. W. Rieman, "Group mental health consultation with public health nurses," in *Consultation in social work*, L. Rapoport (ed.). (New York, National Association of Social Work, 1963).

health specialist may assist the caretaking agents of the community so that the latter within the framework of their usual professional roles, can better utilize mental health principles."[11] Haylett and Rapoport state that "all mental health consultation is directed toward helping the consultees to understand and cope with selected work problems . . . all consultation is consultee-centered and task oriented."[12]

Those defining the consultation function in elementary school guidance tend to be general rather than specific. The ACES-ASCA committee defined consultation as "the process of sharing with another person or group of persons, information, and ideas of combining knowledge into new patterns and making mutually agreed upon decisions about the next step needed."[13] In a similar manner Dinkmeyer defines consultation as a "process by which significant adults in the life of the child communicate about him." Its goal is to increase "the effectiveness of their relationship with the child or group of children."[14] Hume sees consulting "as a generalist function in the sense that it includes not only consultation with the school staff and parents regarding pupils receiving counseling but also involves consultation oriented toward a primary prevention and development of all pupils."[15] McGehearty's concept of consultation is similar to that of Caplan's. "The consultant . . . is an expert in a specific area, ready to work with the consultee about problems he is having in relation to a third person, the client."[16] A variation of the Caplanian theme is found in

---

[11]C. D. Spielberg, "A mental health consultation program in a small community with limited professional mental health resources." In *Emergent approaches to mental health problems,* E. C. Cowen, C. A. Gardner, and M. Zax (eds.), (New York, Appleton-Century-Crofts, 1967).

[12]Haylett and Rapoport, *op. cit.,* p. 330.

[13]ACES-ASCA Joint Committee Report on Elementary School Counselor, April 2, 1966. In *Guidance and counseling in the elementary school: Readings in theory and practice,* Don Dinkmeyer (ed.), (New York, Holt, Rinehart & Winston, 1968), p. 101.

[14]*Ibid.,* p. 96.

[15]K. E. Hume, "Counseling and consulting: Complementary functions," *Elementary School Guidance and Counseling,* Vol. 5 (1970), pp. 3-11.

[16]L. McGehearty, "Consultation and counseling," *Elementary School Guidance and Counseling,* Vol. 3 (1969), pp. 155-163.

the writings of Faust. He believes that consultation is always focused on some unit external to the consultee. "In the case of the consultant to a teacher, the external unit may be a child, instructional method, course content, etc."[17] Consultation can also take place with children, parents, administrators, and referral agencies.

Most definitions of consultation tend to be more descriptive than delimiting. To some degree, each definition contains elements of problem solving, teaching, and helping functions. The balance between cognitive emphasis (i.e., imparting technical information) and affective emphasis (i.e., concern with relationships) is affected by the professional concerns of the consultant and the setting in which he operates. His involvement with problem solving, teaching, and helping may be direct or indirect. The general goal of consultation appears to be the enhancement of the professional effectiveness of the consultee.

DIFFERENTIATION AMONG TYPES OF PROCEDURES

One can infer from the various definitions of consultation that this procedure has much in common with professional education, in-service training, collaboration, supervision, and psychotherapy. Caplan has pointed out that each of these procedures has an educative and helping facet in its methodology; however, he believes that in order to attain a high level of professional functioning, it is necessary to differentiate among these professional activities.[18] The bases for differentiating could be purpose, authority, role relationships, rather than techniques, knowledge, or skills.[19]

The primary purpose of *professional education* is to prepare an individual for a profession by means of a learning experience that is formal, orderly, and sequential in nature. Mahoney sees consultation "as a resource used by a person already trained in his profession."[20] He sees the process of mental health consultation

---

[17]Faust, *op. cit.*, p. 40.

[18]G. Caplan, *op. cit.*, p. 53.

[19]C. H. Haylett and L. Rapoport, *op. cit.*, p. 331.

[20]S. C. Mahoney, "Mental health consultation," (Unpublished manuscript), cited in *Psychiatry in the American community*, H. G. Whittington (ed.), (New York, International Universities Press, Inc., 1966).

as starting with the immediate problem (with transfer of learning as a secondary result) while formal education proceeds from general procedures to specific applications. Caplan contrasts consultation and education, pointing out the latter's emphasis on a predetermined curriculum while the former is more opportunistic in nature.

The aim of *in-service training* is "to provide specific new material and new content related to the agency's expectations of the individual receiving training."[21] "In-service training utilizes educational measures to maintain or improve competencies in a job; presumably, the minimum professional requirements have already been met."[22] But differences between consultation and in-service work can be blurred if the goal of each is to improve the professional competence of the staff. Haylett and Rapoport suggest that the differentiation between the two should be on the basis of the degree of focus on current work problems, level of training of participants, and the extent of systematic coverage of the subject.

The degree of responsibility is the essential factor in differentiating between consultation and *collaboration*. "In collaboration, persons who have a joint responsibility for some case or professional activity interact for such purposes as identifying problems, sharing information, or considering various alternatives and plans for cooperative action."[23] The consultant does not assume any direct responsibility for a client even though he may interview, psychologically appraise, or propose alternative courses of action. If at any point during the consultation, the consultant assumes any responsibility for the client, then the consultation becomes a collaboration.

Supervision is distinguished from consultation in that the supervisor has administrative authority and power. The supervisor has a responsibility to the agency and to the client. Since the supervisor is accountable for the quality of outcome, he must see to it

[21]*Ibid.*, p. 205.

[22]C. H. Haylett and L. Rapoport, *op. cit.*, p. 335.

[23]J. F. Gorman, "Some characteristics of consultation." In *Consultation in social work*, L. Rapoport (ed.), (New York, National Association of Social Work, 1963).

that the agency is investing its resources into its primary tasks and that the supervisees are working at their assigned tasks. Supervision and consultation are similar in that both focus on work-centered problems and on enhancing the competency of the professional workers.

The essential difference between consultation and *counseling or psychotherapy* is that the latter is concerned with personal problems while the former is concerned with work problems. The diversity of goals and techniques of psychotherapy precludes categorical comparison with consultation. Insley believes that consultation resembles case work in that both utilize much of the same content. "This content is based on knowledge of psycho-social factors in individual and family situations, and community resources to meet the needs of these individuals and families."[24] Gorman points out that although consultation uses many of the same techniques as case work, the consultant uses them more selectively. She is of the opinion that "both casework and psycho-therapy are direct services, whereas consultation is an indirect service vis-a-vis the clientele of a professional person or agency."[25]

TYPES OF CONSULTATION

Many proposals have been made to classify in some orderly manner the many kinds of consulting activities. Mannino and Shore are of the opinion that these typologies are empirically de-rived in that they are based "mostly on personal experience, clinical practice, or a general intuitive feeling for what is going on in the field."[26] The various classification systems have value in that they permit the summarization and comparison of consulting experiences in different professional fields. Communication is facilitated by characterizing the consultation by means of anal-ysis of selected activities. According to Haylett and Rapoport,

---

[24]V. Insley, "Social work consultation in public health." In *Concepts of mental health consultation.* (Washington, U. S. Department of Health, Education, and Welfare, 1959).

[25]Gorman, *op. cit.,* p. 42.

[26]F. V. Mannino and M. F. Shore, "Consultation research," in *Mental health and related fields.* Washington, Public Health Monograph, Vol. 79 (1971).

criteria used to classify activities in mental health consultation are:

(1) method used (such as group work or group consultation); (2) the content of the work problems presented by the consultee (such as case material, program considerations, or administrative matters); (3) the problem area on which the consultant focuses (such as problems of the client, problems of the consultee in dealing with his client or with other professional tasks, or the problems of the organization in relation to policies and procedures as they affect the mental health of the client).[27]

Caplan used focus and problem to derive a fourfold classification of mental health consultation: (1) client-centered case conference; (2) consultee-centered case conference; (3) consultee-centered administrative consultation; (4) program-centered consultation.[28] Haylett and Rapoport developed a threefold classification of mental health consultation: client, consultee, and program. In addition to the above typologies, psychiatric consultation activities have been grouped into syndrome, situation, and community factors.

The activities of elementary school consultation have not been classified in any systematic manner. The tendency of most writers is to list or describe the activities that are undertaken by the counselor consultant. Dinkmeyer and Caldwell, and Faust formulate a heirarchy of consultation roles.[29] Preference is given to work with teachers in groups over work with children. Faust recommends that in-service training and case consultation be the predominant activities. Parent and curriculum consultation are also recommended. The focus of parent consultation is on specific parental concerns. Many writers suggest that the counselor become involved in diagnosing learning difficulties. The major recommended activities of elementary school consultation appear to fall into consultee and program analysis categories.

---

[27]C. H. Haylett and L. Rapoport, *op. cit.*, p. 335.

[28]G. Caplan, "Types of mental health consultation," *American Journal of Orthopsychiatry*, Vol. 33 (1963), pp. 470-481.

[29]D. Dinkmeyer and E. Caldwell, *Developmental counseling and guidance: A comprehensive school approach* (New York, McGraw-Hill, 1970).

ROLE AND FUNCTION

Analysis of various typologies of consultation suggests that the roles and functions of consultants cover a wide range of activities. Although the goals and techniques of consultation appear to be similar in many professional fields, the roles and functions are not. The comparison of goals with functions and roles is complicated by the lack of goal specificity.

Caplan suggests that the consultant has different roles for different situations.[30] If the request for consultation is task centered, the consultant becomes a technical expert and a teacher. The client-consultee request usually requires the consultant to use his human relations skills in helping the consultee free himself of the stereotype he has formed of the client. Cohen, in reviewing the work of community mental health consultants, identified the following roles: resource person, program reviewer, program promoter, innovator, teacher trainer, human relations mediator, and supervisor.[31]

Gilmore states that "giving consultation is a professional role, the essence of which is problem solving."[32] She postulates that the function of social work consultation may be to "(1) reinforce, corroborate, or validate; (2) clarify, analyze, or interpret; (3) inform, supplement, or advise; (4) motivate, facilitate, or change." Different work settings give rise to different patterns of emphasis. Gorman describes social work consultation in terms of problem solving and change agent process. As such the consultant must be a technical expert and a process expert. The functions of problem solving include "study or fact finding, diagnosis or evaluating the facts, and treatment or formulating and implementing a plan of action."[33] In assisting with change in an organization the consultant roles are those of diagnostician, technical assistant, ad-

---

[30]G. Caplan, 1959, *op. cit.,* p. 57.

[31]L. D. Cohen, *Consultation: A community mental health method.* A report of a survey of practice in sixteen states (Bethesda, Md. Southern Regional Education Board and National Institute of Mental Health, 1964).

[32]M. H. Gilmore, "Consultation as a social work activity," in *Consultation in social work,* L. Rapoport (ed.), (New York, National Association of Social Work, 1963).

[33]J. F. Gorman, *op. cit.,* p. 42.

viser, and educator. As a teacher, the consultant facilitates staff development. In social work, the consultant role is seen as a staff role rather than a line role. As a consequence, the consultant has no responsibility for implementing the plan to solve the problem. The consultant's function is to provide technical and special information to the staff.

The differential aspects of consulting functions in elementary schools are not as explicit as they are in other fields. Descriptions of activities tend to emphasize process and techniques to be employed by the consultant. The content of consultation is usually stated in nebulous terms. From the various statements about function and role of the elementary school consultant the following role description emerges: teacher, guide, evaluator, program promoter, enabler, case problem solver, resource person, and human relations mediator. Because of the diversity of roles, the elementary school counselor has problems of relating his functions to goals.

Many activities of the elementary school counselor that are classified as consulting are not classified as such in other professional fields. Elementary school consultation is similar to mental health consultation in that its emphasis is on preventative goals. It differs from mental health consultation in that it does not focus on community organization or social planning. Staff development rather than assisting with specific work or home problems appears to be the major goal of elementary school consultation. In specific situations, the immediate goals are improved organizational functioning, human relations concerns, or presenting technical information about child behavior. The differences in practice stem from lack of agreement as to which function goes with what ends. This lack of conceptual clarity precludes a meaningful description of roles undertaken during the consultation process.

EVALUATION OF CONSULTATION

The evaluation of consultation activities in various fields has been handicapped by several factors. First, the lack of a standard nomenclature hinders recording and reporting of consultative activities in a manner that can make comparison among different settings or professional fields. Even descriptive studies demand that observations be accumulated in a systematic and orderly manner. Second, the lack of clarity in stating ultimate goals and the lack of specificity in delineating immediate goals has handicapped the evaluation of outcomes. For example, in mental health consultation the ultimate goal may be "to improve the mental health components of service to clients" and an immediate goal may be "to strengthen and improve the knowledge and skill of the consultee."[34] As Haylett and Rapoport observe, it is one thing to appraise the gain in knowledge and skill in the consultee, but how can you demonstrate that this gain led to improved services to clients? Third, the numerous and varied forces in the consultee's milieu compound the work of the consultant. Organizational goals, administrative procedures, and personnel policies have a direct bearing on the outcomes of consultation. Mannino and Shore have made a comprehensive review of consultation research.[35] Using Mannino's 1969 reference guide to consultation literature, they classified 75 of the 646 articles as evaluating some aspect of consultation. The Mannino and Shore monograph will be used as a basis for reviewing the research articles.

Medical-psychiatric consultation research tends to be descriptive and superficial. Poor nomenclature, lack of conceptual clarity, and inadequate analysis of dynamics of consultation characterize the reported research. Two reported studies of patient opinion of the value of psychiatric consultation indicated that patients do not necessarily benefit from the procedure. One of the studies reported that 30 percent of the patients saw little or no value in the consultation while the other study reported 52 percent of the patients were neither better nor worse after psychiatric consultation. In general the patients who were prepared for consultation tended to gain more from it.

Mannino and Shore use the studies by Iscoe, *et al.* and Pierce-Jones, *et al.* as examples of program analysis and outcome evalu-

---

[34]Haylett and Rapoport, *op. cit.,* p. 355.
[35]Mannino and Shore, *op. cit.,* p. 38.

ation.[36] These studies review the results of a two-year mental health consultation program conducted in 14 schools. The change agent was an in-service education program. Generally speaking, the program had little effect on the teachers' attitudes or orientations. "The only statistically significant finding in the study was an increase in rapport between consultant and consultee which occurred between the beginning and end of the consultation program."[37]

Schmuck reports on the effects of a two-year consultation program on classroom teachers and students.[38] The following are examples of some of the procedures used: sensitivity training, didactic discussions, problem solving techniques, analyses of diagnostic data and role-playing. Cognitive and attitudinal changes occurred in teachers but "it was clear that there were not accompanying behavioral changes, changes in classroom group process, or changes in students' attitudes."[39]

Evaluation studies of elementary school consultation have many of the same deficiencies found in other studies. Lack of clarity and specificity of goals, inadequate role definitions, and incomplete descriptions of the functions characterize the reported research. The major thrust of the studies is to compare the effectiveness of counseling with that of consultation. In contrast to other professionals who use consultation as one aspect of their work, researchers in the elementary school area assume that one activity can be substituted for another because each has as its ultimate goal helping children. Faust makes the following observation on this point:

---

[36]I. Iscoe, *et al,* "Some strategies in mental health consultation. A brief description of a project and some preliminary results." In *Emergent approaches to mental health problems,* E. I. Cowen, E. A. Gardner, and M. Zax (eds.), (New York, Appleton-Century-Crofts, 1967).

J. Pierce-Jones, *et al, Child behavior consultation in elementary schools: A demonstration and research program.* (Austin, University of Texas, 1968).

[37]Mannino and Shore, *op. cit.,* p. 38.

[38]Mannino and Shore, *op. cit.*

[39]Mannino and Shore, *op. cit.*

The counselor who is crisis-oriented will find himself being consumed largely by an endless line of children. The new counselor elects to invest himself more effectively.[40]

Kranzler reviewed several studies in which the effectiveness of counseling was compared with the effectiveness of consulting.[41] His analysis indicated that both procedures were equally effective because no statistically significant difference was found between the counseling and consulting groups. Since the amount of gain or loss in sociometric status or social skills was about the same for the controls as for the counseling and consulting groups, Kranzler facetiously recommends that from the point of view of efficiency leaving children alone would be best. He suggests that the terms counseling and consulting "ought to be dropped from our vocabulary in favor of more precise descriptions of specific procedures to be followed when helping specific types of children make specific types of behavior changes."[42] This conclusion is unwarranted. From the perspective of other professional fields the activities cited by Kranzler as consultation would not be so identified. They fall in the realm of group guidance, in-service training, and teaching. Consequently, the conclusion about the value of consultation should be similar to that made by Mannino and Shore: Group procedures may bring about cognitive and attitudinal changes but not necessarily behavioral changes.

A study that compared counseling with teacher-consultation under experimental conditions was conducted by Anderson.[43] Consultation was defined as a process whereby through individual conferences teachers were assisted in finding new ways of better understanding child behavior. The focus of the counseling process was on self-exploration and problem-solving. Self-ratings, teacher ratings, and two peer ratings were used as indicators of change. It was concluded that (1) counseling was more effective

---

[40]Faust, *op. cit.*, p. 35.

[41]G. D. Kranzler, "The elementary school counselor as consultant: An evaluation," *Elementary School Guidance and Counseling*, Vol. 3 (1969), pp. 285-288.

[42]*Ibid.*, p. 286.

[43]E. C. Anderson, "Counseling and consultation versus teacher consultation in the elementary school," *Elementary School Guidance and Counseling*, Vol. 2 (1968), pp. 276-287.

than consulting in the fourth grade; (2) consulting was more effective than counseling in the sixth grade; (3) counseling and consulting were equally effective in the fifth grade; (4) counseling and consulting were effective when compared with no counseling. However, one may question if the results from the two procedures are comparable. Can change in a child who is counseled be measured in the same manner as in a child whose teacher has been the object of a consultation?

Outcome studies of the effects of consultation on the client generally report a favorable influence on the client. In studies cited by Mannino and Shore, seven of the ten studies showed consultation to have had a positive influence on the client. In the study conducted by Hunter and Ratcliffe of persons seen in mental health consultation in a community mental health hospital, consultation was found to be as effective as direct clinical services.[44] Poor instrumentation of the data-gathering instrument precludes generalizations about the findings. On the negative side, Bolman reported no statistically significant differences on criterion measures between those college students who attended group meetings and those who did not.[45]

Some studies have reported the effects of consultation on the consultee, client, and the system. In general, the findings indicate that consultation has a positive effect although not necessarily to the same degree on all three elements. It is easier to show gain in the consultee than in the client. This is a basic finding in the Iscoe and Pierce-Jones studies. These studies indicate that although teachers used the consultation they tended to rank it low when they compared it to other pupil personnel services. The main use of consultation by the teachers was to confirm a decision already made about the child. Identifying problems and gaining a better understanding of child behavior was secondary.

---

[44]W. F. Hunter and A. W. Ratcliff, "The Range Mental Health Center: Evaluation of a community oriented mental health consultation program," in *Northern Minnesota Community Mental Health Journal,* Vol. 4 (1968), pp. 260-267.

[45]W. M. Bolman *et al,* "An unintended side effect in a community psychiatric program," *Archives of General Psychiatry,* Vol. 20 (1969), pp. 508-513.

These observations are supported by Splete.[46] He reports that teachers believe that consultation may be beneficial in that it gives them an opportunity to find psychological support for what they are doing. Teachers also like help in understanding children but do not want any help in understanding themselves. This teacher attitude may interfere with consultation. Caplan believes that at times the object of consultation should not be to increase the consultee's skill or knowledge but to help the consultee achieve a free emotional relationship with the client.[47] That is to say, the consultant should help the teacher see her student as a human being rather than as a stereotype. The tendency to group individuals into categories and then to associate behaviors with those categories is a natural human tendency. The stereotyping of children creates difficulties for teachers particularly when they mislabel the child and then use improper corrective procedures. For a further exploration of this type of consultation problem and techniques for resolving it see Kaczkowski.[48]

Data from the outcome studies indicate that consultation does have some positive effect. The lack of controls in many of the studies, inadequate experimental designs, and the lack of acceptable definitions of consultation preclude broad generalization from the data. A label is not a working definition. The incompleteness of the definitions has hindered the identification of the changes that were to be brought about through the consultation process. Consequently, global evaluations have characterized outcome studies of consultation. It is necessary to know what is changed and how it is changed before change from what to what can be appropriately evaluated. The same remarks pertain to comparing the efficacy of consultation and counseling. The researchers have generalized that since both procedures are equally effective they must be identical; however, they have failed to rigorously define consultation and counseling. Is the lack of a statis-

---

[46]H. Splete, "The elementary school counselor: An effective consultant with classroom teachers," *Elementary School Guidance and Counseling*, Vol. 5 (1971), pp. 165-172.

[47]Caplan, *op. cit.*, p. 55.

[48]Kaczkowski, *op. cit.*, pp. 103-111.

tically significant difference between the two approaches due to the treatment or to difference in groups? The one group receives a direct service while the other group receives an indirect service. Are the children in the consulting group the same (on certain psychological characteristics) before the experiment as those in the counseling group? Since both groups show improvement on the criterion measures, should it be inferred that either procedure could produce the same rate of change? These and other questions suggest that trying to compare the efficacy of each procedure is a complex research design problem.

IMPLICATIONS FOR THE WORK OF THE COUNSELOR

The influences on a child in school are multiple. "The administrator needs to remember, therefore, that the determinants of behavior emerge from a matrix composed of management philosophy, organizational structure, group membership, and individual personality."[49] The influence of this matrix is felt by all who are associated with the school because of the hierarchical organization of the school. Bogue believes that this organizational pattern impedes "(1) the achievement of individual self-actualization; (2) the occurrence of change and innovation; (3) the effective use of specialists in decision making; and (4) the development of an organic view of the organization."[50] On the basis of Bogue's remarks it can be inferred that the attainment of humanistic goals in education will be limited by the administrative structure. However, the limitations imposed by the organizational structure of the school can be mitigated if consultation is used as a vehicle for helping those associated with schools communicate about their concerns. In this respect consultation is seen as a professional activity whose focus is work problems and which is task oriented.

This limited view of consultation is accepted because of the desire to focus on the enhancement of the professional effective-

---

[49]E. G. Bogue, "The context of organizational behavior: A conceptual synthesis for the educational administrator," *Educational Administration Quarterly*, Vol. 2 (1969), p. 59.

[50]*Ibid.*, p. 74.

ness of the consultee. It does not preclude the counselor from working in behalf of the pupil or teacher. This view of consultation is used so that it can be differentiated from such activities as professional education, in-service training, program development, and counseling. Other professional fields such as mental health and social work have made distinctions among these activities. Consequently, if a counselor is to work among other professional specialists he must use terms in a manner that facilitates communication with others.

Consultation is an indirect service in that it tends to focus on the work problems of the school staff. The methods used to assist the school staff contain elements of problem solving, teaching, and helping functions. The frame of reference may be internal or external. The latter focus is on factors outside of the person, group, or system who desire the consultation. For example, the third grade teachers of a school may wish to discuss the impact of the proposed new readers on the mental health of their pupils. On the other hand, if the principal desired that his third grade teachers know something about mental health then a course from a university or a workshop in-service training program could and probably should be utilized. These two activities may provide the teachers with general information about mental health which they may or may not use.

The consultation focus that has an internal frame of reference emphasizes the direct work concerns of an individual or group. For example, a third grade teacher wishes to talk to a counselor about a problem that a pupil is having in reading. On the other hand, if a third grade teacher wished to talk about a marital problem because it was affecting her teaching, counseling rather than consulting should be employed.

The performance of an individual in a work situation is a function of his competencies and of expectations of others. The interaction between these two elements may cause dissonance. It is the task of the consultant to help the consultee examine his job related concerns. The consultation may have a cognitive emphasis (i.e. imparting technical information) or an affective emphasis (i.e. concern with relationships). The goal of this type of consultation, whether it explores the attitudes and feelings or discusses plans of action, is the enhancement of the professional functioning of the consultee. The focus is the efficiency and effectiveness of the consultee. This view represents the traditional perception that the school staff has of the counselor's role. The counselor through individual contact or group procedures can help the staff clarify the expectations of others, generate interest in new ideas, or develop new skills. However, it is our position that, when discussions about technical information or skill development have been systematized and extend over a period of time, then this experience should be labeled in-service training. We are differentiating between in-service training and consultation in terms of duration, systematic coverage, and focus but not in terms of content, procedures, or tasks. This differentiation will be further discussed when we review program consultation.

When the counselor works in behalf of a pupil or a teacher, the distinction between consulting and counseling becomes blurred. This situation arises when the object of consultation becomes a client or when the counselor believes that in order for a pupil or teacher to be helped, he must have the assistance of significant others. For example, a boy may continue to be a reading problem as long as his mother maintains her expectations about his achievement. In this situation the modification of the mother's expectancies is a necessary step if the boy is to be helped. This might be achieved either through consulting or counseling. Very often beginning teachers have a feeling of inadequacy because they lack an awareness of the expectations of others. Here the consultant may provide a group counseling or encounter group experience, or may seek out another staff member to provide a counseling or encounter group experience. In working in behalf of a client the counselor assumes some responsibility for a course of action. This responsibility is extended to others when they collaborate with the counselor in resolving the problem. In working in behalf of others, the counselor, to a certain degree, predicts that a certain course of action is beneficial for the client. This prediction is based on mutual understanding of the situation.

Consultation provides a vehicle for helping a teacher gain an understanding of the relationship between the instructional process and the needs of children. The focus of consultation is the improvement of the quality of teaching behavior. Counseling can also enhance the quality of teaching behavior by making the teacher more sensitive to his needs and how they can be satisfied within the context of teaching. By becoming aware of the structure of his needs, the teacher can come to understand the manner in which he selects the experiences for the class. Are the selections in terms of his needs or in terms of the needs of the children? This type of self-examination helps the teacher understand how his personal dynamics affect the learning and teaching process. The goal of counseling, whether individual or group, is to help the teacher improve his professional functioning in the classroom, not to reconstruct his personality.

Although the focus has been counseling the teacher, most of the remarks can pertain to other staff members. For example, the principal, examining his needs, can become aware of how they are satisfied by some of his administrative actions. He can also become aware that the satisfaction of some of his needs can interfere with the effective functioning of the school.

Should the goals of counseling of teachers and staff be restricted to role behaviors within the school and the improvement of instructional effectiveness? There is no doubt that some teacher and staff problems whose origin lies outside of the school setting interfere with their functioning within the school. For example, a teacher's marital problems may affect him to a point that he no longer provides effective instruction in the class. Should the counselor help this teacher because the quality of instruction has been growing poor? It can be said that any concern whether it has its origin within or ouside the school has some impact on the teacher's behavior within the school.

What are the types of teacher problems and the range of teacher problems that are suitable for counseling by the elementary school counselor? There is no ready answer to this question. Many administrators restrict the counseling of teachers by the counselor because they are of the opinion that (1) the counselor's time should be primarily devoted to the needs of the pupils; (2) most counselors lack the expertise in counseling with adults. They believe that marital problems and certain types of personal dynamics problems (e.g. phobias and neuroticism) are best handled by an outside counselor or therapist or an agency other than the school. There is some merit to this position. It is not a matter of recognizing the need of helping the teacher or staff members but a matter of the consequence of rendering the help to teachers. Since the counselor works with many different teachers, being privy to some confidential information about a teacher may affect his work with teachers and pupils. For example, during a consultation the question may arise as to why Mr. Smith behaves the way he does when he supervises the playground. The counselor may be aware as to a possible reason for the behavior but since this information was obtained during counseling, the counselor may hesitate to present it to other staff members. Such factors as availability, competency, and confidentiality should be considered when a policy statement about counseling of teachers and staff members by the counselor is being formulated. The policy statement should be published because it provides a means of protecting the rights and interests of counselors and teachers. The position taken by us is that the matter of counseling of teachers whether it is individual or group, is a decision that should be made by the superintendent with consultation of other staff members.

In some school districts the traditional function of consultation is being supplanted by program consultation. Its goal is to increase the skills and understandings of the staff so that the number of problems among the pupils is reduced. Its focus is on prevention and control of problems through program and staff development. Programs are evolved around a series of interventions whose purpose is to modify and control behavior towards some stated goal. Interaction among the staff is used to generate interest and understandings in the program.

Program consultation assumes that the goals have evolved from administrative concerns about problems within the school or community. In some instances the statement of goals and possible course of action is developed by a task force of staff members. The function of the pupil personnel worker in program consultation is fourfold: he (1) collects and processes information about the extent of unmet needs of the pupils; (2) generates interest in the possible consequences of not meeting the needs; (3) advocates a program to meet the needs; (4) trains the staff in intervention techniques used to meet the needs. Pupil appraisal and in-service training play an important role in program consultation. Participation in program consultation should be open to all professional specialists associated with pupil personnel programs rather than restricting it to counselors. However, one can question the wisdom of investing most of the professional effort of pupil personnel workers in this type of activity. Generally speaking, our review of research findings indicated little, if anything, was gained through these types of programs. There is no doubt that modifying organizational structures or policies can reduce the incidence of problems whose origin lies in these elements. What is questioned is the premise that increasing the knowledge that teachers have about pupil behavior leads to a reduction in problems pupils have. Teachers may, through a better understanding of how problems develop and an increased range of methods of coping with them, be of greater assistance to some pupils than they have been in the past. However, this may also lead to an increase in referrals to specialists because of the awareness of competencies needed to help pupils. Program consultation should be an adjunct rather than the primary mode of operation. In many respects, an in-service training program can supplant many facets of program consultation.

Gallessich developed a systems consultation model for schools predicated on mental health consultation.[51] She believes that the consultant should be an "outsider" rather than some staff member. The consultant should be given a "contract" that outlines the expectancies of the school district. The first step is to "scan the system." This may be done by means of a formal analysis or informal analysis of the school district. The procedure should discover the "covert structure, the complex norms, processes and social patterns that shape and direct the staff's energy."[52] The second step is to examine the objectives of the school district. A lack of understanding of objectives and priorities leads to a breakdown

---

[51]June Gallessich, "A systems model of mental health consultation," *Psychology in the Schools,* Vol. 9 (1972), pp. 13-15.

[52]*Ibid.,* p. 13.

of communications. This prevents the district from making full use of problem-solving and decision-making resources. The task of the consultant is to help the staff to remove the blocks to communication. The third step is to study the school district's effectiveness in implementing its goals. This step consists of restructuring the administrative policies as they relate to problem-solving and decision making. The last step is to help the staff develop an on-going evaluation system so that it can monitor the effectiveness of its program in relationship to its goals and the changing environment.

The question arises whether "system consultation" can be undertaken by a staff member. Inherent in this kind of consultation are the following ideas: (1) it assumes that the consultant is without goals; (2) it relies on the skills and competencies of the helping process; (3) the focus is on examination of communication patterns. Most staff members would find it difficult to accept the assumption that the staff member serving as a consultant could be neutral in the analysis of the system. Since he is part of the system, he has some opinion as to its goals and priorities. An examination of the communication patterns of the system poses a threat because it explores the underlying feelings and attitudes toward the system. Consequently, if the total school system is to be studied it would be better to have it done by an individual who is outside the system rather than by someone within the system.

It is our opinion that the more traditional role of consultation should be used as the model on which the counselor should focus his energy. Program and system consultation, though of value to a school district, should be used on a need basis rather than on a systematic basis. Traditional consultation focuses on the relationships between personal competencies and expectations of others. Its ultimate goal is self-actualization for it attempts to enhance the current professional functioning of an individual. The counselor's role during consultation may be that of teacher, problem solver, facilitator, catalyst, model, or explorer of feelings and attitudes. Generally speaking, permitting communication of feelings about work and personal inadequacy is as important as imparting information about child development. Berlin offers the following suggestions for conducting a consultation:

> The consultant's encouragement of verbal expression of all feelings of the teacher about his work is greatly enhanced in my experience as the consultant progressively clarifies that he is not there to analyze the teacher, pry into hidden motivations, or to uncover skeletons about the teacher's personal problems.... Another mental health principle the consultant can demonstrate effectively is that every person has limitations both professionally and personally. Unreal self-expectations and their aftermaths of tension and exhaustion from increasing conflict may seriously interfere with teaching.... A third vital principle that can be demonstrated by the consultant centers around authority. Workers in a hierarchical setting need to be able to accept constituted authority and to work under regulations without undue conflict.[53]

The central theme that is reflected in Berlin's suggestions is that the consultee's concern can be resolved by an assessment of reality and an analysis of the ways by which the concern can be resolved.

SUMMARY

Consultation is a professional activity that provides an indirect service to clients or pupils. Its focus is work centered. The consultant concentrates on how he can help consultees rather than on why they need assistance. Although there is much flexibility in the roles and functions he undertakes, the dual role of problem solver and listener predominates. The ultimate goal of consultation is to assist an agency or school in raising its effectiveness with the clients they serve. The immediate goal is to provide technical knowledge or personal insights in a manner that enhances the professional functioning of the consultee. The content may be a client, staff development, program development or administrative concerns. Because the consultant undertakes multiple roles and functions, he must differentiate between other procedures par-

---

[53]I. N. Berlin, "Mental health consultation in schools as means of communicating mental health principles," *Journal of the American Academy of Child Psychiatry*, Vol. 1, (1962), pp. 671-679.

ticularly those of in-service training, counseling and consulting. These clarifications help set limits on the activities of the consultant and tend to minimize misconceptions of his role. The failure to do this in the elementary school has precipitated confusion as to the value and utility of consultation. Agreement as to the nature of consultation would help those who are implementing or expanding elementary school guidance programs.

SUGGESTED READINGS

Faust, V.: *The counselor-consultant in the elementary school,* Boston, Houghton-Mifflin, 1968.

Muro, J. J.: *The counselor's work in the elementary school,* Scranton, International Textbook Co., 1970.

Chapter 10

THE
SOCIAL ENVIRONMENT
AND THE SCHOOL

THE SCHOOL AND THE CLASSROOM AS SOCIAL SYSTEMS

IF THE COUNSELOR and other student personnel workers are to work intelligently and effectively with teachers and administrators they must understand the social environment of the students. This includes viewing the school and the classroom as social systems. Thus, this chapter examines this area. Beginning with a brief treatment of the general process of socialization, it moves to a consideration of the school as a social system, then to the classroom environment, and then moves into the area of behavior modification as an element in the socialization process in the school and the classroom.

The work of the counselor and other pupil personnel specialists is seen by staff members as centering on problems of individual children. Because of the nature of problems encountered, some children can be helped through group procedures. When group procedures are used in the classroom, the focus is the enhancement of individual development. The social worker attempts to mitigate some of the environmental influences, but only as they affect individual children. In general, the pupil personnel specialist tries to understand the child as he functions in a setting, but does not attempt to gain an understanding of the context of the setting.

This chapter examines the social influences on the child, the teacher, the administrator, and the school. The values and attitudes of those associated with the schools, as well as those of the pupil affect the whole process of learning. No matter what type of teaching method is used, whether textbook, individual programmed instruction, or computer-assisted instruction, there is an interpersonal component in the learning process. In some instances this social interaction generates problems. If the teacher sees the classroom as a social group, many of the problems she encounters can be put into proper perspective. Insight into many problems encountered by the school can be gained if the school is viewed as a social system. Principles obtained from social psychology and behavior modification can be used in resolving the problems. The latter can be used in helping individuals with their social control problems, while the former helps individuals with their transactions among themselves.

THE PROCESS OF SOCIALIZATION

Man's skill in intereacting with others is not instinctual but learned. The ways in which his biological needs are satisfied are also learned. Transforming an infant into an effective member of society is done through the process of socialization. Brim defines socialization as

> . . . a process of learning through which an individual is prepared with varying degrees of success, to meet the requirements laid down by other members of society in a variety of situations. These requirements are always attached to one or another of the recognized positions or statuses in society such as husband, son, employee, and adult male.[1]

In learning the prescriptive behaviors the individual acquires a set of habits, beliefs, and motives that structures his interaction with others. Essentially he learns that there are sets of reciprocal requirements based on positions in the social system that regulate the behavior of individuals toward each other.

---

[1]Orville G. Brim, Jr., "Personality development as role-learning," in Ira Iscoe and Harold Stevenson, (eds.), *Personality development in children* (Austin, University of Texas Press, 1960), p. 128.

Thus the positions, which are the smallest elements—the construction blocks—of societies and organized groups, are interrelated and consistent because they are organized to meet common ends. . . . Since every position is a part of an inclusive system of positions, no one position has any meaning apart from other positions to which it is related.[2]

The socialization process develops individuals into social system members by inculcating in them the idea that "a given position has prescriptions concerning how people in other positions should behave toward him, as well as understanding of what the others expect of him."[3]

By interacting with different people in many types of circumstances, an individual learns the reciprocal requirements of a situation. This learning is acquired by developing the ability to take the role of the other. "His knowledge of these social situations, his ability to discharge successfully his role in each situation, and his motivation to perform up to the level which the situation requires are all variables explaining individual differences in behavior."[4] Social maturity is a reflection of the efficiency and effectiveness of an individual in a social system. Becoming socially more mature means, "for one thing, expanding one's repertoire of statuses, by learning imaginatively to take the role of a greater range of others and thus being able to interact with them confidently on the basis of one's ability to understand their symbolic definitions."[5] The degree to which the role repertoires are organized into a coherent whole can also be used to infer social maturity. Since socialization is role-learning it occurs throughout an individual's life. Thus, social maturity is relative in terms of age and position in the social system.

---

[2]Theodore M. Newcomb, *Social psychology* (New York, Dryden Press, 1951), p. 277.

[3]Brim, *op. cit.,* p. 128.

[4]William H. Sewell, "Some recent development in socialization theory and research." *The Annals of the American Academy of Political and Social Science,* Vol. 349 (1963), p. 164.

[5]Harry C. Bredemeier and Richard M. Stephenson, *The analysis of social systems* (New York, Holt, Rinehart, and Winston, 1962), p. 89.

The initial socialization of the child comes through social conditioning of biological needs. The mother is the primary agent in linking the satisfaction of biological needs to a cultural context. "In the process, the child's discriminatory and selective capacities are conditioned and canalized so that he comes to focus his attention on what is culturally defined as reality, and to base his selections on what is culturally defined as pleasurable and moral."[6] As the child matures he is able to sample from an increased environment different ways of satisfying his biological needs. However, he also learns that his mother expresses feelings about the way he obtains satisfaction of his biological needs. This association of pleasure or lack of it with gratification or deprivation by another is the first step in self-control. It forces the individual to reflect on the consequences of his actions. He becomes aware that the attitude of another person affects his satisfaction. In his interaction with his mother he learns that "by controlling his own actions, he can control her attitudes. All he has to do is to figure out what she wants him to do and then do it."[7] Essentially, the child has become aware of normative behavior and the need for the approval of others. Trying to "figure out what others want" requires the individual to become sensitized to the goals of the family and society. Failure to become aware of the expectations of others can impede the individual's quest toward self-actualization.

Norms and the expectations of others, although they place limits on the behavior of the individual, can serve as a means through which one gains a sense of identity. By comparing his behavior to the evaluations of others and assessing himself against standards, the individual learns a need for self-approval. He comes to realize that to have a meaningful interaction with others he must follow the prescriptions for reciprocation. Failure to follow the prescription may lead to a certain amount of psychological discomfort. The degree to which a person chooses not to conform is, in part, a function of how much pain he can tolerate.

---

[6]*Ibid.*, p. 63.
[7]*Ibid.*, p. 65.

This relationship between conformity and pain gives rise to a sense of personal identity for it determines the degree to which a person is open to new experiences. When a person restricts his range of experiences he, in part, restricts his own being. One of the functions of counseling is to help the individual explore new ways of behaving with a minimum amount of psychological discomfort.

Through the use of norms and expectations an individual is able to objectify himself in the world. That is to say, he can differentiate between the demands of the physical and social environments in a manner that helps him predict the consequences of his actions. To carry out these predictions, he must be aware of the various relationships that exist in the social system. To have meaningful transactions, the individual must incorporate into himself the demands of the various positions and his personalized ways of meeting them. There is diversity in the manner in which prescribed role relationships are carried because of the variation in the characteristics of the socializing agent and in the personal characteristics of the individual. Although the intent of socialization is to incorporate the individual into a social system, the end product is an individual, who reflects many of the modal patterns of the system, but has a unique style of relating to himself and to the world in which he lives.

As one examines the various types of transactions among people it becomes apparent that there is a certain amount of deviation from societal and personal expectations. A pupil tells his mother that he will do his homework after supper. His announced action conforms to his mother's expectations that homework should be done after supper and to his personal expectations that good students do homework after supper. However, he does not do his homework after supper because a TV special is of greater interest to him. It is rather difficult to evaluate his action as either "good" or "bad" because the evaluation of any action lies in the eye of the beholder. Actions tend to be judged first in terms of expectations and, secondly, in terms of standards. An action is defined as "legitimate if there is conformity (in someone's eyes); if it is defined as illegitimate, there is deviance (in someone's eyes).["8] In this context deviation can be seen as a failure to conform to norms governing goals and means.

Using the above idea of deviance, Bredemeier and Stephenson identify four forms of deviation. First, a pupil may strive for a prescribed goal but utilizes unprescribed means. This deviation is present when a pupil copies his homework assignments in order to get a passing grade in arithmetic. Second, a student may accept the means but fails to strive for the prescribed goals. He may do his assignments and raise his hand to respond to a question asked by the teacher, but he has given up trying to understand the subject matter. Third, a student may reject or fail to internalize the goals and means of the school. This type of pupil, if he is present in school, is classified as "unmotivated" if he is passive or "emotionally disturbed" if he is aggressive. If he fails to attend school he is called a truant or dropout. Fourth, the pupil may excessively conform to the goals and means of the school. His behavior is seen as deviant because excessive conformity reduces the range of new experiences he is willing to undertake. The deviation may be induced by inadequate socialization, or the organization of the social structure. The last category is a source of strain to pupils because people in the organization make inconsistent demands. Pupils may have internal conflicts because in their interactions with teachers, administrators, and pupils they are unable to resolve what they perceive as inconsistent demands. The counselor may be of service to pupils by helping them clarify the conflicting demands. The use of task-oriented groups for this purpose is discussed in the chapter on group work. In addition, the counselor working in behalf of the pupils can ask the principal to review the consequences of certain administrative policies.

Many of the federally supported projects in the elementary school are focused on problems of inadequate or inappropriate socialization. The lower-class child may be a deviant in the suburban school because many of his actions are inappropriate. On the other hand, a child who has been raised in a fatherless home may not be inadequate in his role relationships with adult males.

Ibid., p. 122.

The school has always been concerned with those who have been inadequately or inappropriately socialized because of their position in the social system. It should be remembered that the visiting teacher concept grew out of the need for the school to explain its goals and means to the community. This was especially true in those communities where compulsory education was introduced and in communities which had a large influx of immigrants. The school's function in the socialization process was to help with the assimilation of the immigrants into the mainstream of American life. However, the thrust of some of the current projects is not assimilation, but the development of an ethnic or minority identity. Guskin and Guskin have compared the effect of these two styles of socialization and suggest that the ineffectiveness of some of the projects is, in part, due to the inability of the program directors to differentiate between these two approaches.[9] A counselor's contribution to these programs is to help the staff become cognizant of societal norms and values and how the cultural patterns of the minority groups differ from them. More important, the counselor should help the staff evolve a program which makes cooperative understanding among the various groups possible. The program should be focused on the expectancies of the subgroups so that meaningful communication among the various groups is possible. Improved interaction helps individuals to learn the reciprocal requirements of a situation thereby gaining a greater understanding of one another. The goal of the program should be not only to foster association and interaction, but cooperative understanding so that all can work together towards a common goal.

The counselor's understanding of the socialization process helps him broaden his perspective of the child. It helps him become aware how external influences affect the behavior of a child, in particular the influence of parental expectations and group norms. These understandings can be used to generate intervention programs that help pupils in their quest for self-actualization.

---

[9] Allan E. Guskin and Samuel L. Guskin, *A social psychology of education* (Reading, Addison-Wesley, 1970).

THE SCHOOL AS A SOCIAL SYSTEM

School is more than a place where children acquire basic skills. It is a place where the process of socialization is continued under another form. Although it appears as though the school's socialization process is distinct from those of other institutions such as the home and church, in practice it is strongly linked to other societal institutions. Miles challenges the assumption that schools are "locally controlled."[10] Increased funding from state rather than local sources, nationally marketed textbooks, and standardized testing are cited by Miles as some of the forces that structure the function of the school. However, most communities do not acknowledge the existence of these external forces and operate from the belief that schools "not only 'ought' to be but *are* locally controlled."[11] As a consequence, many school problems have a deep political connotation to them. Because of the influence of political orientations and external agencies on the affairs of the school, educational goals are vaguely stated, multiple in nature, and conflictual.[12]

The expectations generated from educational goals make conflicting demands on pupils. The first-grade pupil is not only confronted with the demand that he learn to read but that he behave "like a pupil." Children readily internalize the idea that they should become subject-matter oriented but are slow in perceiving the role behaviors required of them to function as pupils. Essentially, the child must discern what the teacher wants and then do it. Some of the demands of the teacher can be in direct conflict with what he has done at home. The teacher, as the mother did earlier, shapes the behavior of the children by means of a system of rewards and punishments. This shaping of chil-

---

[10]Mathew B. Miles, "Some properties of schools as social systems," in *Social and cultural foundation of guidance,* Esther M. Lloyd-Jones and Norah Rosenau, (eds.). New York, Holt, Rinehart, and Winston (1968), pp. 124-146.

[11]*Ibid.,* p. 126.

[12]*Ibid.,* p. 128. For example, the school is expected to cause children to 'achieve' mastery of academic subject matter, *and* to develop and maintain physical and emotional health in children, *and* to socialize children into industrial society (e.g., make them neat, obedient, prompt, achievement oriented). There are many circumstances under which these goals may prove mutually interfering.

dren is a prerequisite for many activities undertaken in the school, for it inculcates the required role behaviors. It helps to establish the teacher as an authority figure and minimizes the child's choices for action. The shaping process can be detrimental to some first graders in that it fosters the idea that in order to be promoted one must please the teacher. The force of this idea is mitigated by third grade by the need for peer approval. In spite of its existence, there are some educators who find the shaping process repugnant and demeaning. But controlling the behavior of children is not intrinsicly good or bad. It depends on the reason for wanting to control their behavior.

> Our desire is not to fix the kind of pattern in life that children for whom we have responsibility will follow; rather it is to bring children to the point where they eventually can make rational choices for themselves. As educators we have completely failed the child who has a desire, and the basic capability, to become an engineer if we do not do whatever we can to help create within and around him conditions to achieve his goal.[13]

The structure of the school should reflect the educational goals on which it is predicated and the means by which they are reached should reflect the philosophical assumptions of the educational goals. Because many decisions about schools are affected by the political orientations of the decision makers, the activities within the school are disjointed and discontinuous. This is due, in part, to the fact that the concerns of special-interest groups are interjected into programs of instruction. Drug abuse programs, sex education, and programs for the culturally disadvantaged are but a few of the programs whose origin was from the outside of the school setting. This is not to suggest that the programs cited in the examples have no value or that special-interest groups have no right to impose their concerns on the school but to point out that what goes on in the school is subject to many diverse forces. Because of the presence of these external forces, the school has evolved an administrative structure whose task is not to make the school impervious to pressures but to minimize their

---

[13]Roger Reger, Wendy Schroeder, and Kathie Uschold, *Special education: children with learning problems* (New York, Oxford University Press, 1968), p. 66.

influence. But, although the administrative structure helps reduce the strain placed on the staff, it is detrimental to innovation
and change. The support for many new ideas is withheld by the
staff because they have learned from experience that many programs are short lived. New ideas are rejected not because they
are "bad" but because they require a change in normative behavior. The constant demand for change in behavior generates
a psychological strain because individuals strive for consistency
in behavior.

The quest for consistency and continuity is augmented by the
community's expectations that the school be held responsible for
mastery of subject matter by its students. This expectation fosters the development of a hierarchical organization where the
teacher plays a dominant role in the learning process. Generally
speaking, the hierarchical structure permits the development of
a series of experiences that enhance the learning of subject matter. Concomitantly, the structuring of the learning experiences
affects the social interaction in which social influences occur. The
structure also helps the two major groups in school (i.e., teachers and pupils), "each of which has its own moral and ethical
code and customary attitudes toward members of the other
groups," to evolve a set of role behaviors in which the conflict
between the two groups is held to minimum.[14] The cohesiveness
that evolves from the interactions between teachers and pupils
plays an important role in the learning process.

> The school is further marked off from the world that surrounds it
> by the spirit which pervades it. Feeling makes the school a social
> unity. The we-feeling of the school is in part a spontaneous crea-
> tion in the minds of those who identify themselves with the school
> and in part a carefully nurtured and sensitive growth.[15]

Another advantage of the school's hierarchical organization is
that it permits the school to deal with the problems of compulsory education in a rational manner. Compulsory education
places a strain on the instructional process in that it requires that
the school accept children with a wide range of ability and moti-

---

[14]Willard Waller, *The sociology of teaching* (New York, Wiley, 1965), p. 10.
[15]*Ibid.*, p. 12.

vation. Since all children must be in school, how do you take care of them? The school typically meets the challenge by developing a hierarchy of goals. Essentially, the immediate educational goals reflect the ordering of subject matter so that children with different abilities and motivation can acquire some of the basic skills and knowledges. In addition, the school attempts to vary the starting point of instruction, the tempo of teaching, and the materials used in class. This adaptation of the school to the child, although useful in assisting acquisition of basic skills, is not necessarily useful in helping the child attain some of the goals of socialization. A highly controlled instructional process limits the quality of interaction that is so essential in developing meaningful reciprocal relations among the pupils. Some of the recent controversy among educators centers on this very point. As Reger, Schroeder, and Uschold have suggested, there are problems in designing an instructional program whose end goal is "to bring children to the point where they can make rational decisions for themselves and about themselves and their relationships with their environment."[16] Goal diversity, variability in children, emotional feelings of parents, and the political orientation of the community are some of the factors that must be considered when the instructional program is being developed.

Since the school is made up of a hierarchy of individuals and groups whose network of interrelationships permits it to accomplish a set of tasks, system analysis can be used to resolve many of its problems. According to Lighthall, the school has the following nine principal roles or elements: individual student, informal student group, classroom group, teacher, administrator, curriculum specialist, specialist in personal or mental health, parent, and curriculum materials.[17] The problems that arise among these nine elements reflect conflicting relations between people —"unwillingness to accede to another's demands, envy of another's power, failure to comprehend another's expectations, sparse communication amidst a quick succession of events that

---

[16]Reger, Schroeder, and Uschold, *op. cit.*, p. 70.
[17]Frederick F. Lighthall, "A social psychologist for school systems." *Psychology in the Schools*, Vol. 6 (1969), pp. 3-12.

leads to unilateral decisions, policies that do not take account of local conditions or capabilities, or unfamiliar terminology that makes it seem as though a basic conflict of values is present where no such conflict exists."[18] Lighthall believes that the task of the personnel specialist is to help the school staff interact in such a manner that they become aware of problems and devise ways of resolving them. He does this by facilitating the group process of setting and reviewing priorities among problems and by assisting groups in working on priority problems. In order to keep minor problems from developing into major conflicts among the major role elements, personnel specialists should help the staff devise a program for analyzing how well present activities are achieving their goals and what alternative activities could be attempted to achieve them better.

CLASSROOM BEHAVIOR

The teacher, because of her position in the organizational heirarchy, is a dominant force in the learning process. During the course of the day she not only controls what is learned but how it is learned. She controls the classroom mainly through verbal activity. Research has shown that during the course of a day more than a thousand different interpersonal transactions take place between the teacher and her pupils. To achieve the goals of the classroom, the teacher must orchestrate the content of the subject matter with the interpersonal dynamics of the class. This is accomplished by helping the pupils become aware that the classroom has two distinct curriculums: The official curriculum whose focus is the basic three R's and is imbedded in the study guides and workbooks, and the unofficial curriculum whose focus is another set of three R's and is imbedded in rules, regulations and routines.[19] The pupil must have a degree of proficiency in both if he is to avoid psychological pain.

The two curriculums place different demands on a pupil. In the unofficial curriculum, he must become skillful in the role be-

---

[18]*Ibid.*, p. 6.

[19]Philip W. Jackson, "The student's world." *The Elementary School Journal,* Vol. 66 (1966), pp. 345-357.

haviors that are demanded in specific situations. Jackson suggests that these role behaviors help him cope with the delay, denial, interruption, and social distraction that characterize classroom activities. Through patience and, at times resignation, he can overcome the multiple social demands that are placed on him. The official curriculum asks the student to be probing, inquiring, and achievement oriented. At times he must question and challenge authority. This is anthetical to the docility that is normally required in the class. To survive in the class, the pupil must be able to differentiate the demands of a situation and act accordingly.

The teacher's behavior in the classroom is complex because not only must she help the pupils meet the demands of the two curriculums but she must structure her personal activities so that they satisfy her personal needs, conform to faculty norms, and meet community expectations. The teacher functions as ringmaster in a three-ring circus. Concepts developed by Smith and Geoffrey are useful in explaining the complexities of the behavior of teaching.[20] A critical skill that a teacher must develop is that of situational thinking. "The weighing of alternatives in a particular situation, the social skills involved in teacher-pupil interaction, and the repercussions upon the individual and the group seem to strike at the heart of the 'process problem' in teaching."[21] Situational thinking is reflected when a teacher in her lesson plans prepares for contingencies that may arise during the course of a day. She is in a position to vary time, materials, and activities to reach group goals. Advance preparation provides continuity to activities for it provides for appropriate sequencing between lessons and pupil interaction. Planning helps the teacher identify the size and direction of the steps required to shape the behavior of the pupils so that the desired goals can be reached. The multiple and simultaneous events that occur in the classroom require the teacher to be proficient in a variety of role behaviors. Jackson identifies the following as being most im-

---

[20]Louis M. Smith and William Geoffrey, *The complexities of an urban classroom* (New York, Holt, Rinehart, and Winston, 1968), pp. 96-128.
[21]*Ibid.*, p. 127.

portant to the second curriculum: (1) *gatekeepeer:* directs the flow of interaction by deciding who will speak and when; (2) *supply sergeant:* allocates space and materials so that activities can be conducted; (3) *privilege dispensor:* who can do what and when (examples: make up quiz, run movie projector, safety patrol, etc.); (4) *official timekeeper:* what begins when (examples: reading, spelling, recess, etc.).[22] The art of teaching consists of blending the cognitive elements of learning with social interaction so that the needs of the individual and group can be satisfied.

The managerial skills used by the teacher to manipulate the functions of the class are tempered by the expectations of pupils, staff and community. Since the teacher is a dominant force in the learning process, she is held responsible and accountable for what goes on in the classroom. In recent years public interest has been focused on the question of holding the school and its staff accountable for the achievements of its pupils. Although school administrators have attempted to inculcate this idea into their evaluation of the staff, the predominant factor in the appraisal of the teacher continues to be how well she controls the class.

> The teacher who has 'lost control' of his class, as the expression goes, cannot compensate for that deficiency by doing an especially good job of evaluation or by spending extra time with his remedial reading group. In an educational sense, when group control is lost all is lost.[23]

The fear of losing control of the class very often influences the choice of activities the teacher undertakes in the class. Since misconduct can be used by the principal as a sign of ineffectiveness, teachers try to limit its occurrence. This avoidance of misbehavior does at times limit what pupils learn. Tanner and Lindgren believe that the fear of losing control of the class has the following negative effects on the teacher: "(1) anxiety which teachers try to hide because they are afraid of being judged negatively; (2) being unable to function as a professional; (3) teacher drop-

---

[22]Jackson, *op. cit.,* pp. 161-163.

[23]Philip W. Jackson, *Life in classrooms* (New York, Holt, Rinehart, and Winston, 1968), p. 106.

out."[24] The counselor can help beginning teachers deal with this fear by developing task-oriented groups whose focus is the professional problems of teachers.

The multiple and simultaneous events that take place in the class mandate that the pupil be flexible in meeting many of the demands without overloading his capability for adaptation. In the initial phases of his socialization, the pupil learns that he must control some of his behaviors if he desires that his needs be gratified. He learns that one of the basic rules of survival is to be able to discern the priorities in the multiple-demand situation. For example, watching the cartoon show on TV, putting toys away, washing his hands, and coming to the table for supper have definite piorities attached to them. In school he recognizes the need to conduct himself with a certain amount of civility if he wants to avoid conflict in his transactions with others. His awareness of social control and structure in life makes it possible for him to view (in a favorable light) the hierarchy of status and role obligations inherent in the school's organization. It helps him develop a priority, thereby relieving him of potentially conflicting choices. For example, not informing on a pupil takes precedence over placating the teacher. Many of the rules and regulations structure the interaction patterns in order to prevent the occurrence of strain or to inhibit the strains from leading to deviance.

Educators have taken different positions about the manner in which self-control can be achieved. The traditional educator believes that the child learns self-control by being controlled by the teacher. The modern educator believes that self-control comes about through the practice of self-discipline. There is agreement that children must be restrained in their behaviors. Rules developed by teachers and parents are designed to help children become aware of the specific demands that the adults are making on them. If the expectations and consequences are clear the child is able to associate his behaviors with the criteria used to assess

---

[24]Laurel N. Tanner and Henry Clay Lindgren, *Classroom teaching and learning* (New York, Holt, Rinehart, and Winston, 1971), p. 357.

his performance. Hopefully, the end-goal of self-control is achieved.

There is no doubt that an educator's values enter into the decision about the role that structure should play in the school. Those who wish to limit the role of structure in the lives of pupils argue that rules and regulations lead to rigid and inflexible practices, and that many of these practices inhibit creativity and foster role learning. Furthermore, since most of the rules are developed by administrators, the principles of democracy are violated, and as a consequence, the child never is able to acquire the true meaning of democracy. The argument against structure is further distorted by claiming that all misbehavior is a product of punishment and that pupils have a moral right to reject rules which were written without their participation. It is our position that structure is needed to help children develop guidelines for rational behavior. The purpose of these guidelines is not conformity, but to help children formulate rational decisions for themselves and about themselves so that classroom events can have personal relevance. On the relationship of democracy and discipline Ausubel has made the following observation:

> Democratic discipline is a form of discipline that is as rational, nonarbitrary, and bilateral as possible. It provides explanations, permits discussion, and invites participation of children in the setting of standards whenever they are qualified to do so. Above all, it implies respect for the dignity of the individual and avoids exaggerated emphasis on status differences and barriers between free communication. Hence it repudiates harsh, abusive, and vindictive forms of punishment and the use of sarcasm, ridicule, and intimidation.[25]

Our position is similar to that of Ausubel's in that if the school is to help children in their quest of self-actualization pupils must become aware of the social limitations on their classroom behavior. Without this awareness most of their interpersonal relations will be characterized by conflict rather than by civility.

[25]David P. Ausubel, "A new look at classroom discipline," *Phi Delta Kappan*, Vol. 43 (1961), p. 28.

"In a democratic society nobody is so important that he is above apologizing to those persons whom he wrongfully offends."[26]

A teacher's lack of understanding of the group process may contribute to the production of classroom difficulties. Redl is of the opinion that the teacher, because he is a group leader, needs not only an understanding of group dynamics but must be skillful in group analysis.[27] His basic thesis is that the structure of the group contributes more to classroom misbehavior than the idiosyncratic behavior of an individual. "When something is wrong with the group, even the most normal individual member is likely to produce confused action leading to problem behavior."[28] Redl, in his analysis of classroom difficulties, grouped them into the following six classifications: (1) dissatisfaction in the work process; (2) emotional unrest in interpersonal relations; (3) disturbances in group climate; (4) mistakes in organization and group leadership; (5) emotional strain and sudden change; (6) the composition of the group. He believes that any one of the six group-psychological factors in discipline problems may coexist with any other. The task of a counselor is to help the teacher to think through the problem. He facilitates the helping process by looking past the surface behavior and looking at the interaction system of the class to identify the strains. To expedite the analysis the counselor can use the six group-psychological factors as guidelines. The consultation should help the teacher develop a program that modifies the existing pattern of interaction. The goals may be either surface behavior or basic attitudes. In some cases the teacher may have to modify her own behavior, teaching materials, or the goals that she has set up for the class.

Long and Newman suggest that there are four major alternatives in handling surface behavior in the classroom.[29] They are

---

[26]*Ibid.*

[27]Fritz Redl, *Discipline for today's children and youth* (Washington, Association for Supervision and Curriculum Development, National Education Association, 1956), pp. 45-57.

[28]*Ibid.*, p. 45.

[29]Nicholos J. Long and Ruth G. Newman, "Managing surface behavior in school," in *Conflict in the classroom*, N. J. Long, W. C. Morse, and R. G. Newman (eds.), (Belmont, Wadsworth, 1971), pp. 442-452.

permitting, tolerating, interfering, and preventive planning. Each tactic has its own merits and it is incumbent on the teacher to find the right combination of techniques for each child. However, Redl has pointed that no amount of advance planning can prevent misconduct from taking place in class because the teacher does not have total control of the multiple and simultaneous events that take place in the classroom. Although the teacher may be skillful in "situational thinking" and plan for what she believes is "appropriate" sequencing of content and public interaction, the structure of the class, individual pupil needs, and social distraction affect the degree to which the goals of the plan are attained. In order to minimize the effect of these and other influences, the teacher must become a skillful behavioral manager. By knowing how to use various intervention tactics, the teacher can interfere with surface behavior in a manner that maintains the dignity of the pupil while minimizing his disruptive influence on the class.

Some educators believe the behavioral management has no place in schools because it violates the premises of democracy. This argument would be valid if the school were in a position to control every facet of the child's life. Societal expectations limit the types of activities that the school can undertake. Since the school has certain demands placed on it by society, it must exercise some control over events within the school so that goals may be reached. Ideally, the school should provide an environment where the pupil can explore alternative perspectives from which to view society so that he can evolve a schema for himself about himself and the world. In order to gain a better understanding of himself and the world, the pupil must undertake tasks which he may find irrelevant and uninteresting. There is no assurance that situational thinking can prevent bored and disinterested students from disrupting the class. The teacher must accept the idea that some content, no matter how manipulated, is not relevant to the immediate needs of some pupils. It is during these times that the teacher's behavioral managerial skills are put to the test.

Another source of disruptions of the instructional process is the interpersonal relationship network of the class. Expectations of others and self-expectations affect the transactions between class members. "What is expected of me?" "Can I do it?" "What will happen if . . . ?" "Will they like me if I do it?" "How will the teacher feel about it?" These questions deal with the child's position in the classroom's socio-emotional structure. Lippit and Gold believe that the child's position in this structure "becomes a very important determinant of his mental health, and of his motivation, and ability to participate in classroom interaction."[30] Their research has shown that a child who has a low position in the socio-emotional structure tends to have the following characteristics: (1) negative self-evaluation; (2) hostility toward others; (3) unskilled or unrealistic behavior output; (4) insensitivity or defensiveness about feedback from others about his own behavior. Their work supports Redl's opinion that the structure of the class can precipitate misbehavior in a pupil. Class-induced misbehavior occurs because of "(1) a very rapid evaluative labelling of a child and a strong tendency to maintain this evaluative consensus in spite of further information about the individual child as a stimulus; (2) very inadequate skills of the group in providing the member with feedback which communicates sympathetic guidance rather than rejection or ignoring; (3) a lack of group standards concerning acceptance and support of deviancy."[31] The teacher can contribute to the child's low position in the socio-emotional structure by failing to practice good human relations, ignoring interpersonal grouping practices, and inadequate modeling.

The Lippit and Gold study has implications for the counselor and teacher. It implies that the teacher must be skilled in both individual and group managerial skills in order to minimize the difficulties generated by transactions among class members. Teachers who lack these skills tend to be ineffectual because they spend more time dealing with disruptive behaviors than with instructional concerns. To the counselor, the study should reaffirm the idea that the pupil, the class, and the teacher are his

---

[30]Ronald Lippit and Martin Gold, "Classroom social structure as a mental health problem," *The Journal of Social Issues,* Vol. 16 (1959), pp. 40-49.
[31]*Ibid.*

clients, and that he must use a variety of tactics in order to help them. The reliance on one procedure restricts the type of help he renders his clients. By the same token, focus on one specific goal of guidance, such as developmental concerns of children, is unrealistic in that it restricts the type of problems with which the counselor comes in contact. The counselor should not only be familiar with the tactics of behavior management but he should also use them in his work.

BEHAVIOR MODIFICATION IN THE SCHOOL

The advocacy of the use of behavior modification is not inconsistent with our position that the goals of the school and counseling should be the self-actualization of the individual. It should be remembered that we believe that self-actualization is a general goal of life. In the process of defining self-actualization we listed its characteristics and manifestations. Inherent in the elements of self-actualization are a series of specific goals. It is in the area of specific goals that the techniques of behavior modification can be used. For example, if on the basis of observation, it is concluded that a pupil's disruptive tactics (e.g., out-of-seat behavior) can best be controlled by means of a behavior modification technique, then the tactic should be employed. Although individual counseling is helpful, it should not be used indiscriminately. Generally speaking, behavior modification techniques are useful in situations where the teacher or counselor can exert precise control over specific behaviors. When the goals become more general, then behavior modification should be used in conjunction with other procedures.

Behavior modification is based on the premise that all behavior, whether adaptive or maladaptive, is learned according to the same principles. These principles stem from classical and instrumental learning theory. The basic difference between these two learning theories is that the focus of the latter is on voluntary behavior while the focus of the former is on involuntary behavior.

Pavlov's experiments in the conditioning of dogs to salivate to a bell is an example of classical conditioning. This type of conditioning depends on forming associations between some external event and an internal body process according to the principle of contiguity. The association can be formed by either chance or plan. Classical conditioning procedures can be used to control emotions and many bodily functions. Under such circumstances, a specific emotional reaction (e.g., fear of dogs) can be learned in only one exposure to an external event. The process of conditioning emotional responses to words is called "semantic generalization." In this process a specific emotion is aroused by an irrelevant word. "Love of God, of country, of tribe, or party, or of principle; fear, distrust, and contempt for strangers, minorities, majorities, races, religions, doggies, and harmless little garter snakes—all have been taught, in every human society, by classical conditioning, in which words take their connotations from emotions aroused in connection with their use."[32] Some classroom problems are a direct result of emotional reactions to words. Children can be provoked into irrational behavior by such words as "nigger," "Polack," and "dummy." Counterconditioning can be used to replace the inappropriate behavior with a constructive one. Joseph Wolpe has developed a number of techniques based on counterconditioning. Among them are (1) *discriminative training* by which an individual is taught to discriminate between those stimuli that cause fear and those that produce gratification; (2) *assertive training* by which an individual is taught to become more expressive in his relationship with others; (3) *conditioned avoidance* which is used to help an individual eliminate a behavior he deems inappropriate. [33]

E. L. Thorndike developed many of the ideas that are inherent in instrumental conditioning, whose focus is such voluntary behavior as habits, skills, and problem solving. According to this theory, responses are learned through the reinforcement principle. A reinforcer is something that follows a response and increases the likelihood of occurrence of that response. Experimental studies have shown that positive reinforcement (rewards) is more effective than negative reinforcement (punishment) in

---

[32]Perry London, *Behavior control* (New York, Harper and Row, 1969), p. 88.
[33]*Ibid.*, pp. 60-62.

conditioning behavior. It should be noted that what is "rewarding" or "punishing" is determined by an individual's needs. For example, a teacher can increase the hand-raising response (e.g., you raise your hand before you speak in class) in pupils by praising them when they do it. In this situation, the need for approval by others is rewarded by praise.

The principles of extinction are used to eliminate or reduce the occurrence of a response. Extinction is the opposite of reinforcement in that it involves the withholding of reinforcement in order to reduce the strength of response. For example, a teacher may ignore those who enter a classroom discussion without raising their hands. By not reprimanding them or not calling attention to their failure to raise their hands, she is systematically applying extinction principles. Extinction is differentiated from punishment in that the latter involves the application of negative consequences. Teachers tend not to use some forms of extinction because they tend to be misunderstood by the class. For example, ignoring those who failed to raise their hands may be construed by some pupils that you no longer have to raise your hand.

B. F. Skinner has incorporated some of the ideas of instrumental conditioning in his concept of operant conditioning. Operant behavior is seen as being emitted by the person rather than being evoked by stimuli. That is to say, operant behavior operates on the environment without being controlled by any specific stimuli. For example, a pupil reaching for food (an operant response) is not only controlled by his sight of it but also by such factors as hunger, other people eating, and the fact it is his lunch period. Skinner, like Thorndike, assumes that if some type of reinforcement follows an operant, then that response is more likely to occur, even though the stimulus for the operant is unknown. He differs from other conditioning theorists in that he does not believe that behavior is made up of specific stimulus-response connections. Behavior is seen as being dependent on the total pattern of external and internal stimuli.

Skinner has integrated many of his techniques so that it is possible to control the development of complex acts. This form of behavior modification is called shaping. The complex behavior pattern is learned through the utilization of the principles of reinforcement and successive approximation. The complicated behavior pattern is reduced to a series of steps which are gradually learned by selective reinforcement of appropriate responses. The learning is so arranged that each successive step comes closer to the desired level of performance.

Modeling is a technique adopted in behavior modification that is based on the assumption that the probability that a pupil will perform a behavior increases if he observes another pupil (model) performing that behavior. Many social skills are acquired by imitation and identification with appropriate models. There is some research evidence that suggests that modeling tactics are more effective in establishing new responses in children than are reinforcement techniques. Bandura identifies three types of effects when a child is exposed to a model: (1) *modeling effect* by which a pupil acquires a new response; (2) *inhibitory or disinhibitory effect* by which a pupil controls his own behavior by seeing what happens to another pupil; (3) *elicitation or response facilitation effect* by which a pupil structures a previously learned response to meet the demands of the situation.[34] The probability that a pupil will imitate a model depends on such factors as need for approval, perception of appropriate responses in the model, and awareness of the demands of the situation.

Of the various behavior modifiction procedures that have been reviewed, operant conditioning, with its emphasis on shaping behavior, is seen by teachers as having the greatest utility in the school. Their interest in operant conditioning stems from the fact that (1) it deals with voluntary behavior; (2) identifiable reinforcers are used to control consequences; (3) most behavior in school is operant behavior; (4) operant conditioning can be learned more readily than other types of behavior modification. In part, this preference for operant conditioning by teachers supports the contention that the counselor is a specialist in ef-

---

[34]A. Bandura, "Behavioral modification through modeling procedures," in L. Krasner and L. Ullmann (eds.), *Research in behavior modification* (New York, Holt, Rinehart, and Winston, 1965).

fect. Consequently, he should be well versed in helping students control some of their emotional reactions through classical conditioning.

Specificity is the basic principle that underlies most of the procedures used to shape the behavior of a pupil. The first task is to define the goals toward which operant conditioning is to be directed. The problem must be defined in a manner that reduces any ambiguity about what is to be changed. For example, changing the child's maladaptive behavior is too global, while reducing the occurrence of out-of-seat behavior is not. The second step is to identify those elements in the classroom that are associated with the target behavior. The third step is to identify the specific ways that can be used to modify the implemented target behavior. In the fourth step, the specified modification program is implemented. The last step is to evaluate the consequence of behavior modification in terms of level of performance. If the shaping process fails to reach the desired level of performance, then alterations must be made in the reinforcement schedule and behavioral contingencies. The shaping process requires considerable ingenuity and imagination in establishing and manipulating the relationships among the operant behavior, reinforcers, and the pupil's needs. It is not an easy task to induce a pupil to perform at a level that is satisfying to the child and the counselor or the teacher.

The essential elements of a behavior modification program are observation, plan, implementation, and evaluation. However, the use of the operant conditioning techniques or any of the other types of behavior modification is affected by terminology used to describe the process. Terms such as contingency, reinforcement, and successive approximation tend to block, rather than facilitate the use of operant conditioning. Lindsley has suggested that the term *reinforcing stimuli* be replaced with *acceleration.*[35] He points out that if the reinforcing stimulus or consequence increases the probability of a response on future occasions you

---

[35]Ogden R. Lindsley, "Theoretical basis for behavior modification," in C. E. Pitts (ed.), *Operant conditioning in the classroom* (New York, Thomas Y. Crowell, 1971), pp. 54-60.

know it. There is no point in asking, "How can you tell if a consequence is accelerating?" because it is obvious that the consequence is either accelerating or decelerating the rate at which the response occurs.

> The reason *acceleration* and *deceleration* or *accelerating* and *decelerating consequences* are good terms to use with teachers is that they are functional. They mean something from the teacher's point of view and they mean something from the child's point of view. The teacher and the child are immediately aware of the effect. I find it very easy to teach functional behavior analysis in one hour or two hours to parents and teachers for two reasons: (1) if the teacher or if the child, himself, chooses the consequence that is meaningful for him, then there is a high probability that it is going to work; (2) if it doesn't work, then we know something else is happening.[36]

The implication of Lindsley's remarks is that two other factors in addition to specificity affect the success of operant conditioning. They are the quality of the relationship between the teacher or counselor and the pupil and the ability to discern behavior in the classroom. Many of our remarks about the function of a relationship in individual counseling are germaine to the role that the interaction between the teacher or counselor and pupil plays in setting contingencies or consequences. Of particular interest is the pupil's recognition of the need for help, his willingness to engage in activities that will help him modify his behavior, and assistance in the development of consequences. The rate at which the consequences affect the behavior of the pupil is determined, in part, by the personality and attitudes of the teacher and her relationship with the pupil. When this relationship is combined with reinforcement, modification of behavior occurs.

Observation plays a key role in specifying the behavior to be changed and the effect that the consequences have on the rate of occurrence of the new behavior. After the teacher or counselor has identified the environmental events that support the old behavior, data are gathered to determine the rate at which it occurs. These baseline data serve as a reference point from

---

[36]*Ibid.*

which to measure the effects of the introduction of new consequences or contingencies. The type of data that is gathered depends on the ingenuity and imagination of the teacher or counselor. The data-gathering process must reflect what is to be changed, how frequently it occurs, or in what situations it occurs and what happens to it when consequences are applied to it. Keeping a record of the data presents a problem, but a review of the literature shows that teachers have overcome this obstacle in many ingeneous ways. For example, counts of maladaptive behavior have been kept by means of the wrist counters used by golfers and the counters used to record purchases in supermarkets. In addition, asking the pupil to keep his own record, especially after the base rate has been established, serves as an additional consequence in shaping the behavior.

The type of reinforcement or consequence used in a classroom poses a problem. Although primary reinforcers, such as candy and food, have been used with success in shaping behavior, their use in a large class can be disruptive. Secondary reinforcers, such as checkmarks or tokens that can be exchanged for toys or candy, have been used with success in a large classroom. However, they pose a record-keeping problem for the teacher. Forness suggests that teacher attention and high-frequency behaviors can be used as consequences.[37] He suggests that for teacher attention (such as praise, encouragement, friendly looks, or smiling) to be effective, it must be used in a systematic manner. Teachers can use those activities in which a pupil engages the most often (such as games or reading comic books) as reinforcers for behaviors which he does not willingly perform (such as doing arithmetic problems). Forness supports Lindsley's position that what constitutes positive reinforcement is whatever works. Teacher or counselor observations can identify what behaviors the pupil engages in most frequently in relatively unstructured situations and use those behaviors as reinforcers. Some may object to this procedure because it has the earmarks of blackmail. It should be noted that

---

[37]Steven R. Forness, "Behavioristic approach to classroom management and motivation," *Psychology in the Schools,* Vol. 7 (1970), pp. 356-363.

usually the child and teacher mutually agree to the use of the high frequency behavior as a consequence.

Meacham and Wiesen, in their review of the effectiveness of reinforcement procedures, evolved seven principles which they believe are essential to the systematic modification of classroom behavior:

1. Reinforcers are determined by their actual effect on the learner, not by their supposed effect.
2. Reinforcers affect behavior automatically.
3. Reinforcers should be linked to the behavioral criteria of accomplishment.
4. Reinforcement should be administered consistently.
5. Reinforcement should follow immediately the behavior to be modified.
6. Reinforcement should be frequent and appear early in the learning sequence.
7. Reinforcement should be applied at each step of the learning sequence.[38]

When new behavior is being acquired, a continuous schedule of reinforcement should be used. However, to maintain newly established behavior patterns, a variable or an unpredictable reinforcement schedule should be employed. One of the common problems that a teacher or counselor should guard against is that of inadvertently reinforcing the wrong behavior. They should also be aware of the fact that the effectiveness of some reinforcers tends to "run out"; that is, some pupils become satiated because of the overuse of one type of reinforcer. Most teachers are aware that pupils seldom tire of attention and approval.

The various concepts and procedures of behavior modification can be set into proper perspective by referring to the diagram in Figure 10-1. Hewett developed this model for generating behavior modification programs predicated on operant conditioning.[39] The diagram shows the three essential ingredients found

---

[38]Merle L. Meacham and Allen E. Wiesen, *Changing classroom behavior* (Scranton, International Textbook, 1969), p. 46.

[39]Frank M. Hewett, "Educational engineering with emotionally disturbed children," *Exceptional Children*, Vol. 34 (1967), pp. 459-467.

in all classroom behavior modification programs: (1) selecting and defining the appropriate task; (2) providing reinforcers or consequences after task completion; (3) maintaining a suitable structure by the teacher to control pupil behavior. The elements of the diagram can serve as a useful checklist for developing and maintaining a behavior modification program.

Intervention Procedures in the Schools

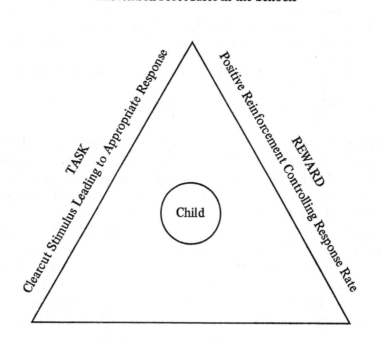

Withholding of Positive Reinforcement or Administration of
Negative Reinforcement Following Inappropriate Responses

Scheduling of Positive Reinforcement

Setting of Contingency for Receipt of Reinforcement

STRUCTURE

Figure 10-1. The Learning Triangle

A procedural guide for establishing a token system of behavior modification has been prepared by Sattler and Swoope.[40] This guide indicates how Hewett's model can be operationalized. The token system is designed to expand the reward or consequence dimension in order to provide a broader reinforcement base. The token system involves the use of some object or symbol that a pupil can later trade in for something he wants. Experimental studies have shown that the token system is a useful vehicle for implementing operant principles. Listed below are ten procedural considerations that Sattler and Swoope believe are necessary for implementing a token system.

1. Select a method for choosing desirable behaviors.
2. Select the kind of token to be awarded.
3. Choose back-up reinforcers for which tokens can be exchanged.
4. Select a cueing method for informing which behaviors will be reinforced.
5. Choose a mode for awarding tokens.
6. Construct a master control sheet for recording tokens awarded.
7. Schedule a time for exchanging tokens for back-up reinforcers.
8. Select a method for making back-up reinforcers available.
9. Devise a method for bringing the reinforcing activity period to an end.
10. Select the appropriate type of contingency to be used when awarding tokens.

Sattler and Swoope suggest that the token system be paired with teacher attention. They believe that after the pairing has been accomplished, teacher attention, in and of itself, can become a strong reinforcer. The token system reinforces not only the task, but the need of approval by others.

It is beyond the scope of this book to list all of the various types and methods of behavior modification and their application to the classroom. A large number of articles and books have been written on this subject. We hope that our review of the theoretical rationale for behavior modification can provide an adequate background for understanding the process and its use

---

[40]Howard E. Sattler and Karen S. Swoope, "Token systems: a procedural guide," *Psychology in the Schools,* Vol. 7 (1970), pp. 383-386.

in the school setting. Those who are interested in additional information should read some of the material listed below.[41]

THE SOCIALIZATION PROCESS REVISITED

One of the unfortunate conclusions that can be reached about operant conditioning and other forms of behavior modification is that their sole concern is with reinforcers or consequences. "How did you get Jim to do that?" typifies the concerns that some practitioners have about the process. What is important is that the probability of the occurrence of a specific behavior has increased, not that some type of reinforcer worked. The essence of behavior modification is to provide an environment that brings about some desired change in the pupil. This means more than identifying a set of reinforcers or consequences that "work." It means the identification of a specific goal that is of mutual concern to the teacher and the child. The goal helps to identify the means that can be used to "control" the individual to the point that he has "self-control" over whatever behavior is the object of modification.

The pupil is not "programmed like a machine" but is seen as a unique individual whose voluntary behavior is shaped because of mutual cooperation. In order for a behavior modification program to succeed, the pupil must exhibit some degree of willingness to participate in the program. He must feel that he is going to get something out of it. This "something" may not necessarily be what the teacher or counselor has specified. Without personal commitment to "participate," the behavior modification program will not succeed.

Behavior modification programs have much in common with the process of socialization. Each is concerned with controlling

---

[41]John D. Krumboltz and Helen B. Krumboltz, *Changing children's behavior* (Englewood Cliffs, Prentice-Hall, Inc., 1972); John D. Krumboltz and Carl E. Thoresen, *Behavioral counseling: cases and techniques* (New York, Holt, Rinehart, and Winston, 1969); Meacham and Wiesen, *op. cit.*; Nicholas J. Long, William C. Morse, and Ruth G. Newman. *Conflict in the classroom* (Belmont, Wadsworth, 1971); Carl E. Pitts, (ed.). *Operant conditioning in the classroom* (New York, Crowell, 1971); L. P. Ullmann and L. Krasner (eds.), *Case studies in behavior modification* (New York, Holt, Rinehart, and Winston, 1965).

the behavior of the child to the point that he has achieved self-control over some aspect of his behavior. Each makes systematic use of reinforcers to enhance the frequency of occurrence of some specified behavior. In the case of socialization, the reinforcers are in the form of gratification and deprivation of specific personal needs, while the reinforcers in behavior modification tend not to be directly related to basic needs. However, both emphasize the need for approval by others. An additional difference between the two is that in behavior modification the child tends to be aware of the goal while in socialization he must figure out what his mother wants him to do and then do it. This requires that the child become proficient in "reading" his mother's behavior. This emphasis on the stimulus suggests that some forms of socialization utilize classical conditioning. This is reflected in conditioning the child to have strong feelings about certain words (e.g., semantic generalization). The implication that can be made from these comparisons is that the child has some understanding of behavior modification when he enters school. His behavior has been shaped by many of its techniques since infancy.

The socialization process is not restricted to the home. Since the home cannot provide the child with all of the ways he can adapt to the demands of society, the school helps the pupils to acquire additional means of coping. The classroom interaction provides a vechicle for integrating many of the societal forces. The social forces of the class can affect what is learned, how it is learned, when it is learned, and at what level of performance. The various subgroups within the class help its members form emotional attachments that affect the interaction network within the class. For effective learning to take place the class must be seen as a group rather than as an aggregate of individuals.

The school has been given the responsibility for altering or modifying behaviors that are the consequences of inadequate or inappropriate socialization. This approach to the problems of the school sees children as being "social deviates" rather than as being "emotionally disturbed." Behavior modification programs based on sociological rather than psychological principles employ reward systems but they use different types of reinforcers.

Bredemeier and Stephenson suggest that established socialized behavior can be modified in the following ways.[42]

1. separating the socializers from former associates so as to minimize self-approval for resistance to change;
2. enlisting peer group support and suppressing prior statuses in order to minimize self-approval for resistance to change;
3. emphasizing the linkage between the old and the new and de-emphasizing the discontinuity so as to maintain consistency in self-conceptions;
4. down-grading previous sources of gratification;
5. 'de-grouping' so as to diminish the saliency of old associations.

Although the above procedures reflect some of the extinction principles of instrumental conditioning, they focus on the social aspect of the environment and the direction of the modified behavior is controlled by gratification (not satisfaction). The need for approval by others and self-approval are the reinforcing elements.

If the school desires that the pupils acquire new socialized behavior, Bredemeier and Stephenson suggest the following procedures.[43]

1. developing anticipatory socialization in a structure of ranked or graded statuses;
2. making desired rewards contingent on conformity to new statuses;
3. socializing to a pattern of deferred gratification;
4. structuring or countering reference groups so that the estimates of relative gratification and deprivation decrease conceptions of costs and increase conceptions of profits.

Some of the principles of positive reinforcement are reflected in the above procedures. The behavior is controlled to enable the pupil to make a transition from the old to the new. Self-control is achieved by a systematic application of delayed gratifications. Subgroups within the class can help with the process by providing the pupil with models for the appropriate behavior. The general intent of the process is to help the pupil acquire new modes

---

[42]Bredemeier and Stephenson, *op. cit.*, p. 120.
[43]Bredemeier and Stephenson, *op. cit.*, p. 120.

of behavior so that the strain and the pain of inadequate responses can be minimized.

The appropriate blending of sociological and psychological principles for the purpose of improved classroom functioning requires that the teacher and counselor have an understanding of elements that comprise them. The ways that these understandings are used in the class are affected by the multiple and simultaneous events that take place in the classroom. What may be appropriate for helping the pupil with his behavior if he were the only one in the class, may be inappropriate because of the nature of the subgrouping within the class. The child's reference groups affect whether he is willing to change his behavior. The teacher's skill in situational thinking can help with planning activities that consider the multiple demands of the classroom and the individual needs of the pupils. In the course of a school day the teacher must make modifications in the plan because factors over which he has minimal control have intruded into the instructional process. The teacher continually makes judgments as to which alternatives should be used. Because some decisions are made rapidly, errors in judgment occur. Figure 10-2 shows some of the elements that the teacher must consider when deciding on a course of action.

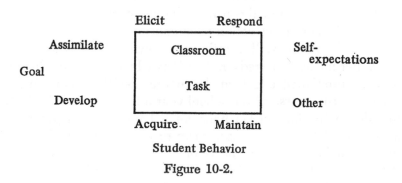

TEACHER BEHAVIOR

Elicit   Respond

Assimilate   Classroom   Self-expectations

Goal

Develop   Task   Other

Acquire   Maintain

Student Behavior

Figure 10-2.

The forces that affect the teacher's decisions are as follows:

1. General goals of education
   a. Behavior patterns that the society wants the child to assimilate
   b. Development of the individual as a unique person
2. Teacher behavior
   a. Teacher activities that elicit a pupil response
   b. Reactions of teacher to responses of pupils
3. Expectations
   a. Self-expectations (pupil or teacher)
   b. Expectations of others (pupil, teacher, parents, community)
4. Pupil behavior
   a. Acquisition of some type of behavior
   b. Maintaining of some type of behavior
5. Task
   a. Affective
   b. Behavioral
   c. Cognitive
6. Classroom
   a. Norms
   b. Roles
   c. Cohesion
   d. Subgroups

The six dimensions do not represent all of the forces that influence the decision-making process, but represent those forces that typically influence on-the-spot decision making. For example, the school district's policies, principal's opinion, and staff norms influence the planning. However, once the lesson plan is implemented, modifications must be made because factors over which the teacher has minimal control influence what has been planned. Some of the corrective action must consider the personal development of the pupil. Will a smile or a frown enhance the learning? A teacher makes hundreds of decisions which over the school year have a cumulative effect on the mental health of her pupils.

During the course of the school year a teacher should take time to reflect what impact her behavior is having on her pupils. It is at this point that the counselor can provide an invaluable service to the teacher. Not that he resolves the teacher's misgivings, or that he provides the teacher with a decision-making model that is error free, but he provides the teacher with an opportunity for self-evaluation with a minimum of threat. If a number of teachers express similar concerns, the counselor can use group procedures to help the teachers with their concerns. The focus of these procedures is to help the teachers express their concerns and feelings about how their actions affect the mental health of their pupils. What is not needed is an in-service training program on the principles of mental health. Understanding of self is the need to be met here, not the understanding of the pupil.

The counselor's role in the school is to help those associated with the school with their concerns. Children, parents, teachers, administrators, and special-interest groups are among those who can benefit from his service. Essentially, the counselor's clientele are the constituents of the community. Most of his time should be devoted to helping individual pupils meet their needs so that their personal development can be enhanced. Traditionally, this has meant that the focus of the relationship is the intrapersonal dynamics of the pupil. However, the child's position in the interaction network and the process of assimilating cultural requirements can generate concerns for the pupil. In addition the teachers and administrators realize that these factors induce problems for children. They, too, would like assistance. Thus, the function of the counselor is to help all of these individuals in a manner that reduces the psychological stresses, strains, and pains they are currently feeling so that in the future they can be open to new experiences. The counselor must employ a variety of tactics in helping these individuals. No one procedure can be used to resolve all concerns. It should also be apparent that other personnel specialists must participate in the helping process. Because of the complexity of the problem, no one counselor can possess the necessary skills to help all those who have asked for assistance. The counselor and personnel specialist play an important role in helping the school and the pupils achieve their goals.

There is no question that methods of behavior modification can be used to induce conformity behavior, or to train pupils to behave in ways that suit the convenience of teachers and administrators. The methods can be used for good or ill. But control of behavior is now exerted, and the effectiveness of behavior modification offers an opportunity to examine our goals and objectives in the classroom. The methods can be used, as suggested in this chapter and in Chapter 12, as a means of socialization and of providing a stable, consistent and predictable environment in which pupils can function more effectively and more efficiently in learning.

Behavior modification is no panacea for all classroom problems or problem children. It can be overdone, particularly the token economy involving tangible rewards. Pupils have been known to ask, when requested to do something in classrooms when this system has been used to induce desirable behaviors, "What do I get if I do it?" As noted above, the method loses its effectiveness when the reinforcers no longer constitute rewards. Finally, the methods may lead to the development of dependent behavior, including dependency on extrinsic rewards rather than intrinsic satisfactions. Problems arise in attempting to move from external to internal controls. In the development and maturation of the individual there should be a movement from the need for external controls as inner controls are established. The goal of maturity, or of self-actualization, is the reduction of dependency on external controls. The individual becomes aware of the broad demands of the physical and social environment, and of their imposition of consequences for his action, and responsibly chooses his actions on the basis of this knowledge of consequences.

SUMMARY

The basic thesis of this chapter is that self-control can be achieved by controlling the individual's behavior up to the point that he can make decisions about himself by himself. *Controlling*, in this instance, does not mean the total control of the individual but structuring those elements in the environment that would assist the child in learning requisite behaviors. Although many methods of behavior control were described, no single method was singled out as being best. The method used for controlling an aspect of behavior should be selected in terms of the goal and the unique attributes of the child. All methods are predicated on the use of some type of reinforcement. The process establishes a relationship between the controller and the child in terms of relating the reward to some need of the child. In the course of developing the response pattern, the child establishes an association between the use of reinforcers and the need for approval by others. After a period of time this need for approval by others generalizes into a need for self-approval. Thus, when the child transcends from the stage of reliance on the approval of others to that of approval by himself, he begins his quest for self-actualization. Although he respects the opinion of his fellowmen and sees the value of their standards and norms, he must, as Polonius said, "to thine own self be true."

The socialization process, as reflected in the school and home, is not free of problems for the socializer and socializee. Change in values and goals, inadequate communication patterns, and poor interpersonal skills are among the factors that generate problems. Many different procedures were cited as being helpful in reducing the psychological strains and stresses. The task of the counselor is to provide assistance in a manner that reduces the strains and stresses and at the same time induces the willingness to try new experiences. The end goal is not to produce a problem-free individual but one who is willing to take occasional risks in order to become himself.

SUGGESTED READINGS

Clarizio, Harvey F.: *Mental health and the educative process*, Chicago, Rand-McNally, 1969.

Jackson, Philip W.: *Life in classrooms*, New York, Holt, Rinehart and Winston, 1968.

Pitts, Carl E.: (ed.), *Operant conditioning in the classroom*, New York, Thomas Y. Crowell, 1971.

Chapter 11

THE COUNSELOR
AND THE
CURRICULUM

TRADITIONALLY THE GOAL OF EDUCATION has been to teach the three R's, or, somewhat more broadly, to transmit the culture to the young. In recent years disagreement regarding the nature of curriculum has become commonplace. Changes, modifications, and revisions in school programs are taking place at an ever increasing pace. This emphasis on speed of change without considering the ramifications on the existing organization of the school has brought about a lack of coherence in the activities of the school. It is rather difficult to have a unity of goals and procedures when diverse groups are attempting to change a school program without regard for one another's proposals. Many of the proposals do not put into proper perspective the relationship between the characteristics of the learner, the teaching behaviors, and the learning process. In this chapter, we shall try to establish a frame of reference for considering the content and activities of a school program in relation to those individuals who are associated with it.

THE NATURE OF THE CURRICULUM

One of the more difficult words to define in education is the term *curriculum*. When defined from the perspective of the school, curriculum refers to the manner in which the environment is organized, while a definition from the pupil's point of view emphasizes the responses he has to make to the environment. Some definitions of curriculum describe the school's program for pupils. These descriptions may include "all courses in a particular field, a group of related courses, a sequence of courses, the courses at a particular grade level, and the total school program including studies as well as student activities."[1] One of the "anomolies" in education is the inconsistency between descriptions of curriculum which appear in the literature and the comprehensive definition of it. "Curriculum conceived to be the total educational process is difficult indeed to deal with in descriptive or research terms."[2]

Cuban makes this terse observation:[3]

> After all, curriculum is considered by many to be what a school teaches and what children are expected to learn; it is textbooks, basal readers, and course syllabi, and course outlines. It is the school's slice of reality. The Board of Education, the superintendent, principals, and special interest groups determine the reality. Teachers teach it. Kids endure it. That's all.

Inherent in all descriptions or definitions of curriculum are the notions of goals and products. It is a plan of action whose purpose is to change the behavior of children in some type of systematic manner. "It is based on tradition, conventional wisdom, sound planning, and expediency" and reflects "what should be taught, in what order, and to what purpose, what has priority, and what has value."[4] In other words, "curriculum is assumed to be content (data, concepts, and /or modes of inquiry) and the vehicles by which it is contained for student confrontation and interaction."[5]

---

[1]Gerald R. Firth, "Youth education: A curricular perspective." In Raymond H. Muessig (ed.), *Youth Education* (Washington: Association for Supervision and Curriculum Development, 1968), p. 86.

[2]Helen L. Wardeberg, "Elementary school curriculum and progressive education," in James R. Squire (ed.), *A new look at progressive education* (Washington, Association for Supervision and Curriculum Development, 1972), p. 75.

[3]Larry Cuban, *To make a difference: Teaching in the inner city* (New York, The Free Press, 1970), p. 84.

[4]Wardeberg, *op. cit.*, p. 207.

[5]Firth, *op.cit.*, p. 89.

A formal definition of curriculum will not necessarily help the counselor understand the concept. An explication of the various views of curriculum would be helpful in that the review would trace the development of various ideas about the nature of curriculum. Shane, Shane, Gibson, and Munger have made an interpretive review of the viewpoints of curriculum written during the past 35 years.[6] Their discussion follows the concept of curriculum as content, organized as experiences sponsored by the school, derived from the needs of society, and with psychological implications. After the review they observe that there are two fundamentally basic concepts of the curriculum: the *subject*-centered and the *learner*-centered. The focus of the latter type of curriculum is activities and answers the questions of why and what while the focus of the former is the ordering of cognitive tasks, and answers the questions of how and when. Shane, et al., believe that "the pointless argument over whether one teaches children OR subjects may be boiled down at present to an acceptance of the point that one begins to teach children effectively only when he has developed insights into the transactional relationships which exist among these children, their environments, and the learning experiences toward which a balanced curriculum directs our efforts."[7] They provide several guides by which a counselor can identify his position on the curricular continuum by analyzing his beliefs about the nature of the child, the environment, and the learning process. The purpose of the guidelines is to help the counselor to clarify his thinking as to where he stands regarding certain curriculum issues.

The process of curriculum development must put into proper perspective the relationships among structure and freedom, cognitive and affective domains, and the learner and what he learns.[8] The content of any subject matter can be related to pupils and their affective concerns. However, the pupil must be taught how to utilize the various activities in a manner that satisfies his needs.

---

[6]June Grant Shane, Harold G. Shane, Robert L. Gibson, and Paul F. Munger, *Guiding human development* (Belmont, Wadsworth, 1971), pp. 126-146.

[7]*Ibid.*, p. 140.

[8]Wardeberg, *op. cit.*, p. 226.

Firth believes that the curriculum should be so constructed that not only the teachers understand it but that it makes sense to the pupil so that he can use it constructively for his own learning.[9] This requires a systematic approach to curriculum development in order for the various elements to be integrated into a meaningful whole. In this way both the staff and the pupils can utilize the various activities for their own personal development.

The counselor's role in curriculum development is twofold. First, he can provide data about students so that various activities can be arranged into appropriate sequences. Second, when the staff is planning the curriculum he can serve as a process consultant. In this role he observes how the interpersonal networks among the staff affect the planning. He helps the staff to clarify their attitudes, expectations, and understandings, so that the blocks to curriculum development can be reduced.

RELATIONSHIPS AMONG CURRICULUM, INSTRUCTION, TEACHING AND LEARNING

If the curriculum can be seen as a statement that provides a guideline for selecting learning experiences in the school, it has incorporated into it answers to what, why, how and when the school should undertake to teach. There is some question as to whether a curriculum statement should contain a detailed account about materials and procedures. Discussion about details very often obscures the general purpose of the curriculum; however, a lack of details prevents a systematic integration of effort of the staff. The arranging and identifying of curricular tasks has value in that it helps teachers in their preparation for teaching a unit of instruction.

Differentiating curriculum from instruction can help alleviate the argument as to how much detail should be found in the curriculum statement. Gagne defines instruction as "the institution and arrangement of the external conditions of learning in ways which will optimally interact with the internal capabilities of the

---

[9]Firth, *op. cit.*, p. 100.

learner, so as to bring about a change in these capabilities."[10] The basic function of instruction is to control the external conditions of the learning situation. Among the external conditions are sequencing of tasks, identification of essential stimuli, and the development of verbal directions. In an earlier chapter we discussed the role that *situational thinking* played in teaching. The teacher must be skillful in anticipating the consequences of some of the activities that the pupils undertake. Gagne would call this type of teacher behavior instruction for its purpose is to control the external conditions of learning. The basic difference between instruction and curriculum is that the latter's focus is long range while the former's focus is short range. Another basic difference between the two is that instruction is planned and designed by the teacher while curriculum planning is undertaken by various groups and individuals such as faculty committees, citizen advisory groups, principals, and curriculum specialists.

Teaching can be distinguished from instruction in that its focus is the teacher's behavior in the classroom with the purpose of facilitating the achievement of learning. Instruction is concerned with the development of sequences of tasks that help control the external conditions of learning. Teaching is a polymorphus concept because it includes a variety of operations.

> Teaching is not just placing things before people for their consideration, or informing, or telling, or conversing, or narrating, but taking such measures as will bring it about that something envisaged by the teacher is learned, by which I mean that it is both understood and remembered. What we teach is intended not just to be registered, but kept in mind: teaching involves the deliberate equipping of a person in some way, whether in respect of knowledge, skill or settled habit.[11]

Teaching is an intentional activity whose purpose is to facilitate change and to provide situations for realistic stimulation and feedback. The teacher's task is to arrange situations in the environ-

---

[10]Robert M. Gagne, "Instruction and conditions of learning," in Laurence Siegel (ed.), *Instruction: some contemporary viewpoints* (San Francisco, Chandler Publishing Co., 1967), p. 295.

[11]R. F. Dearden, "Instruction and learning by discovery," in R. S. Peters (ed.), *The concept of education* (London, Routledge and Kegan Paul, 1967), p. 137.

ment so that the pupils' interaction with them will lead to optimal learning.

Learning can be differentiated from teaching in that its focus is the change in behavior of the pupil. The degree to which a pupil has learned is inferred by observing the pupil's level of performance before and after teaching. This suggests that teaching alters the pupil's internal capabilities and that this change can be called learning. Learning, like teaching, is a polymorphus concept.

> Learning is the comprehensive activity in which we come to know ourselves and the world around us. It is a paradoxical activity: it is doing and submitting at the same time. And its achievements range from merely being aware, to what may be called understanding and being able to explain.[12]

This comparison of curriculum, instruction, teaching, and learning suggests that integrating teaching and learning with the general goals of education is a complex task. It appears that it is easier to order cognitive tasks than to arrange activities that facilitate the self-development of pupils. Biber believes that the dictum "fit the school to the child" is easier said than done.

> To fit the school to the child now requires knowledge of developmental stages in terms of intellectual and psychosexual changes; understanding of Hunt's theory of "match"; the impact of life environment conditions on learning style and attitudes; and, awareness of cognitive-affective interaction processes.[13]

The task of fitting the school to the child requires the cooperation and skills of all personnel of the school. The pupil personnel specialists can contribute their understandings and skills to the planning of meaningful educational experiences. Their contributions can be in direct involvement in the planning, or in critiquing the plans to insure that all facets of pupil development are considered. In addition, the counselor can serve as a process observer during

---

[12]Michael Oakeshott, "Learning and teaching," in R. S. Peters (ed.), *The concept of education* (London, Routledge and Kegan Paul, 1967), p. 156.

[13]Barbara Biber, "The 'whole child,' individuality, and values in education," in James R. Squire (ed.), *A new look at progressive education* (Washington, Association for Supervision and Curriculum Development, 1972), p. 66.

the planning phases of the curriculum. As a process observer his task is to inform the group as to the manner of their communication styles and point out the various blocks to meaningful communication. He does not act as a mediator of disputes among the group members but acts as a facilitator of effective communication.

In recent years the development of curriculum plans has been facilitated by the use of several conceptual formulations. Among them are (1) the Tyler rationale;[14] (2) the taxonomy of educational objectives; (3) the stating of goals in terms of behavioral objectives. Macdonald has made the following observation on the fusion of these three conceptual formulations.[15]

> The taxonomy of educational objectives has provided for locating the kinds of goals within any substantive area. The Tyler rationale—(a) stating objectives; (b) selecting experiences; (c) organizing experiences; and (d) evaluating experiences—provides an intellectual phase analysis for a curriculum of the learning cycle which can carry out the fulfillment of objectives.

In addition to considering the long range effect of the curriculum plan, the designers of the curriculum plan must also consider variables in the learning situations and within the learner. It becomes apparent that in order to plan an effective curriculum or to plan for effective instruction, data are needed about the nature of the pupils and the learning situation. Standardized tests are a contribution to meeting this need.

STANDARDIZED TESTING IN THE SCHOOL

The use of standardized tests in the schools has been under criticism for a variety of reasons. In order to put the various criticisms into proper perspective, the counselor should answer the following question: "Is standardized testing an appropriate technique to be used in a school setting?" Some of the factors that the counselor should consider in exploring the answer to the

---

[14]Ralph W. Tyler, *Principles of curriculum and instruction* (Chicago, University of Chicago Press, 1950).

[15]James B. Macdonald, "Curriculum development in relation to school and intellectual systems," in Robert M. McClure (ed.), *The curriculum: Retrospect and prospect* (Chicago, National Society for the Study of Education, 1971), p. 107.

question are (1) the nature of testing; (2) the nature of man and his use of symbolic language; (3) methods of classifying test performance; (4) values; and (5) role of the school in social issues. In this section we will review how these and other factors affect the use of standardized testing in the school.

The traditional use of intelligence tests in schools has been challenged by a variety of sources. McNemar has recently catalogued some of these objections:[16]

> Among the supposed strikes against general intelligence are the following: The earlier false claims about IQ constancy; prediction failures in individual cases; unfounded claims that something innate was being measured by the tests; equally unfounded assertions that nothing but cultural effects were involved; the bugaboo that IQ tests reflect middle class values; the notion that an IQ standing fosters undesirable expectations regarding school achievement; the idea that IQ differences are incompatible with democracy and lead to educational determinism; and, finally, the great stress on general intelligence caused us to ignore other possible abilities.

In order to minimize the controversy generated by the use of intelligence tests, it has been suggested that achievement tests be used in their place. This does not resolve the problem but rather complicates it. It is rather difficult to differentiate between achievement, intelligence, and aptitude tests on the basis of content (what the test covers) and process (what the examinee has to do). Wesman suggests that the best way to differentiate between these types of tests is by the function of the test results. To what end or purpose do we wish to use the performance on the test? For example, a score on the arithmetic section of the Iowa Basic Skills Test can be used to predict success in algebra (i.e., aptitude), or it can used as an indicator of arithmetical skill (i.e., achievement).[17]

Some of the controversy regarding the utility of standardized tests may be minimized by looking at the definition of a psychological test. "A test is a systematic procedure for comparing be-

[16]Quinn McNemar, "Lost: Our intelligence?" *American Psychologist*, Vol. 19 (1964), p. 871.

[17]Alexander Wesman, "Aptitude, intelligence, achievement," *Test Service Bulletin*, No. 5 (New York, The Psychological Corp., 1956).

havior of two or more persons."[18] A test is only a sample of behavior in a given area. A sophisticated test user examines the
test as to the adequacy of the sample and the methods of making
comparisons between individuals. This procedure is undertaken
to see if the kind of data given by the test yields sufficient information for a specific purpose. Failure to do so will lead to misuse
of test data.

An example of the misuse of test data can be found in the manner that the high relationship between performance on an intelligence test and school achievement has been utilized in the
schools. Many educators equate performance on an intelligence
test with the ability to learn. "It is indeed curious that we use
intelligence tests to predict capacity to learn and yet, none of
our tests involve any learning; instead they give us a cross section of what has been learned."[19] Vernon, after reviewing the
work of Thurstone, Anastasi, and Guilford, concluded that " . . .
there is no general learning ability common to all types of tasks.
Rather, there seems to be a number of poorly defined factors in
learning and there is little indication that these possess any useful diagnostic validity; however the findings tend to be more positive when complex tasks are learned."[20] It is difficult to infer
how well a student will learn from his performance on an intelligence test because psychologists have not discovered a factor that
indicates general learning ability.

The operational dilemma that the counselor finds himself in is
the demand by the principal and the teachers for inferences from
standardized tests that transcend the available data. The failure
of the principal and teacher to comprehend that test scores reflect a pupil's behavior in a specific situation has led to a distrust
of test data. Recent psychological studies have shown that the
type of situation affects the level of performance.

---

[18]Lee J. Cronbach, *The essentials of psychological testing* (New York, Harper &
Row, 1960), p. 21.

[19]P. E. Vernon, *Intelligence and cultural environment* (London, Methuen, 1969),
p. 42.

[20]*Ibid.*, p. 43.

As a rule, one looks for performance at its best and infers the degree of underlying competence from the observed performance.... If performance is treated (as it often is by linguists) only as a shallow expression of deeper competence, then one inevitably loses sight of the ecological problem of performance. For one of the most important things about any "underlying competence" is the nature of the situations in which it occurs. Here lies the crux of the problem. One must inquire, first, whether a competence is expressed in a particular situation and, second, what the significance of that situation is for the person's ability to cope with his life in his own milieu.[21]

Cole and Bruner imply that an individual may have competence in some aspect involving the use of a skill but may not be able to express that competence in the context in which it is expected to be shown. The counselor very often is asked to make a statement about an individual's competence in many areas based on performance in a highly structured situation. In order for the counselor to extrapolate the test performance, he must have a good understanding of the validity of the test and the situations to which it can be applied.

Cronbach suggests that the developers of general ability (his label for group intelligence) tests attempt to achieve two diverse goals: (a) they attempt to "predict school success and therefore include measures of educational skill in their tests" and (b) they "ask the same test to measure a psychological attribute which is distinct from educational attainment."[22] As a consequence, these types of tests usually do not yield information about either area. The utility of data from tests of general ability is dependent on the test user's familiarity with research findings. Even tests with low-predictive validity are useful in particular situations.

The use of achievement tests in conjunction with mental ability tests is supported by Levine. He observes that "intelligence tests are more pervasive in scope and measure for the most part crystallized learnings from early life" while achievement tests

---

[21]Michael Cole and Jerome S. Bruner, "Cultural differences and inferences about psychological process," *American Psychologist*, Vol. 36 (1971), p. 874.
[22]Cronbach, *op. cit.*, p. 235.

"measure residuals of later learning and consequently are not as highly correlated with each other as the verbal and quantitative reasoning tests."[23] Levine suggests that an appropriate achievement test combined with an intelligence test will augment the validity obtained from the general mental ability test alone. "In a practical prediction problem, aptitude tests (i.e., general mental ability tests) may be compared to a coarse adjustment on a microscope and achievement tests to the fine adjustment."[24] A counselor should keep in mind that intelligence tests have certain additional characteristics that affect the interpretation of an individual's performance. McNemar calls attention to two basic considerations:[25] First, responses to test questions go beyond the mere stimulus-response paradigm. A test performance is not a summation of S-R responses. The philosophical and psychological nature of man must be considered in evaluating the performance. Second, the test results do not deal with the *process* by which an individual makes an intellectual response. The test performance is only an indication of the degree of interaction between innate ability and motivated learning. The test score gives only inferential information rather than an exact measure of intelligence. Mackworth further suggests that intelligence tests "pick out the efficient verbal reasoners rather than intuitive observers." However, he does point out that "problem finders (as contrasted to problem solvers) are scarce because this kind of basic thinking is very difficult to undertake."[26] The counselor should keep in mind that intelligence tests do not measure "creativity" or "originality" although each of these factors is dependent on intelligence.

To a certain extent the way tests are used by a teacher, counselor, or administrator reflects their ideas on what role a school should play in social matters. Among the roles that a school can play in social issues are: (a) promote the *status quo,* (b) stress those factors that a majority of the society feel are important at

---

[23]A. Levine, "Aptitude versus achievement tests as predictors of achievement," *Educational and Psychological Measurement,* Vol. 18 (1958), p. 518.

[24]*Ibid.,* p. 520.

[25]McNemar, *op. cit.,* p. 185.

[26]N. Mackworth, "Originality," *American Psychologist,* Vol. 20 (1965), p. 53.

the moment, (c) stress those factors that "experts" feel are important, and (d) promote the self-development of students so that as adults they can shape their own destinies. A school that believes in the promotion of the status quo would use intelligence tests of the abstract type so that it can assess the facility with which its students can use symbolization. A student who would score "high" on this type of test is held in higher esteem (from a societal point of view) than one who scores "low." Schools that are affected by public opinion can have a variable testing program. If a community feels that going to college is important then the focus would be on scholastic aptitude tests. On the other hand, if basic skills are deemed important, then achievement tests will be emphasized. Schools under the influence of "expert opinion" would also have a variable testing program. A "liberal expert" would remove tests that measure individual differences and retain those that promote similarity between people. The "conservative expert" would place special emphasis on achievement testing to see how well the students have mastered the traditional elements of a school program. A school interested in the self-development of its students would not have a rigorous testing program. Tests would only be used when a student desired to have some "objective" evidence regarding certain aspects of his self-concept.

Limiting the use of intelligence tests in school reflects some of the liberal thinking in social matters. The promotion of "equality of opportunity" is in part impeded by evidence of innate differences between individuals. Those who plan to bring about the "equalization of opportunity" by means of environmental manipulation must of necessity play down inherited aspects of development. The political disregard for the uniqueness of man and his preexisting and predetermining factors can have a formidable impact on the utility of certain psychological theories. Although it is impossible to keep one's religious and political views out of research, one should be cognizant of the effect they have on the interpretation of results. The molding of a psychological model of man solely on a political orientation can lead to dangerous consequences. One of the reasons for low yields of crops in Russia in the 1960's can in part be the adherence to the Lysenko point of view on plant development. Essentially it denies genetic transmission of characteristics according to Mendellian principles but stresses environmental adaptation as a means of developing new strains. The Lysenko viewpoint is compatible with the doctrine of dialectic materialism which stresses the equality of all matter.

The appropriate use of intelligence, achievement, and aptitude tests in schools is a complex matter. The counselor must be aware of the social implications of this technique. He must be willing to evaluate its impact on social issues of the day. The abstractness of the technique, the incompleteness of research and inadequate communication on the part of the schools, has confused the general public on this matter. At times it has the impression that the test user is some type of soothsayer who can by some magical power translate pencil markings into predictions of the future. By the same token, the counselor should not assume that the testing approach as it applies to schools is needed. However, the educator should not structure his research activities so that they favor the political orientation in power. His personal values and ethical concerns should guide the implications he makes regarding his research findings.

Is standardized testing an appropriate technique to be used in a school setting? The answer to this question depends on what use will be made of the test data. If the chief use of the tests is to classify the students in a manner similar to that of grading beef, the answer to the above question is "no." A louder "no" can be voiced if test results are used to support or promote a particular political orientation. If test data are used to enhance the self-development of students or help the school reconstruct its course of studies, the answer is "yes."

In one sense it does not matter if the test carries the label "intelligence" or "achievement." In either type of test some aspect of the individual's symbolic repertoire deemed essential by society is being appraised. What is important is the interpretation that is placed on the test. In any type of standardized test, students are either compared or judged. This procedure is inherent in the technique. Test scores require a frame of reference to be meaningful. When used appropriately, testing procedures help the school to answer two basic questions: "Who can profit from additional instruction?" "What should the nature of instruction be so that students can profit?"

Standardized tests should be so constructed so that they will yield usable answers to the above questions. Centering attention on test content, process, or classification mechanisms detracts from the original purpose of giving a test. Tests are like lampposts: you can either lean on them or use them for enlightenment.

APPRAISING STUDENTS FOR INSTRUCTIONAL PURPOSES

In essence, the original use of the IQ score to identify and select children for programs within schools forced educators to use grade-point averages and grade equivalents as criteria of successful identification. As a consequence, a premium was placed on achievement rather than other products of instruction. Only in recent years have educators become aware that intelligence is only one facet inherent in cognition and thought. Concern for how information was perceived, processed, stored, and retrieved brought about changes in methods of identifying and educating the gifted.

Many factors precipitated the change in the programs for the gifted. Among them are the work of Piaget, computer technology, the writings of Bruner, teaching machines, Bloom's taxonomy, Guilford's structure of the intellect, etc. The change in ideas brought about change in perceptions. As Bruner suggests, "We perceive and think in a fashion that depends on techniques rather than upon wired-in arrangements in our nervous system."[27] He further suggests that techniques serve as amplifiers for skills and modes for self-generation of new ideas. With appropriate teaching strategies, linkages between skills and ideas could be generated so that the quality of learning and growth far exceeds what was possible under traditional methods. Hunt, Harvey, and Schroder among others have proposed methods for linkage formation. Trow points to some of the variations in teaching procedure: (1) assign-test-mark, (2) refer-diagnose-treat, (3) en-

---

[27]Jerome S. Bruner, *Toward a theory of instruction* (New York, Norton, 1966), p. 26.

rich environment-permit-pace, and (4) assess-teach-evaluate.[28] Trow is of the opinion that the last strategy is the most viable because it can promote skill acquisition as well as social learning.

An instructional program should focus not just on scholastic achievement but should enable the student to invest his cognitive energy in an ideational flow that generates many alternatives. The end product would be a student who is interested in accomplishments outside the academic area while at the same time exhibiting clear relationship to academic achievement itself.

In its simplest form, the instructional program would interrelate the following elements:

$$goal \times \frac{subject}{matter} \times \frac{teaching}{strategy} \times \frac{learner}{characteristics} \times \frac{information}{processing}\ strategy$$

The above outline suggests that assessment is a key factor to success of the instructional program. Assessment must be made of the component parts, feedback mechanisms, and outcomes.

The traditional mode of classifying the gifted is not viable for the proposed instructional program. In the traditional mode, the identification program gave little consideration to the nature of the instructional program. Since the main outcome was increased achievement, the identification process was concerned with those attributes that are typically associated with achievement. The identification process in outline form looks like this:

$$g \times s \times \textit{level of attainment} \times \textit{effort}$$

The students were placed in programs that stressed achievement. The programs used various means to achieve this objective: ability grouping, enrichment programs, special classes, acceleration, special sectioning, etc. The total process reflected the premise that tested intelligence, ability to learn, and level of attainment were identical constructs.

The suggested approach to teaching requires the development of the program before identification would be undertaken. The objectives of the program would help formulate the attributes

---

[28]William C. Trow, "An educational model for social learning," *Psychology in the Schools*, Vol. 7 (1970), pp. 237-241.

needed to meet the requirements of instruction. The specifications would not only include the nature of the student but type of environment, teacher characteristics, and nature of information processing.

The identification process would be based in part on a hierarchical view of factors.[29] Since the goal of instruction is to maximize the interaction between accomplishment outside the academic arena and achievement itself, factors inside the school as well as outside the school would have to be considered. The Vernon factor (v: ed) would be included in the identification process. "This verbal-educational complex refers to the ability to handle tasks like those encountered in schools."[30]

General Outline for Identification

General fluid g

Verbal-education (v: ed)
    Verbal, spelling
    Reading, number

Number ability

Verbal reasoning

Conceptual development
(Human Information Processing)
    Fluency
    Induction
    Ideational flow
    Linkages

Creative abilities

Personality
    Flexibility
    Submissiveness
    Independence

Interpersonal skills

Home background

Motivation schema

Information obtained from procedures used to identify various pupil characteristics provides useful data to curriculum planners and teachers. This type of information is useful in schools that feature individualized instruction programs. These types of programs need information about pupils so that appropriate place-

---

[29]Vernon, *op. cit.*, p. 189.
[30]Cronbach, *op. cit.*, p. 260.

ment in the instructional sequence can be made. Lindvall and Cox state that two other types of tests are needed: (1) diagnostic tests for given units, and (2) curriculum-embedded tests for monitoring pupil progress. They suggest that the placement tests[31] should provide a general profile of individual competence over many areas of work. The function of diagnostic tests is to identify the level of a pupil's competency in a specific instructional unit which he is about to study. The function of a curriculum-embedded test is to measure the performance of a pupil on one particular objective in the sequence. This type of testing procedure avoids one of the major pitfalls of test interpretation: drawing inferences that transcend the available data. The error is avoided by constructing tests for the various sequences and objectives in the program. This test construction is undertaken by test construction specialists. The counselor and other personnel specialists play a minimal role in this aspect of the instructional program.

Lindvall and Cox are fundamentally concerned with the appraisal of products of instruction. The focus of their evaluation is to identify where a class or an individual is in respect to a sequence of instructional activities. This type of evaluation concentrates on the cognitive abilities of the child.

Thelen believes that the focus on the products of instruction detracts from looking at the whole child in the classroom.[32] If the classroom is seen as a miniature society, then the teacher needs assessment skills that can capture the feelings, language, and action of the class. Thelen believes that the teacher must be skillful in diagnosing, trouble-shooting, and feedback in the group process so that he can make judicious interventions in the social systems of the classrooms. The several paragraphs that follow are based on Thelen's concept of evaluation of group instruction.

---

[31]C. M. Lindvall and Richard C. Cox, "The role of evaluation in programs for individualized instruction," in Ralph W. Tyler (ed.), *Educational evaluation: New roles, new means* (Chicago, *National Society for the Study of Education,* 1969), pp. 154-180.

[32]Herbert A. Thelen, "The evaluation of group instruction," in Ralph W. Tyler (ed.), *Educational evaluation: New roles, new means* (Chicago, National Society for the Study of Education, 1969), pp. 115-153.

When the classroom is seen as a social system, the pupil's role is more than that of a producer of instructional products. He is a member of a group and as such is expected to coordinate a large number of internalized roles: student, baseball player, friend, brother, helper, boy scout, and so on. The role expectations not only include academic tasks but also define procedural choices for the child, boundary lines for action, deadlines, and common purposes for the class. The pupil realizes that the expectations are inherent in the situation rather than a reflection of a teacher's whim. A pupil who violates group standards and common expectations is noticed, and corrective action is undertaken by the class or the teacher. By the same token, the teacher uses overt participation as a method of assessing the effectiveness of the on-going process of learning.

Thelen points out that, as the teacher observes tell-tale behavior, he attempts to make sense out of it. When the teacher diagnoses the group process, he "attempts a theoretical reconstruction that explains why everyone in the group feels and acts the way he does."[33] He differentiates diagnosis from trouble-shooting in that the former is concerned with "where we are and where we ought to be" and the latter attempts to see what caused the discrepancy and what action should be taken to remove it. "Trouble-shooting is a built-in feedback that enables the teacher and the group to see how they need to modify their activity to bolster or soft-pedal events in the various subsystems.[34] The focus may be on learning tasks, group management, or personal feelings.

The manner in which diagnosis and trouble-shooting are used depends on how the teacher views the group. According to Thelen, the group may be seen as (1) a collectivity, (2) an interpersonal network, and (3) a micro-society. He describes how each of the tactics can be used with the different perception of the group. Some of the suggested procedures are (1) clarification, examination, and demonstration of task procedures; (2) discussion of what class members expect from the teacher and from

---

[33]*Ibid.*, p. 125.
[34]*Ibid.*, p. 148.

each other; and (3) examination of attitudes about what "ought" to be done in class.

Thelen's chapter on the evaluation of group instruction is more than a primer on how to undertake this type of evaluation. It attempts to persuade the reader that evaluation should be made of the "whole child" rather than of his role as a producer of educational products. Evaluation of the whole child deemphasizes the progress made towards educational tasks and examines the pupil's ability to cope with molar tasks. It also examines the child's repertoire of roles such as group-member, ecologist, citizen, consumer, and so forth. From this standpoint of evaluation, a pupil or class can show little gain in achievement but considerable amount of gain in personal development or group membership skills. Thelen laments the fact that there is more interest in achievement gains than in gains to cope with the world. Did one ever hear of a teacher who was denied tenure because his pupils scored low on a measure of mental health?

One conclusion that can be reached regarding Thelen's article is that it is naive to assume that the only two types of behaviors that occur in the classroom are the teaching and the learning of subject matter and that the only outcome is educational achievement. The classroom has a social environment and its impact on the teacher and the pupils can transcend the stated educational objectives of the class. Thus, the teacher and the pupil must not only be aware of the social environment but also understand how it affects their behavior.

The Thelen approach stresses a more informal approach to the group instructional process. A formal approach of the observable characteristics of the classroom phenomena is presented by Biddle and Adams.[35] The model presented by them is divided into four variable classes: teacher behavior, pupil behavior, the social environment, and the physical environment. They discuss the various types of coding systems that have been used for achieving reliable observation. They suggest that, for the best results, the

---

[35]Bruce J. Biddle and Raymond S. Adams, "Teacher behavior in the classroom context," in Laurence Siegel (ed.), *Instruction: Some contemporary viewpoints* (San Francisco, Chandler, 1967), pp. 99-136.

classroom observations should be separated into examining the communication structure (e.g., pattern of symbolic exchange among actors) and the spatial structure (e.g., physical location regarding one another). The work of Biddle and Adams describes methods and concepts for conducting field research on teacher behavior and the social environment. It is not intended to provide a teacher with a frame of reference for conducting a classroom. It is their intention to evolve a theory of instruction that is predicated on the evidence obtained from their observations of teachers at work.

The counselor will probably find the work of Thelen more useful than that of Biddle and Adams. The latter article is concerned with discovering the principles of effective teaching, while the former is concerned with the personal development of pupils. The remarks of Biddle and Adams have value to curriculum planners in that they provide a framework for examining the interrelations among many variables that must be considered when the curriculum is designed. Thelen's chapter can help a counselor in the following ways: (1) serve as a foundation for an in-service training program for teachers and administrators; (2) provide an impetus for developing an evaluation program whose focus is the "whole child;" (3) furnish a frame of reference for consulting with teachers who are having problems with group instructional procedures. The counselor's understanding of interactional problems can be enhanced by becoming familiar with the writings of Herbert Thelen.

THE CURRICULUM AND THE SELF CONCEPT

The curriculum can be seen as a plan for modifying behaviors of teachers and pupils in the classroom. It provides a frame of reference for selecting activities when a number of alternative courses of action are present. In essence the curriculum modifies the behaviors of teachers and pupils by controlling their choices. Usually evidence of control is seen in statements that describe cognitive and behavioral outcomes. However, emotional control is also necessary. Biber suggests that "emotional arousal must be controlled if the children are to be engaged intellectually in thinking about issues being opened to them by the teacher."[36] She believes that emotional arousal is necessary for deepening learning but it must be controlled in a manner that makes it possible. She cites Jones to support her opinion. "One cannot aid in the development of emotional and imaginal skills without reference to their integral cognitive counterparts . . . neither . . . can one hope to effectively aid in the development of cognitive skills without reference to their integral emotional and imaginal counterparts."[37]

Biber believes that the end goal of control should be the freedom of the individual. Using Dewey as a point of departure, she makes the following observation:

> Individuality emerged not through sporadic, passive, "doing" activity, but as the consequence of engaging in a sequence of experiences that involved questions, knowledge seeking, new accomplishments, and further questioning. . . . Though Dewey chose content that was intellectual, he expected well-organized learning experience to have broader developmental impact. "Disconnected activities," he wrote, "do not provide for development of an integrated self." If we were to paraphrase this concept today, we would say an integrating intellectual experience is not just cognitive, but resonates toward other aspects of the self.[38]

Biber's opinions suggest that the quality of classroom interactions affect the pupil's self-concept. From these interactions an individual develops an awareness of self and an awareness of how others feel about him. He not only becomes cognizant of his abilities but also of the relevant behaviors that affect them. School achievement plays an important function in the development of the self-concept of a pupil because it serves as a sign of self-worth.

Purkey, in reviewing the research on the relationship between self-concept and academic achievement, concludes that the view "that the successful student is one who is likely to see himself in

---

[36]Biber, *oj. cit.*, p. 60.

[37]R. M. Jones, *Fantasy and feeling in education* (New York, New York University Press, 1968).

[38]Biber, *op. cit.*, p. 65.

essentially positive ways has been verified by a host of studies."[39]
He does observe that some research evidence points out that
all those who profess high self-concepts do not necessarily perform at comparable levels. He suggests "that confidence in one's
academic ability is a necessary but not a sufficient factor in determining scholastic success."[40] Purkey further states "that unsuc-
cessful students, whether underachievers, nonachievers, or poor
readers, are likely to hold attitudes about themselves and their
abilities which are pervasively negative."[41] His general conclusion is that there is a reciprocal relationship between the self-
concept and academic success and that improved scholastic performance can be induced through the enhancement of the self-
concept.

The self-concept is a dynamic summation of such elements as
seeing, remembering, imagining, feeling, and emoting. Purkey
observed that "once we have acquired an idea about ourselves,
it serves to edit all incoming information and to influence our
future performance."[42] Seeman employed a similar concept when
he described the personality to be an internal communication
network whose function is to provide information on which to
act and to synthesize experiences.[43] The emotionally mature individual is one who tries to maximize the availability of information and who can synthesize the information effectively. "These
processes would lead to behavior which, on the one hand, has
high variability and complexity, and on the other hand, has
clear boundaries and adequate control."[44] In applying this model
to children, he found the high adjusted pupil to be stable, self-
assured, organized without finicky attention to detail, and accepted by other children while the low adjusted pupil was highly

---

[39]William W. Purkey, *Self-concept and school achievement* (Englewood Cliffs,
Prentice-Hall, 1970), p. 18.

[40]*Ibid.*, p. 19.

[41]*Ibid.*, p. 22.

[42]*Ibid.*, p. 23.

[43]Julius Seeman, "Toward a concept of personality integration," *American Psychologist*, Vol. 14 (1959), 633-637.

[44]*Ibid.*

distracted by his environment or impervious to it. The highly adjusted pupil could be characterized as having high environmental contact, high internal communication, and high stability.

Many of the above ideas were used by Prescott Lecky in helping pupils who were failing in school.[45] In his theory of self-consistency he assumed that an individual's idea or concept of himself was organized in a manner that had a high internal consistency. The self was not based on objective evidence but was essentially subjective, private, and wholly individual. As such, the self resists any attempt to modify itself. Lecky believed that a pupil fails because he expects himself to fail and that this expectation is continually renewed so that it is forged into an almost unbreakable cycle. In order for remedial procedures to be effective the pupil's self-concept must be altered. This is done by demonstrating to the pupil how his personal standards interfere with his functioning in the classroom. The counselor should point out that this is the pupil's problem and not the school's; however, the counselor is willing to help the pupil without jeopardizing his internal consistency.

Lecky notes that some pupils who can do arithmetic cannot read. These pupils "think of themselves as unable to read, and maintain this standard by rejecting the ideas necessary for reading, for these ideas are inconsistent with their self-conception and consequently cannot be assimilated."[46] He suggests that standardized tests or observations, when used with this type of pupil, are not only indicators of his present level of ability but also can be thought of as expressions of his internal standards. The pupil as well as the test show a high degree of reliability. Identification and treatment of pupils who have problems functioning in the class because of the structure of their internal frame of reference are difficult. No one procedure or system of diagnostic tests can discover them. A multivariative analysis of behaviors hopefully can yield additional information about the status of various pupils.

The function of testing and observation is highly variable and

---

[45]Prescott Lecky, *Self-consistency: A theory of personality* (New York, Island Press, 1951), pp. 245-255.

[46]*Ibid.*, p. 250.

complex. Generally speaking, the data obtained from these procedures are used to design activities that modify the behaviors of teachers and pupils. The data can also be used to measure the effectiveness of various procedures and methods. In addition, tests and observations can be used for diagnosis and troubleshooting. The role that the counselor plays in the assessment and appraisal process is variable. When attempting to identify students whose self-concept interferes with performing in the school, the counselor may find a minimal utility from standardized testing procedures. On the other hand, testing procedures are helpful in placing students in various types of programs. Thus, the program of evaluation must evolve from the needs of the school district and not from the competencies of the staff.

CAREER EDUCATION IN THE ELEMENTARY SCHOOL

To date, our discussion on curriculum has focused on planning, designing, instruction, testing, and evaluation. It is not our pur pose to review specific content, materials, and procedures. However, there is one aspect of content or, to be more precise, a subgoal of education, that should be discussed because it has become a relevant topic in education.

Career education has come to the foreground because of interest in it by federal agencies. Sidney P. Marland, U. S. Commissioner of Education, outlined the basic premises of career education in a speech to the National Association of Secondary School Principals in 1971.[47] He suggests that the term career education should supplant vocational education because the latter expression has a restrictive meaning that denotes training for a skilled type of occupation. Career education is a more pervasive term in that it includes all of the individuals in the school and assumes that many of the school's activities can be related to career development. Most of the current discussion on career education is focused on the secondary level.

The role that the elementary school should play in career education is not clear. Many educators agree that occupational in-

---

[47]Sidney P. Marland, "Career education now," *Vocational Guidance Quarterly,* Vol. 20 (1972), pp. 188-192.

formation should be made available at the elementary level but disagree as to the form in which it should be presented. Should the occupational information be in the basal readers, in supplementary readers, in units of study, or for individual study? Another point of disagreement is the purpose of the occupational material. Should the material be used for exploratory purposes or as a basis for decision making?

It should be noted that career education is not equivalent to providing occupational information. The focus of career education is on making the pupil aware of the fact that someday he will become a worker and that his choice of a career is influenced by many factors. One of the factors that influence a pupil's choice is his attitude toward work. There is some research evidence that suggests that some attitudes toward work become established by grade eight. Hales and Fenner, in examining the work values of fifth, eighth, and eleventh grade students, concluded that "children develop values toward the world of work early and, within a specific cultural setting, these values appear to be relatively similar for students of different ages."[48] Perrone, using the Readiness for Vocational Planning developed by Gribbons and Lohnes, evaluated the impact of an in-service training program and curriculum modifications on pupil vocational planning.[49] The results indicated that the average-achieving pupil in an inner core school and the low and average-achieving students in the suburban school benefited the most. Perrone believes that information about vocations and self should be presented continuously and should take into consideration the different levels of comprehension. In addition the school should work with parents in helping them assess the pupil's knowledge regarding his knowledge of school, work and self.

Hill and Luckey suggest that the school should begin early in helping children understand the relationship between education and employment.[50] According to these authors the school should

[48]Loyde W. Hales and Bradford Fenner, "Work values of 5th, 8th, and 11th grade students," *Vocational Guidance Quarterly*, Vol. 20 (1972), pp. 199-203.

[49]Philip A. Perrone, "Teaching vocational aspects of development in eighth grade," *Vocational Guidance Quarterly*, Vol. 20 (1972), pp. 204-209.

[50]George E. Hill and Eleanor R. Luckey, *Guidance for children in elementary school* (New York, Appleton-Century-Crofts, 1969), pp. 359-361.

help pupils develop the attitude that all forms of work are worthy of respect. They believe that the pupils should be made aware that their interactions with other people, in particular adults, help shape how they feel about themselves. However, this self-concept should have a degree of flexibility about it because the rapid changes in technology and society may demand that the pupil become retrained to meet the demands of the new situation. Thus, the child should become aware that the process of choosing a vocation is complex and that factors beyond his control may affect what he will do as an adult.

Arbuckle challenges the basic assumption that the world of work should be seen as the center of life rather than the individual.[51] He believes it is wrong to perceive the environment as some vague outside-of-the-person force to which an individual must adjust. Arbuckle is of the opinion that most theories of vocational choice reflect this assumption. He cites Super as an example of this type of thinking and uses the following quotation to back his judgment: "(vocational counseling) . . . is the process of helping the individual to ascertain, accept, understand, and apply the relevant facts about himself to the pertinent facts about the occupational world, which are ascertained through incidental and planned exploratory activities."[52]

Arbuckle prefers to view man from an existential perspective. To match a child's abilities to someone else's plan is an unwarranted restriction of man's freedom to choose and to become.

> "Environment" is not something outside of me to which I must, in order to get along, learn to adjust, but it is, rather, a reflection of me. I have a responsibility, not to adjust to a fixed environment, but as a result of my living, to do something to modify and change both it and me. Indeed, one may question whether one could actually say "it" and "me," since they are both entwined with each other.[53]

Because of his existential orientation, Arbuckle believes that most of the occupational information made available to elemen-

[51]Dugald S. Arbuckle, "Occupational information in the elementary school," *Vocational Guidance Quarterly*, Vol. 12 (1964), pp. 180-186.

[52]Donald E. Super and John O. Crites, *Appraising vocational fitness* (New York, Harper and Row, 1962), p. 2.

[53]Arbuckle, *op. cit.*, p. 183.

tary school children has little personal meaning to them. He agrees with Kowitz and Kowitz who say that "on the elementary level the selection is too often limited to about a dozen service occupations such as milkman, postman, and policeman."[54] Lifton supports this observation by citing his research which showed that primary grade texts emphasized the service occupations while the upper grade texts stressed the professional occupations.[55] Additional evidence of bias and distortion in elementary school textbooks was found by Tennyson and Monnens.[56] The reading series that was analyzed emphasized professional, managerial, and service occupations but gave only scant attention to skilled or clerical occupations. The results of these and other studies seem to indicate that there is a need for more and better occupational information. These studies do not resolve the question as to the type of information that should be made available to elementary school children. Perhaps the emphasis should be on helping the children acquire a personal meaning of work and how this personal meaning can be extended into the world of work.

It is difficult to prescribe a program of vocational or career education for the elementary school because any plan would reflect the designer's ideas about how theories of vocational choice, personality development, and cognitive development should be blended so that a viable career education program could be written. Vocational development, like any other type of development, proceeds sequentially so that the pupil becomes more aware of himself, his environment, and the world about him. Our discussion of group work (Chapter 5) makes a detailed analysis of this process. The task of the school should be that of a provider of a variety of exploratory situations, not necessarily about the world of work but about life in general, that in some way challenge the child. In this way the child may generate a personal meaning

---

[54]Gerald T. Kowitz and Norman Kowitz, *Guidance in the elementary school* (New York, McGraw-Hill, 1959), p. 154.

[55]Walter Lifton, *The elementary school's responsibility for vocational misfits* (Chicago, Science Research Associates, 1960).

[56]W. Wesley Tennyson and Lawrence P. Monnens, "The world of work through elementary readers," *Vocational Guidance Quarterly*, Vol. 11, (1963), pp. 85-88.

for a variety of different types of situations and the ways of coping with them. The purpose of these experiences "is to bring children to the point where they can make rational decisions for themselves and about themselves and their relationships with their environment."[57] A career educational program that features the classification of pupils into job categories and predictions about their success has a limited view of man. The pupil should have a right to explore the world about him in a manner that allows him to "window shop" without becoming committed to any definite life style. Information about the world of work should be integrated into the instructional process so that the knowledge obtained is a natural consequence of learning rather than something that the pupils are "forced" to learn.

Career education in the elementary school should focus on helping the child understand the world about him and how different individuals live in it. From the exploratory experiences the child should develop respect for the diverse ways by which others cope with the demands of the environment. He should be able to generalize from these exploratory activities that people can satisfy their needs in many different ways. As he matures he can extend this generalization to include himself. To become an individual means to move about in the world in a manner that brings personal meaning and satisfaction to what is done. Thus, career education should help the child to live in the world rather than to fit him into some occupational niche.

The counselor in the elementary school should be concerned about and involved in the development and implementation of a career education program.

SUMMARY

The counselor's role in curriculum development can be direct or indirect. He may participate directly in the planning of the curriculum by providing information about the nature of pupil characteristics. Of particular interest to the planners would be knowledge about cognitive development and information process-

---

[57]Roger Reger, Wendy Schroeder, and Kathie Uschold, *Special education: Children with learning problems* (New York, University Press, 1968), p. 70.

ing in children. The counselor may also assess the impact of the procedures and materials on group instructional procedures. His indirect contribution may be that of data giver and process observer. In the latter role the counselor reports to the planning group how their interpersonal relations affect the planning process. As a data giver he informs the planning group about the characteristics of the student body. Information obtained from various sources is used to determine the appropriateness of procedures and materials. Of particular interest is the relationship between intelligence and the ability to learn from a test of intelligence. However, intelligence tests are useful in that they give us information about the individual's ability to process certain types of symbols. One of the tasks of the counselor is to help the staff become informed about the relationship between learner characteristics and teaching strategy.

The role of the counselor in evaluation is varied in that he may directly participate in the process or serve as a technical consultant. The focal point of the evaluation should be the "whole" child rather than the products of instruction. If the school is to fit the child, then the school should provide the child with opportunity to explore the world about him in a manner that enhances his quest for self-actualization. Career education can be readily incorporated in the program since its fundamental purpose is to enhance the being of the whole child.

SUGGESTED READINGS

Cronbach, Lee J.: *Essentials of psychological testing.* New York, Harper & Row, 1970.

Shane, Jane Grant; Shane, Harold G.; Gibson, Robert; and Munger, Paul F.: *Guiding human development.* Worthington, Charles A. Jones, 1971.

Squire, James R. (ed.): *A new look at progressive education.* Washington, Association for Supervision and Curriculum Development, 1972.

Tyler, Ralph W. (ed.): *Educational evaluation: New roles, new names.* Chicago, National Society for the Study of Education, 1969.

Chapter 12

PSYCHOLOGICAL
EDUCATION IN THE
ELEMENTARY SCHOOL

IN CHAPTER 2 IT WAS NOTED THAT THERE has been increasing concern with prevention rather than remediation of problems. In some instances it appears that those who have advocated prevention would abandon all attempts to help those who need help. In addition, it is seldom clear just how prevention is to be achieved.

The developing field of community mental health has become concerned about prevention, in the face of an inadequate number of treatment facilities and personnel. It is again not particularly clear just how prevention is to be achieved. Discussions talk about "planned intervention into a social system," such as the family, neighborhood, peer group, school and church, with emphasis on the larger social systems.[1]

The importance of childhood is recognized, especially in terms of difficulties in progressing successfully through the developmental tasks.

While it is of course desirable, even necessary, that intervention occur at every level and every social system, it would seem

---

[1] J. Glidewell, "Priorities for psychologists in community mental health," in G. Rosenblum (ed.), *Issues in community psychology and community mental health* (New York, Behavioral Publications, 1971), pp. 141-153.

that, with the exception of the family, the system most important in the lives of children is the school. It is one of the purposes of this book to attempt to change the social system of the elementary school by the encouragement of a broad pupil personnel program which will provide children a psychologically healthy environment and assistance in meeting the developmental tasks which they face.

One specific aspect of this intervention is consultation with teachers and administrators. This approach, as are most interventions in social systems, is indirect, insofar as the goal or target—the child—is concerned. Again, while such efforts, by community psychologists and counselors, are useful and important, a more direct approach should not be overlooked. Such a direct approach is education. Good consultation is or should be educational, concerned with more than the specific incident or situation which initiates the consultation. In addition, the counselor should be involved in the psychological education of teachers through in-service training. The education of teachers seldom prepares them for interpersonal relationships with children. If teachers are to function in the manner described in Chapter 4, they will need preparation and assistance.

While the in-service education of teachers is important, the psychological education of children is perhaps even more important. The focus of this chapter is upon this neglected area. It is often emphasized that the counselor should be involved in curriculum planning and development, and, while he is not, and should not be, a specialist in curriculum, he should be knowledgeable about the psychological effects of the curriculum. In the area of psychological education he is or should be more than this: he should be an expert in curriculum content.

EARLY ATTEMPTS IN PSYCHOLOGICAL EDUCATION

Concern with psychological education is not new. The introduction of "mental health materials" into the curriculum has been advocated for a quarter of a century. Henry E. Bullis and

Ralph H. Ojemann[2] have worked hard and long in fostering education in human behavior and human relations, and in developing curriculum materials.

The extent to which such instruction is included in school curriculums is extremely limited, and seldom is such content introduced into elementary school education. There is little evidence, moreover, that such instruction is effective. This is probably related to the fact that the curriculum materials may have little relevance to the interests and needs of students. It may even be questioned that the content of the curriculum is relevant to actual human behavior and interpersonal relationships, in many cases. Some have even questioned whether we know enough about human behavior or mental health to be able to develop any content to teach.

In addition, instruction in this area, as in other subject matter areas, is cognitively oriented. Instruction is thus concerned with information rather than with experience, with the result that students learn—if they really learn anything—*about* human behavior or human relations, rather than learning how to behave or how to relate to others. The purely cognitive approach would appear to be doomed to failure in this area. The Delaware Human Relations Teaching Program (developed by Bullis) was highly cognitive and highly structured, with guided discussion to predetermined conclusions. The atmosphere of the lessons may be surmised by the two rules for their conduct by teachers: each student who desired to speak was required to raise his hand, and, on speaking, the student had to stand. Perhaps this is a model for a formal democratic procedure, but not for informal human relationships. Ojemann recognized the importance of the teacher as a model, and thus was concerned about the behavior of teachers, who were trained in practicing the approach they were teaching. As a result partly of this, and also because of the

---

[2]H. E. Bullis and E. E. O'Malley, *Human relations in the classroom* (Wilmington, Hambleton Co., 1947); R. H. Ojemann, "Research in planned learning programs and the science of behavior," *J. Educ. Res.*, Vol. 42 (1948), p. 96; R. H. Ojemann, *Developing a program for education in human behavior* (Iowa City, State University of Iowa Preventive Psychiatry Program, 1959).

breadth of the programs, evidence of its effectiveness, at least in immediate results, both on tests of knowledge and in behavior, has been obtained.[3]

In general, however, instruction in mental hygiene or mental health has not been particularly effective. The method of instruction has often, as in the case of the Bullis method, been inconsistent with the content. The method has been structured and highly didactic. The instructors, not being psychologists or familiar with the subject matter, or involved in it themselves, have taught from manuals or lesson plans which had little meaning to them. The approach has been subject-matter rather than person oriented; this is perhaps another instance of how educators—or curriculum writers—can make a subject matter which should be highly relevant and interesting just the opposite. Thus the content itself has not usually been interesting or particularly relevant. There has been little agreement on what should be taught; there is no commonly accepted theory of desirable human behavior or of positive mental health.

AFFECTIVE EDUCATION

The emphasis of this book has been upon the development of the pupil as a whole person, a self-actualizing person. Education, if it is to contribute to this development, must go beyond the training of the intellect. We are feeling as well as thinking beings; the education of feelings is as important as cognitive education. Pupil personnel services are concerned with the feeling aspects of pupils, but, except in the group situation (see Chapter 7), are not directed toward the specific affective development of all pupils. Psychological education should be a part of the curriculum for every child. Psychological education recognizes the nonintellective or noncognitive aspects of the person as the object of education in their own right, not only as incidental to or as they affect cognitive learning.

Affective education is concerned with attitudes, emotions, feel-

---

[3] R. H. Ojemann, "Investigations on the effects of teaching in understanding and appreciation of behavior dynamics," in Gerald Caplan (ed.), *Prevention of mental disorders in children* (New York, Basic Books, 1961), pp. 378-397.

ings, and values about the self and others. Such attitudes and feelings are important in the development of the self, and relations with other persons.

Affective education is concerned with the development of self-awareness. This requires, first, that the individual be permitted to, and be free to, express himself, or disclose himself to others. He must feel free, or secure, in being himself—open, honest, real and genuine. Second, the individual must then be able to look at and explore himself. Part of this process involves genuine and accurate, and nonthreatening, feedback from others on how they perceive him. Third, there then develops a self-awareness or self-understanding, and the development of a self-concept that is realistic in the sense that his self perceptions are not greatly inconsistent with the perceptions of others. Finally, the individual can then recognize inconsistencies between his self-concept and his ideal self-concept, or the self he would like to be. This is the basis upon which he can attempt to change himself, to become more what he wants to be and is capable of becoming.

Affective education is also concerned with the development of awareness of others, and the exploration of interpersonal relationships to foster the development of good interpersonal relationships characterized by empathic understanding, respect and warmth, and genuineness.

These two areas—the self and interpersonal relationships—constitute the core of an affective education whose objective is the development of self-actualizing persons. Three major approaches to affective education may be identified. These, which will be considered in turn, are (1) modeling, (2) didactic instruction, both direct and indirect, and (3) experiential learning.

MODELING

In Chapter 4 we discussed the classroom teacher as the facilitator of learning and personal development. Empathic understanding, warmth and respect, and genuineness were presented as being the facilitating conditions. These conditions, in addition to facilitating cognitive learning, also, through what has been called the principle of reciprocal affect, lead to the development of learning of empathy, warmth and respect, and genuineness in those who are exposed to the conditions. The process by which this occurs is modeling—or, to use the more common terms, example and imitation.

Modeling is currently claimed as a behavioristic method. It is true that behavioristically oriented psychologists have developed this method, or made adaptations of it, for use in changing or modifying behavior. But the behaviorists did not develop or discover modeling. Modeling and imitation—conscious and unconscious—were the earliest ways of teaching and learning; indeed they constituted education in primitive societies. Bandura and Walters quote the anthropologist Reichard who says that in many languages "the word for 'teach' is the same as the word for 'show.'"[4] Even in our own present day society a great deal of learning takes place through imitation of models, particularly at the pre-school level. The importance of this source or method of learning has been underestimated.

Learning through a model is usually acquired as a whole or total pattern, rather than on a piece-by-piece process as is the case in reinforcement (or rewarded) learning. Thus this method is more efficient than part learning through reinforcement, and in addition is not explainable through reinforcement, since learning through modeling often occurs in one trial and the response can be a new or novel response not previously in the learner's repertoire. It is true, however, that the consequences to the model of the behavior exhibited do influence the acquisition by an observer. Thus children who see a teacher punished or criticized (e.g., by an administrator) for humanistic behavior towards others are likely to be inhibited from expressing such behavior. "In addition, models who are rewarding, prestigeful, or competent, who possess high status, and who have control over rewarding resources are more readily imitated than models who

---

[4] Gladys A. Reichard, "Social life," in Franz Boas (ed.), *General anthropology* (Boston, Heath, 1938), pp. 409-486. Quoted in Albert Bandura and Richard H. Walters, *Social learning and personality development* (New York, Holt, Rinehart & Winston, 1963), p. 47.

lack these qualities."[5] Teachers, as well as parents, meet these standards or criteria.

The fact that modeling allows for learning of complex patterns of behavior as wholes, and is particularly effective in the learning of social behaviors, makes it a preferred method for the kind of learning we are concerned with here. Some behaviorists have attempted to break such behaviors down into their elements or components, and to teach these separate elements, often by means of reinforcement. This can result in a long, laborious process, and creates the problem of putting the elements together again, which may be similar to putting Humpty-Dumpty together again after his fall. But, as Bandura notes:

> Fortunately, for reasons of survival and efficiency most social learning does not proceed in the manner described above [gradual shaping through reinforcement]. In laboratory investigations of learning processes experimenters usually arrange comparatively benign environments in which errors will not produce fatal consequences for the organism. In contrast, natural settings are loaded with potentially lethal consequences that unmercifully befall anyone who makes hazardous errors. For this reason it would be exceedingly injudicious to rely primarily on trial-and-error and successive approximation methods in teaching children to swim, adolescents to drive automobiles, or adults to master complex occupational and social tasks. . . . Apart from the question of survival, is is doubtful if many classes of responses would ever be acquired if social training proceeded solely by the method of approximations through differential reinforcement of emitted responses. . . . In cases involving intricate patterns of behavior, modeling is an indispensable aspect of learning.[6]

Modeling is thus a widespread and powerful method of teaching and learning. Its effectiveness is recognized in numerous clichés, folk sayings and in common sense observations. It influences the myths of the good teacher and the high social standards demanded of teachers. We want our teachers to be "good examples" for children. Modeling is particularly useful for teaching the complex aspects of social behavior represented by em-

---

[5] Albert Bandura and Richard H. Walters, *ibid.*, p. 107.
[6] Albert Bandura, *Principles of behavior modification* (New York, Holt, Rinehart & Winston, 1969), pp. 143-144.

pathy, respect, and genuineness. It is difficult if not impossible to teach these in the usual sense, or entirely didactically, although, as we shall see, efforts are being made to do so. The most effective way in which a teacher can teach understanding, respect and warmth, and genuineness is to be empathic, respecting, warm and real.

Michael, discussing the teaching of styles of life, self-actualization, the enlargement of the self, and the avoidance of alienation, writes:

> The only way a teacher can teach these things is to *be* these things. You cannot exhort the student to do it; *you have to be it.* You have to be a model . . . the only way to 'teach actualization' is to be people who are courageous enough, trusting enough, compassionate enough, sympathetic enough, to be vigorously and openly involved in the whole world and to carry that involvement into the teaching environment.[7]

Modeling may not be the only way, but it is probably the most effective way. If a teacher is not the kind of person he is trying to teach students to be, no matter what he does he cannot teach this. But he will teach whatever he is, whether he is aware of it or intends to or not.

This is the problem of much of education in the area of attitudes and values. The principles of democracy are taught in a classroom and a school which are anything but democratic. No wonder students don't learn democracy and respect for others. Borton reports that, at the end of a summer teaching in a special program:

> It became evident that neither I nor the other members of the staff were using the principles we were trying to instill in our students. . . . It is as though we teachers have become accustomed to teaching irrelevant curricula that we can hardly believe it is possible to teach material which actually could make a difference —not only to our students' lives, but to our own. Once that realization comes, once a teacher is growing because of his own ef-

---

[7]Donald Michael, "Tomorrow's sources of actualization and alienation," in Robert R. Leeper (ed.), *Humanizing education: The person in the process* (Washington, Association for Supervision and Curriculum and Development, National Education Association, 1967), p. 40.

forts . . . he . . . will serve as the same example for his students that the math teacher's expert knowledge provides for his young mathematicians.[8]

In short, the teacher will have become a self-actualizing person, and being such, will facilitate the development of his students as self-actualizing persons.

INDIRECT AND DIRECT TEACHING OF FEELING AND HUMAN RELATIONS

Using the Standard Curriculum. Affective education and human relations can be taught through the regular curriculum. There are many opportunities in which the standard curriculum can be utilized or adapted to teach human relations, although attempting to work only through the current curriculum is insufficient. We do not, therefore, agree with Wilhelms, who says: "if we cannot help them with their human becoming in every one of the subjects they are taking, each in its appropriate way, we are not going to help them very much. . . . Most of what we call humanization has to be the long accretion of subtle influences built right into the curriculum."[9] It is true, of course, as Wilhelms goes on to say, that "wholesome human qualities . . . are not going to emerge somewhere else from some extraordinary miracle." That is why we have to include them directly in the curriculum as well as use the existing curriculum to teach them indirectly. And Wilhelms is right in emphasizing that the curriculum must be used to humanize students, and, regarding a subject about which it might be argued that there are no such possibilities, he asks: "What is it doing in the curriculum in the first place?"[10]

To the objection that it is difficult to find subject matter which produces knowledge and skill and also can be used to teach humanization, Wilhelms answers that such subject matter is abundant. The problem is to select out of the vast materials of the

[8]Terry Borton, *Reach, touch, and teach* (New York, McGraw-Hill, 1970), p. 175.
[9]Fred T. Wilhelms, "Humanization via the curriculum," in Robert R. Leeper, *op. cit.*, pp. 21, 24.
[10]*Ibid.*, p. 21.

sciences, the humanities, mathematics, etc., that which has the greatest potential to promote human development. It also is necessary that the teacher actually exploit the materials. Wilhelms provides the example of the English teacher who looks at themes not simply in terms of grammatical exercises, but at what they say, and uses them to understand students, and to encourage creative expression and honest communication. Thus the English curriculum can be used "to teach each young person to be sensitive to his own ideas and feelings, to listen to them, and to honor them. It has become part of the curriculum to teach that all communication rests on honesty and sensitivity and the courage to be one's self, out in the open."[11]

As Wilhelms notes, this is essentially what liberal education, the approach of the classical humanists, was designed to do. Subject matter was conceived of as medium for personal development. But it now has become an end in itself, important only for its content.

The recent new curriculums in the physical and social sciences, and in mathematics did not utilize Wilhelms' criterion of potential to promote human development in the selection of content. Whether because of this lack, or for other reasons, no one appears to have attempted to exploit the social studies curriculum for the education of feelings and emotions.

There have been a number of attempts to introduce affect into education through the curriculum. Lyon describes in summary form some of these attempts.[12]

Most such attempts have been limited, providing illustrations rather than full scale programs of affective education. Two quite different attempts which are rather extensively reported will be considered briefly.

One of these consists of illustrations of how the emotions aroused by a fifth-grade social studies course entitled "Man: A Course of Study" can be utilized educationally, or for the emotional development of the students. This is done by Richard

---

[11]*Ibid.*, p. 24.
[12]Harold C. Lyon, *Learning to feel—feeling to learn* (Columbus, Merrill, 1971).

Jones, who takes Bruner, the developer of the course, to task for his highly cognitive orientation in the course.[13]

The course does deal with human development:

> The content of the course is man: his nature as a species, the forces that shaped and continue to shape his humanity. Three questions recur throughout:
> What is human about human beings?
> How did they get that way?
> How can they be made more so?[14]

The potential for relating the social studies to human development is greater than, say, for mathematics. Any and all subject matter has such potential, and it is clear in the materials in "Man: A Course of Study." But this potential must be exploited, and the teacher should be provided some help in doing this. Moreover, the potential is for more than a cognitive, intellectual understanding of the development of man. The materials arouse feelings and emotions in children. These feelings should not be ignored, but many teachers will not be aware of them unless they are prepared for and sensitized to their occurrence. The feelings—human feelings about the behavior and experiences of other human beings—are a source for affective learning and development.

In his book Jones provides a fascinating account of the failure of one teacher to utilize the potential of the materials, including films, in a unit on the Netsilik Eskimo. The teacher focused upon the cognitive elements, and in fact considered the emotional reactions of the children not only irrelevant but an interference with cognitive learning, and thus ignored or suppressed them. Jones then goes on to show how two young teachers, with the help of a master teacher and a psychologist, were able to utilize the potential of the materials for personal development or affective education.

Utilizing standard curriculum materials for the purpose of affective education is difficult, and the teacher needs special train-

---

[13]Richard M. Jones, *Fantasy and feeling in education* (New York, New York University Press, 1968). (Also Harper & Row Torchbooks.)
[14]*Ibid.*, p. 12.

ing and preparation, and help, in doing so. The materials themselves, no matter how good, are not sufficient. Charlotte Epstein
provides some suggestions for utilizing curriculum materials for
teaching intergroup relations.[15] Other examples will be found
in the following references.

A second example of the attempt to introduce affect into the
curriculum is reported by George Brown. Brown has presented
an extensive program which he calls "confluent education." He
defines confluent education as "the integration or flowing together of the *affective* and *cognitive* elements in individual and
group learning—sometimes called humanistic or psychological
education."[16] The development of the program was supported
by the Fund for the Advancement of Education of the Ford
Foundation. Approaches to affective learning developed at
Esalen which seemed to be appropriate for classroom use were
adapted in workshops at Esalen, and then tried out in the classroom in an appropriate curriculum context.

Forty examples of affective techniques, which were presented
to professionals in workshops at Esalen, are described briefly by
Brown. Brown states: "Ideally, a teacher or leader should have
an extensive repertoire of techniques and approaches and should
also be able to create new techniques the moment the need
arises. Of course, the decision to present a particular technique
is at times arbitrary and will depend on the emerging needs of
the group or situation.[17]

An example of a technique is the trust circle:

> Under Gloria's guidance, the group next worked on the develop-
> ment of communications and trust. Some of the participants went
> around the circle talking to each individual, completing the sen-
> tence 'I want to communicate with you by...' Later, others did the
> same with the sentence 'I think I can/cannot trust you because...'
> After some trust had been established or identified among various
> members of the group, small groups of eight people formed trust cir-

[15]Charlotte Epstein, *Intergroup relations for the classroom teacher* (Boston, Houghton-Mifflin, 1968).

[16]George I. Brown, *Human teaching for human learning: An introduction to confluent education* (New York, Viking, 1971), p. 3.

[17]*Ibid.*, p. 28.

cles. One of the group stood in the center and, letting himself go, fell and was caught and supported by those in the circle, who then passed the person around the circle. Through these techniques, the need for trust and the need for support was demonstrated to the group.[18]

These techniques are actually not related to academic or subject matter content, and can be used as direct instruction in affective education. In fact, this is their use in sensitivity or encounter groups with adults. But in the context presented by Brown, they are to be introduced in the teaching of subject matter. They include a number of Gestalt techniques. Some of these, adapted for classroom use, are included in a book by Janet Lederman, who was involved in the Ford-Esalen project.[19] The techniques presented by Lederman, although used in the classroom, may have no relation to the subject matter being taught, but may be used in response to the emotional reactions of children. This is particularly the case at the kindergarten and first grade level. Here the children are less inhibited and respond to games and exercises more naturally.

Brown's project developed a number of units and lesson plans involving secondary school social studies and English content. One of these was a unit in a course in American Government and World Geography. The presentation included the showing of the pictures in Edward Steichen's "The Family of Man," a lecture on theories of the nature of man, and a brief statement on the unique self and the self as an example of man. Then followed nine affective exercises toward self-discovery, and the writing of two essays, one entitled "Who Am I?," and the second, "What Is Man?" followed by a list of some things common to the two essays. One of the exercises was the following:

> Exercise. (Pass out scratch paper.) Tear those pieces of paper into eight parts. They don't have to be even parts, because you're going to throw them away in a while. Now, on each of those scraps of paper, write one of the words that came into your consciousness a few moments ago—words that describe your character. If I were

[18]*Ibid.*, p. 41.
[19]Janet Lederman, *Anger and the rocking chair* (New York, McGraw-Hill, 1969).

doing this, I might say that I'm usually pretty honest, that I tend to use people to get what I want, that I'm pushy, that I'm...(Etc., whatever the teacher feels at that time. GET INVOLVED YOUR-SELF!) Remember, one word or short phrase on each slip of paper, You are the only one who is going to see these words, so you don't have to be afraid to be honest with yourself. Now read what you have written. Arrange them in order, placing the one you are happiest about or like the most on top, and the one you like least or are least happy about on the bottom. Make a stack of them and place the stack right in front of you. Now for a while confine your eyes to the surface of your desk. Don't look at anyone or anything except the top of your desk and the pieces of paper. Take each piece of paper in order and really spend some time with that word. Stay with it for a few minutes and try on the word just as you try on clothes hanging in your closet. Our characters are like a wardrobe. We are sometimes one way, sometimes another. Today we are going through the wardrobe and examining our clothes and trying them on. Really see how they feel. Become the words you see. Accept them as *you* at one time or another, then do with the word and the piece of paper what you want to do. Put it back in your wardrobe, tear it up and throw it away, or whatever you wish. All right, you may begin. Take plenty of time with each word.[20]

In other units the exercises are woven into the cognitive requirements. The relationship of the exercise to the subject matter content is not always clear nor direct. There is a contrived element present: the units are contrived to allow the bringing in of the exercises, and the exercises sometimes appear to be introduced in a contrived manner. Thus some seem to be natural but others seem to be techniques. The affective elements do not seem always to flow from the materials, as seemed to be true for "Man: A Course of Study." It would appear that the content and materials were selected for their utility in fostering the use of the techniques of affective education, which was the major, even sole, objective, rather than any subject matter achievement. Thus this method approaches direct instruction, utilizing subject matter rather incidentally. This is particularly the case with the individual lessons as compared to the units.

---

[20]George I. Brown, *op. cit.*, p. 57.

Brown, in his evaluation, feels that all the techniques were "extremely successful both in getting across the subject content and in getting the students in touch with their feelings."[21] However, no data are provided to support this evaluation. Teachers in the project report better learning of cognitive material; heightened motivation and response to learning situations; greater appreciation of self, nature and others; greater pupil responsibility; and, at the secondary-school level, lessened desire for drug use by some students. The teachers were obviously pleased and happy, and offer testimonials. One writes: "This year is the first in which I have felt like a real educator and not just a purveyor of information and a 'people-pusher.' I feel that as a result of the Ford Esalen project I have grown as a person and as a teacher . . . the change in the students has also been fantastic. They have grown and matured faster this year than in any other I have experienced. They are more aware, more creative, and better students as a result of this project."[22]

But that all this was the result of the techniques used can be seriously questioned. The teachers were well liked, and in two cases were given elaborate surprise parties by the students. At one of the parties, one girl said to the wife of the teacher: "For me, it's not just the teacher-student bit. It's not all those field trips he took us on, but it's what he did for me as a person. I'm a better person because of him! I mean, I can tell him anything and he listens and understands. I'm a better person."[23] Clearly, this kind of reaction was not created by techniques! The techniques cannot be separated from the person of the teacher, and fade into insignificance in contrast to the person. The teachers were selected (in part, perhaps, self-selected) and were obviously good, dedicated and devoted teachers. They were enthusiastic about the project, about participating in a novel experience. This whole aura partakes of the well-known Hawthorne effect.

Techniques alone could not lead to the responses of the chil-

---

[21]*Ibid.*, p. 96.
[22]*Ibid.*, p. 200.
[23]*Ibid.*, p. 202.

dren which are described. These could only be responses to the person of the teacher—his empathic understanding, his respect and warmth, and his genuineness. While some of the techniques could no doubt be used successfully by other teachers in appropriate situations where they would naturally fit, many of them could not be used successfully by most teachers because they would not be natural to the teacher. Techniques must cease to be techniques, and must be a part of the genuine teacher, before they can be effective in the everyday, continuing teaching situation. Sometimes techniques can be built into a role, so that the teacher becomes a showman, becoming unable to function as a real person without his techniques. Such teachers are sometimes considered to be successful—they hold the children's interest and entertain them. Techniques can also become a crutch.

But when they are simple and natural, exercises and games can facilitate the expression of feelings. Our society encourages the repression rather than the expression of feelings. Inhibition rather than spontaneity or genuineness is encouraged. Thus people need to be given "permission" to be themselves, to be spontaneous, to express their feelings. Thus a simple exercise, such as "For the next ten minutes I want you to talk to each other and say nothing but positive things about each other" gives permission to express feelings which otherwise would not even be recognized, let alone expressed. Games may make it possible for people to touch each other—a taboo in our society except under special conditions.

But exercises and games are not the end, and if they are continued or overemphasized, people are not helped to be genuine and spontaneous in every day life. It is the teacher who is not dependent on such techniques, but who is a real person in all his relationships with students who has an effect on the personal development of the students.

Direct Education: A Curriculum of Affect. If the development of the emotions is a function of the schools, along with the development of the intellect, then feelings, emotions and interpersonal relations are subject matter themselves, in their own right. At the beginning of this chapter we referred to two earlier approaches to such direct education. Here we will consider a more recent approach.

In an attempt to introduce relevance into affective education, Weinstein and Fantini have attempted to develop a curriculum from the basic concerns of students.[24] The curriculum effort developed from the Elementary School Teaching project of the Fund for the Advancement of Education of the Ford Foundation.

The assumption on which the development of relevant content was based was that *"Significant contact with pupils is most effectively established and maintained when the content and method of instruction have an affective basis.* That is, if educators are able to discover the feelings, fears, and wishes that move pupils emotionally, they can more effectively engage pupils from any background, whether by adapting traditional content and procedures or by developing new materials and techniques."[25]

Student concerns are more than a means of arousing interest in traditional content; they are content in themselves. The project attempted to identify the principal concerns of students, "to help teachers to recognize pupil concerns, use them in selecting and developing content, and devise techniques and procedures enabling students to deal with these concerns."[26] Materials and techniques were tried out in actual classrooms.

Concerns, according to Weinstein and Fantini, are more basic than interests or feelings, although they involve and include these. "Concerns are the most persistent, pervasive threads of underlying uneasiness the learners have about themselves and their relation to the world."[27] Three broad classes of concerns were identified: (1) concern about *self-image* (identity); (2) concern about *disconnectedness* (alienation), i.e., about where one fits into the scheme of things; and (3) concern about *control* over one's life (power). The manifestation of these concerns

[24]Gerald Weinstein & Mario D. Fantini (eds.), *Toward humanistic education: A curriculum of affect* (New York, Praeger, 1970).
[25]*Ibid.*, p. 10.
[26]*Ibid.*, p. 11.
[27]*Ibid.*, p. 22.

will vary in different age, socio-economic, geographic, cultural and racial or ethnic groups. Desirable outcomes are not changes in concerns, but in behavior representing an improvement in dealing with concerns.

Subject matter from the standard disciplines, including psychology, may be used to achieve the desired outcomes. In addition, classroom incidents, out-of-school experiences and the children themselves provide content.

Weinstein and Fantini provide units and materials for a study of the self-concept, designed to help children recognize that the self-concept develops out of experiences with others, leads to certain ways of seeing the world and to responses to what he sees that tend to reinforce the self-concept. The technique of "one-way glasses" was used to help children realize that much of our world is created through our perceptions, which then determine our responses as well as our views of ourselves.

Their use of one-way glasses is illustrated in a class of 10-and 11-year olds in an ungraded University demonstration school. The children were very concerned about power and self-concept, which were tied together in their behavior. They seldom listened to each other, and reactions to what others said were generally negative. The objective was to replace the disconnectedness in the classroom with connectedness, so that the children would have feelings of constructive power and positive self-concepts. This would be manifested in the children listening to each others' viewpoints, acknowledging each others' strong points, and in the withdrawn children responding more. Teaching was organized around three ideas: (1) there are many ways of seeing the same situation; (2) perceptions and responses depend on the feelings and thoughts accompanying them; and (3) limited perception constricts the person's view of himself and of the world. No subject matter content was used. An example of the use of "one-way glasses" is the following:

> The teacher now held up two pairs of sunglasses, each with a different color lenses. He explained that these were very special glasses, that each pair colored the wearer's view of the world with a particular feeling.

TEACHER: The first pair of glasses are "suspicious" glasses. When a person wears them, he regards whatever he sees or hears with suspicion. [The teacher asked for a volunteer to put on the suspicious glasses and tell the class what he saw.]

VOLUNTEER (looking at two children who were talking and laughing, as he put on the glasses): I wonder if they're talking about me. Are they laughing at me? [The teacher asked that questions be addressed to the volunteer.]

STUDENT: Who's your best friend?

VOLUNTEER: Why does he want to know that? Are they going to try to take my friends away?

TEACHER (holding up second pair of glasses): I have a second pair of glasses, which are rose-colored. They make whoever wears them see and hear with this feeling: 'No matter what anyone says to me, I know they really care for me.'

[Teacher asked for and secured the cooperation of another volunteer. Throughout the dialogue that followed the teacher sought to clarify the volunteer's responses by asking: "Are you acting suspicious or just curious," "Do you really feel that way, or are you exaggerating your reactions?" "Do you really think they might be trying to do that to you?"]

TEACHER: Let's get some reactions from our volunteer.

STUDENT (to second volunteer): You're just a noisy little pipsqueak!

VOLUNTEER 2: He always calls me a little pipsqueak, but that shows he really notices me and probably likes smaller people like me.

STUDENT: How come you're always hanging around with Betty?

VOLUNTEER: I bet she asked that because she really wants me to try and make more friends.[28]

In the last lesson, the class was asked to put away their put-down and suspicious glasses and wear another pair called "strong-point" glasses, which are very difficult to wear:

TEACHER: Now we'll choose somebody to come to the front of the room and tell us how he sees himself through his strong-point glasses.

At the teacher's request, members of the class dropped slips of paper bearing their names into a hat, and one was drawn. The person chosen went to the front of the room.

---

[28]*Ibid.*, pp. 79-80.

TEACHER: How do you think this person feels?

STUDENTS: Embarrassed.

TEACHER: You can help him overcome his embarrassment by not making faces at him or making fun of him and by looking at him supportively.

The teacher warned the selected person that his strong-point glasses might occasionally slip, in which case he might don his "crack-a-joke-about-me" or put-down glasses. The group was asked to be on the lookout for such lapses. Now the teacher suggested that in the event the target person ran out of positive things to say about himself, he was to feel free to admit it and ask the class for help in finding additional strong points. The class was cautioned once again about the difficulty of its assignment. With this in mind, the teacher, too, was prepared to help students find strong points if necessary.

FIRST PERSON (a strong, quiet, interested, class leader): I'm good in science and in playing baseball and all kinds of sports and at home when it comes to helping around the house. I'm strong in the classroom in writing poetry and discovering and exploring new things. I like to do a lot of reading. I think I can produce a lot of ideas and create things. I think that's all, does anyone have anything else?

STUDENTS:—You're creative.

—You as a person are nice. You're not a boaster, put-down, or suspicious. You're a good worker and compatible— not always criticizing.

—You're good at organizing, like when you were class president.

—You have a good sense of humor. You can hold up against your three brothers. You're tactful.

—You don't always try to be on top.

The strong-points situation was repeated several times, giving as many students as possible a chance to tell about their own strong points. . . .

TEACHER: How do you feel about this whole idea? How do you feel when this is going on? Why are these the most difficult glasses to wear? We're often taught to look at the worst in ourselves and others; to be overly critical. When we wear one-way glasses or only a few pairs of glasses—that is, critical or put-down glasses—we see only a piece of the world. The more different kinds of glasses we are able to wear, the more we are able to see.[29]

[29]*Ibid.*, pp. 91-92, 93.

There were seven lessons, each lasting one to two hours, over a period of three weeks. The teacher felt they were successful:

> As the series of lessons drew to a close, the original participants seemed more attentive to others and less destructive. Positive observations about others were expressed more freely as the students glimpsed more strong points in themselves and others. One student, for example, exclaimed admiringly to the rest of the class about a target person during the strong-points episode: "Gee, I just never thought of John that way!"[30]

Some students objected to the use of real glasses as props. The authors suggest that perhaps use of the glasses should have been discontinued after one or two lessons. Some students felt they were better able to "dope out" other children: "Now I can see through a person better," one said. This evaluative, judgmental or critical attitude would appear to be an undesirable outcome. Some children felt that the lessons didn't help a lot. They were perhaps some of the inhibited or withdrawn ones. Often these children are the very ones who dislike and fail to be drawn into games and exercises which may seen artificial and unreal. Other students gave more positive reactions, for example:

> I've learned how to see people in different ways and to see how other people look at us.
> The glasses have helped me and other people mostly in realizing that different people do not always think the same, and it has helped me look at things as if I were another person.
> It helped me to view other people's strong points and also to realize my own.[31]

Weinstein and Fantini propose their approach as simply a suggestive beginning, open to criticism and change. Several comments might be made regarding it. Weinstein and Fantini attempt to put their contribution in the form of a model. It would appear to be premature to attempt this at this point. The model appears to be simply the usual model for developing a curriculum, and might be seen as a device to appeal to educators who are obsessed with formal statements of curriculum. The

---

[30]*Ibid.*, p. 97.
[31]*Ibid.*, p. 99.

model places emphasis on "diagnosing" student concerns, which is simply another term for the usual "needs." But while it is true that basic concerns may be expressed differently by different groups, they are also expressed differently by each individual in any group. More important, however, is the fact that all individuals, and all groups, share these basic common concerns, and it is not necessary to go through the process of diagnosing before teaching—a point which Weinstein and Fantini incidentally recognize.

A strong impression given by Weinstein and Fantini is that the teacher is always in control. Teaching is a highly structured situation, following a detailed plan—a lesson plan, in effect. The approach is highly cognitively oriented—in effect it is *the teaching of affect by cognitive methods.*

Finally, one is conscious of the technique orientation, as in the case of confluent education. It is almost as if Weinstein and Fantini are afraid to face a class of children without a well prepared program of techniques, and would be uncomfortable in a free, open, unstructured situation. As teachers take refuge in a lesson plan, so they take refuge in techniques. This attitude is apparent when Weinstein and Fantini write: "In the sense that they get children to talk about themselves, the people they live with, and the aspects of their lives which they feel are most significant, these [three diagnostic techniques] are learning techniques for both students and teachers."[32] But techniques are not necessary to get children to talk about themselves, as Herndon, Kohl, Kozol and others have clearly shown. It takes an understanding, warm, real, sensitive human being who will listen.

The use of techniques, including games, exercises, and physical activities is a phenomenon not limited to direct or structured affective education, but, as noted in Chapter 7, is common in many encounter groups. It appears to be related to the difficulty of getting people, especially adults, to relax, loosen up, drop their inhibitions, and express themselves freely in relation to others. This is certainly a problem with adults, as well as older children. It may be questioned whether such methods are the

---

[32]*Ibid.,* p. 123.

best or only ways to achieve more open and spontaneous behavior. The resort to techniques appears to be related to the impatience of teachers, leaders and facilitators of groups, and their
inability to work slowly through the necessary stage where people are getting to know and trust each other. A colleague, using
an analogy with dramatics, has suggested that the need to resort to such techniques or props is in inverse ratio to the skill of
the actor.[33]

It may be that some method of facilitating the development
of spontaneous, relaxed behavior could be useful, even with children who usually haven't developed the inhibitions of adults.
The difficulty with games and exercises is that they are artificial,
and at some point they must be abandoned for real or genuine
behavior. An approach which is more real and natural has been
proposed and used in the Interdisciplinary Model Programs in
the Arts for Children and Teachers (IMPACT) supported by
the U. S. Office of Education under the Education Professions
Development Act. The purpose was to infuse art into the curriculum "as a means of enhancing and improving the quality and
quantity of aesthetic education in the school and as a *principal*
means for expanding the base for affective learning experiences
in the school."[34] The program encouraged individual expression
in different media, emphasizing the arts as central subjects in
elementary education. Dance appeared to be the most effective
subject, involving not only body movement but the nerves,
senses, mind, imagination and spirit. Teachers became involved
with children in a new way through the arts:

> It was the revelation of their own capacity for abstract non-
> verbal communication that was the humanizing, sensitizing agent
> that made the teachers able to empathize with the uncertainties
> and their excitments of creating whether in music, art, theatre, or
> dance; they could now be patient and they were able to see their
> pupils' capacities and subtle expressions which would have escaped

---

[33]Harold A. Moses, Techniques versus relationship. Unpublished paper.

[34]Quoted in Lydia Joel. "The impact of IMPACT." *Dance Scope*, Vol. 6(2),
(1972), pp. 6-25. I wish to thank Diane Frank, then a graduate student and
instructor in dance at the University of Illinois, for calling my attention to this
area.

them previously or which would in the past have seemed meaningless. A new-found respect for the children was an inevitable result and with that came a shift in relationship between teacher and pupil.[35]

The projects under the IMPACT programs involved professionals in the arts who worked in the schools with children and teachers. How successful such a program would be without the involvement of professionals, with their skills and especially their respect, admiration and enthusiasm which they generated, is difficult to say. Certainly some results could be achieved if, as the project evaluator recommended, all elementary school teachers received extensive education in the arts and were permitted and encouraged to make them a central part of the curriculum.

EXPERIENTIAL LEARNING

The contention that learning by experience is the most effective method of learning is nowhere more justified than in the area of interpersonal relations. Such learning obviously cannot take place in the usual classroom, or in independent study. Other persons must be involved. In other words, the learning of interpersonal relations requires the presence of several persons interacting—that is, a group. Thus, the use of encounter groups is an important, even a necessary, part of affective education. Chapter 7 deals with this topic.

SOME CRITICAL COMMENTS

While recognizing that the approaches described briefly in this chapter are tentative beginnings in a new field, it appears to be desirable to make a few comments which might be helpful to those who wish to advance the field of affective education beyond these beginnings.

The overemphasis upon techniques and structured, teacher-controlled procedures has already been mentioned. This would appear to be inconsistent with the goals of affective education, which include spontaneity, student initiated activity, open and free discussion in a natural setting, and self-directed exploration

---

[35]*Ibid.*

and learning. Content and structure can be provided by materials such as films and reading, rather than by the teacher.

The emphasis upon techniques also requires that teachers, and student teachers, must be warned that the adoption of any or all of these and other techniques, games, exercises, etc., will not make a humanistic teacher or facilitate affective learning. It is possible that an approach such as that of Weinstein and Fantini could become the basis for new methods courses in teacher education. It would be a mistake to go in this direction. Current methods courses do not prepare teachers for the teaching relationship, and new methods courses focusing upon new techniques will not do so either. Robert E. Samples, in his review of Borton's book, sounds a relevant warning when he says that "these instructional strategies may well have as many shortcomings as the mechanistic approaches to subject matter that the past ten years of curriculum revision have supposedly replaced. In addition, students are deeply sensitive to contrivances of any sort. . . . Whenever we get rational about needs and feelings, our efforts usually create relatively meaningless and contrived lessons."[36]

Perhaps the greatest difficulty or deficiency in current approaches to affective education is that they are not based on any systematic theory of human behavior, or human development and interpersonal relations. Bruner has empasized that if subject matter is to be taught effectively, it must be organized in terms of basic principles or propositions. It would appear that before we can develop a curriculum of affect or human development or of psychological education, we must have some knowledge, understanding, and agreement upon the psychology of emotional development. Mosher and Sprinthall recognize this when they say: "A major problem confronting psychological education is the lack of an adequate theory of personal or emotional development."[37] They attempt to build their approach to adoles-

---

[36]Robert E. Samples, "Tools for everyone," Review of Terry Borton, *Reach, Touch and Teach, Saturday Review* (September 17, 1970), p. 82.

[37]Ralph L. Mosher, Norman A. Sprinthall, and others. "Psychological education: A means to promote personal development during adolescence." *The Counseling Psychologist*, Vol. 2 (No. 4) (1971), pp. 3-82.

cents upon the work of Piaget, Erikson and Kohlberg. But when they teach counseling to high school students they do not indicate their definition of, or theoretical approach to, counseling.

This book is based upon a systematic theoretical approach to human behavior, which is outlined in earlier chapters. This theoretical system can be used as a basis for the direct teaching of human relations. If the basic conditions for facilitative interpersonal relationships are empathic understanding, respect or warmth, and genuineness, then the development of these conditions should be the objective of a curriculum in interpersonal relations. The direct teaching of these conditions should be a major part of the curriculum. There are many other aspects of personal development which are important, and necessary for the development of these conditions—these include the concerns of Weinstein and Fantini—and these should be included in the curriculum. But they must be integrated into a systematic or theory based approach.

The teaching of counseling is an effective—perhaps the most effective—but not the only way of teaching the core conditions. Counseling or psychotherapy is, or should be, the purest form of a facilitative interpersonal relationship, and thus training in counseling is a highly effective method of education in interpersonal relationships. This is, to some extent at least, implicit in the Mosher and Sprinthall approach. Carkhuff has pioneered efforts to teach these conditions to other groups, including parents.[38]

The counselor and other pupil personnel workers, as specialists in human relations, should be involved in psychological education—planning and developing the curriculum, preparing teachers to function in this area, and assisting and supervising teachers. Whether they should function themselves as teachers is questionable, since their time is required for so many other things, and because it is generally felt that counselors should not be involved in teaching those who are potential counselees. However, the humanistic teaching relationship and the subject matter of psychological education should not be inconsistent with

---

[38]Robert R. Carkhuff, *Helping and human relations: A primer for lay and professional helpers*, Vols. I & II. (New York, Holt, Rinehart & Winston, 1969).

counseling. The matter of evaluation or grading would appear to be the greatest problem. But psychological education should be one area where evaluation and grading should be absent.

Eventually teachers should be prepared to teach in this area, as well as prepared to conduct encounter groups. Then the counselor and other pupil personnel specialists would serve as consultants and supervisors of the teachers who conduct encounter groups.

SUMMARY

In Chapter 1 we argued that the major function of the schools is to produce self-actualizing persons, persons who can understand themselves and others and can relate to others.

In this chapter we have reviewed several attempts to introduce affective education, or psychological education, into the curriculum. One approach is to utilize existing subject matter as a basis for affective education. Subject matter areas vary in their adaptability to this purpose. The social sciences are perhaps most adaptable.

The education of the emotions, and the learning of interpersonal relations through the standard curriculum may be considered an indirect approach. It can even be considered simply as a by-product, although when so considered—as it has been in the past—it is not likely to be effective. On the other hand, when the standard curriculum, especially in the social sciences, is directed specifically toward affective education it can be, and may be, perhaps the most effective approach, since the history of the development of man and the human race provides inherently relevant content. Such content can be inherently relevant if it is used to show the human problems in living together.

However, other approaches are also useful, including the direct approach to education in human relations or psychological development. Currently, such approaches are technique oriented and lacking in systematic or theoretical foundations. It seems that we have lost our basic humanity, since we are unable to relate to students—or to each other—without the intervention or use of techniques. It is interesting in this connection that we are recognizing that the essence of the psychotherapeutic relationship is that it is a relationship devoid of, or without, techniques.

The implication is that teaching should also be a relationship devoid of techniques. Children have—inherently and until we deprive them of it—this ability to relate to others naturally, honestly, trustingly, understandingly. *We don't need techniques to relate to children*—in fact techniques interfere with establishing a relationship with children.

An important aspect of psychological education is group experience. Encounter groups, eventually conducted by teachers, should be a continuing aspect of education from kindergarten through college.

The counselor and other pupil personnel workers should be directly involved in psychological education. Eventually, when teachers are prepared in this area of curriculum, they would function as consultants and supervisors.

SUGGESTED READINGS

Jones, R. M.: *Fantasy and feeling in education,* New York, New York, University Press, 1968. (Also Harper & Row Torchbooks)

Patterson, C. H.: *Humanistic education,* Englewood Cliffs, Prentice-Hall, 1973.

Chapter 13

WORKING WITH PARENTS

WHEN THE CHILD ENTERS SCHOOL, he brings with him a behavior repertoire that has helped him meet the demands of his home environment. Some of the response patterns have been with him since infancy, when his mother socially conditioned some of his biological needs. In our discussion of the socialization process (Chapter 10) we considered the various forces that structure the behavior of the child. It was suggested that an understanding of the dynamics of socialization by the counselor would help him in generating a variety of programs that would enhance the pupil's quest for self-actualization.

The school has long recognized the centrality of the family in society. It is through the home that the child learns to meet many of the requirements of society. The child's ability to function in society depends, to a large degree, on how well he can interact with others in a variety of situations. The quality of that competency is regulated by the family in that it determines the kind of contacts that the child has with the environment. Since child-rearing practices fluctuate from family to family, what each child learns before he comes to school will vary. Thus, the manner and the rate at which a child accomplishes the goals of the school will vary.

The position of visiting teacher was developed to help explain the role of the school in the socialization process to parents. This was especially necessary in those areas with a large influx of immigrants. Concomitantly, the visiting teacher could obtain information from the parents so that the school could better understand the children and thereby make the necessary adjustments in the school program. This early awareness of the relationship between how the child was brought up and what he learned in school initiated the school's commitment to become involved in the affairs of the family. In its inception this commitment took the form of helping the family help the child meet the school's educational objectives. However, in recent years, the school has become interested in raising the quality of life of the parents and their children.

The goal of this chapter is to explore the many ways in which the counselor and various community agencies can work with parents and their children to enhance the quality of their living together. The rapid changes in the patterns of living have forced parents to seek professional help in order to understand and to cope with the problems of living in a technologically changing world. The function of pupil personnel services is to provide a variety of programs that may assist the family so that it and its members may function more effectively.

WHY PARENTS NEED HELP

The focal point of most conflicts between children and parents is that the latter are unable to understand and accept the childishness of children. The child is essentially egocentric and, as such, functions on the basis of the pleasure principle. He derives satisfaction from his actions with little thought about the consequences. On the other hand, the parent evaluates actions from the standpoint of practicality and future consequences. Thus, parents see their principle role as that of curbing instinctual urges in order for the child to function more rationally.

> Being dominated by the primitive pleasure principle, they cannot but see the act only in the present with no reference to the dimension of time. The act, to a child, is sufficient unto itself. To the adult, on the other hand, each act and event is seen as a precursor

and progenitor of future events; and if one is undesirable, a whole train of developments of like in nature are envisioned.[1]

This fear that a young child's current behavior will persist forever influences many child-rearing practices. It gives credence to that theory that the parent must be seen as an absolute monarch and the child must submit to every parental whim. The goal of many of the punitive measures used by parents is to support their authoritarian position rather than to control the behavior of their children. In addition, some parents feel that children must have some sense pounded into them and act accordingly. They forget that the ability to perceive the relationship between cause and effect is dependent on cognitive development and accumulated experience.

Parents who attempt to use a "reasonable" approach in bringing up their children tend to fail for two reasons. First, parents usually do not have an adequate grasp of the time that is required for a child to change from an instinctual mode of behaving to one that reflects a modicum of inner control. As a consequence, parents become impatient when the child fails to "grow-up" according to their schedule. In order to enhance the maturity of their child, parents tend to resort to tactics that in many instances prolong the period of infantalism. For example, toys are bought for the purpose of stimulating the cognitive development of the child rather than enhancing self-exploration. Very often the child does not find the toy stimulating because of a lack of "readiness" but is forced to play with it by the parent. Thus, the child, instead of becoming independent, becomes increasingly dependent on the parents.

Secondly, the "reasonable" approach may fail because parents become too concerned about the "reasons" for the tactics they use with their children. What will other parents think about what we are doing to our children? The evaluation of child-rearing practices by others is a concern of parents because in our society parents are held responsible for helping their children become ac-

---

[1]S. R. Slavson, *Child-centered group guidance of parents* (New York, International Universities Press, Inc., 1958), p. 19.

ceptable members of society. In addition, the self-worth and self-esteem of parents is predicated on how "well" they bring up their children. Since it is the task of parents to make children "behave," parents tend to emulate what other parents do to make their children "behave" although some of the practices may be psychologically unsound. Hence, it is not surprising to find that children in a given neighborhood behave in similar ways.

Parents seldom realize that their emotional concerns over child-rearing practices have a direct bearing on the self-development of the child. If the parents utilize procedures which they do not personally accept or lack the skill in carrying them out, they fail to provide the child with an adequate model for identification. If the child rejects the parents as models, his quest for self-actu-alization is retarded. If he just imitates what his parents do with-out internalizing some of the attitudes and values associated with the skills they are teaching him, his personal development be-comes rather shallow. It is essential that the parents not only provide for the child's physical well-being but his psychological well-being.

> A major handicap to constructive parenthood is the almost universal lack of knowledge that a child's needs for security and love are as definite and imperative as are his needs for physical sustenance. Parents who without question follow dietary requirements and health measures are in most instances unaware of psychologica'. needs of the child, which are not infrequently more important than are his physical needs. It has been demonstrated time and time again that a child cannot assimilate food, nor can he develop physi-cal health unless he is sustained also psychologically. The child does not eat with his mouth alone: he eats with his entire body and psyche.[2]

Parents who believe that they are the sole influence on their child's behavior, have lost sight of a fundamental principle of child development. It is the *total* environment not just his parents that affects the direction and rate of development. Slavson sug-gests that it is "because of his identification with (internaliza-tion of) the parents' self-controls, the demands of peers, also

---

[2]*Ibid.*, p. 22.

the consequences of organic, psychological, and social maturation, and through the demands upon him by the live situation" that the child evolves into a competent and mature adult.[3]

To help children in their quest for self-actualization, parents must come to realize that a given act by a child is transitory in nature and that his over-all behavior is subject to constant change. The nature of the help that parents can give their child is dependent on which stage of development the child has reached. The parents must be able to perceive the stage of development the child is at and recognize the significance of the behavior to the child so that they may be able to respond in appropriate language and manner. The key to successful child-rearing lies in the ability of parents to adopt procedures that are compatible to a particular situation, their personality, and the family setting but which at the same time help the child to meet his psychological needs.

Although the goal of socialization is the same (that of helping the individual become an acceptable member of society) the process of socialization varies among societies. The process of socialization reflects a compromise among the following three factors: (a) What "ought" to be taught; (b) What "should" be taught; (c) How it "should" be taught. Since each family makes its own modifications in the manner in which it combines the three factors, it is not surprising that individual behavior varies as much as it does. The various behavioral sciences have studied the relationships between societal and family influences on the personality formation and social adjustment of the child.

Anthropologists have made extensive studies of the role that the family plays in various cultures and how various types of child-rearing practices affect individual development. In general, the results indicate that the family helps the individual lead a meaningful and productive life. Although in recent years there has been a rise in the number of people involved in communal living (e.g., the *kibbutz* of Israel and the *commune* in China), a historical review of past attempts at communal living indicates

---

[3]*Ibid.*, p. 20.

that it is detrimental to the individual and society.[4] In general, most child-rearing practices tend to enhance the well-being of the child. Those practices that tend to promote some type of self-defeating behavior in an individual reflect some atypical value or goal.

Sociologists have made extensive studies of family life in the United States. Generally speaking, the studies indicate that the pattern of family living has been gradually changing during the past 25 years. There is no agreement among sociologists as to whether this change is positive or negative. The studies further indicate that child-rearing practices vary among different socio-economic levels. In general, the studies suggest that the role the child plays in the family and the quality of emotional support he receives are important determiners of his social adjustment.[5]

Psychological studies of the family have focused on the inter-personal relationships within the home. The studies suggest that the emotional climate generated by the interpersonal relation-ships affect the behavior of all the members of the family. The quality of emotional support is an important factor in helping the child form his self-concept. This is particularly true of the degree to which a child internalizes the values and attitudes of his parents. There is no conclusive evidence as to the specific role that child-rearing practices play in personality formation and social adjustment. There is no doubt that the day to day inter-action in the home helps to shape and mold the behavior of the child. However, there are many speculations as to the role the family plays in personality formulation. The studies do suggest that the child is a resilient and adaptable individual who can ad-just to many of the demands that are made on him. His quest for self-actualization transcends the forces that impinge upon him.

Many of the studies undertaken by behavioral scientists sug-gest that, although many activities within the family enhance the well-being of the child, some practices can hinder the develop-ment of the child. The problems encountered by the family can

[4]M. Mead and K. Heyman, *Family* (New York, Macmillan, 1965).

[5]James Brossard, *The sociology of child development* (New York, Harper and Row, 1960), pp. 108-109.

arise from many different factors. The emotional climate of the home, lack of knowledge about the needs of young children, and cultural taboos can contribute to family tensions and conflicts.

Technological changes have influenced family living because its members must make adaptations to an environment that is more complicated than it was in the past. Although research studies have been helpful in understanding the family, most parents are oblivious of the results. There is some question as to the utility of knowledge about family living and child development in bringing up children. The parent must not only know, but also understand what he is doing.

> Among the chief errors of "parent education" is the assumption that information is necessarily transformed into practice. John Dewey emphasized that ideas cannot be transformed into experiences; only experiences can be transformed into experiences. Education, even in allied fields, does not necessarily help a parent deal with his children. One is surprised to observe men and women trained in fields of education, psychology, psychiatry, and child development, unable to deal with their children appropriately.[6]

Slavson suggests that the reason that knowledge alone is not sufficient in helping parents raise their children is that in order to apply the knowledge one must be sensitive to the needs of children. The parent must be able to perceive significance in apparently insignificant situations. How the parent responds in these "meaningless" situations (not necessarily meaningless to the child) is indicative of the family climate.

> A child's life consists almost entirely of minutiae, and it is with these that parents must deal properly. . . . But education is an empirical function as a parent cannot be theoretical and conceptual for, as already indicated, concepts are too far removed from practice. . . . The aim of parent education is to help each participant learn or evolve ways of dealing with specific situations most suitable for them and for their children.[7]

The implication that can be drawn from the above quotation is that parents need help because in their day-to-day encounters

---

[6]S. R. Slavson, *op. cit.*, p. 28.
[7]*Ibid.*, pp. 33-34.

with their children they lose sight of the ultimate goal: that of helping their children in their quest for self-actualization. In these daily encounters parents rely on expediency in order to maintain harmony within the family. Over a period of time the combination of expediency and authoritarianism leads to tension and conflict. The parent turns for help because he would like to restore harmony in the family milieu. He expects the help to be specific and concrete.

TYPES OF HELP AVAILABLE TO PARENTS

The previous section postulated that the reason that parents seek help about their problems with children is that they are primarily concerned with having harmony in the home. They turn to the professional helper for opinions and advice on how to reach this goal. It was also suggested that, although most child-rearing practices facilitate the development of the child, some procedures have a detrimental effect on the development of the child. The typical consequence of an inadequate child-rearing practice is a pattern of self-defeating behaviors. Children who exhibit self-defeating behaviors are seen by their teachers as either a disruptive force in the classroom or as individuals who need help as persons. From either view, the child whose potential is limited, or where the potential of those around the child is limited, will force the teacher to seek a consultation with a counselor because the situation will eventually create tension or conflict in the classroom. The school is interested in helping parents because what parents do to their children influences what children do in school.

There is disagreement among professional helpers as to what type of help should be given and at what point in time it should be given. Some professional helpers believe that the help should be given to parents during the child's early formative years. Others are of the opinion that the help should be given when the child enters school because through diagnostic procedures those children needing help could be referred to the appropriate pupil personnel services or community agencies. A few recommend that a system of parent education and individual child counseling would be most beneficial. These differences in opinion have precipitated the development of a variety of different helpers and helping agencies. As a consequence, a parent may obtain help for his child from a counselor, a social worker, a school psychologist, a counseling psychologist, a psychoanalyst, a psychiatrist, or a child development specialist, who may work in a school, a mental health center, a child guidance clinic, a community agency, or who is engaged in private practice. One may wonder why, with all this help available, parents continue to have problems in raising their children.

The kinds of help that parents can obtain for their children may be analyzed from the points of view of mental hygiene and guidance. Kaplan states that mental hygiene services can be divided into three categories:

> (1) *Primary prevention,* the promotion of normal, healthy emotional development; (2) *secondary prevention,* the early recognition and management of emotional disorders; (3) *tertiary prevention,* the effective treatment of psychiatric disturbance in an effort to restore the individual to a useful life as soon as possible.[8]

Parents are particularly interested in primary prevention because of its focus on the prevention of maladjustment at its point of origin. They wish to know how to develop a home atmosphere so that life within the family can be constructive. They are of the opinion that "a happy childhood, spent in a serene household with loving care from competent parents" is a prerequisite for mental health.[9] Parents would like to see the school not only as a place where children learn the basic skills but also as a place where children learn how to get along with others.

Parents tend to have mixed feelings about secondary prevention whose focus is the early detection of maladjustment and its management. This reaction stems from the feeling of guilt about being labeled as a failure as a parent. However, mass media, in particular, television, have stressed the fact that emotional disorders can arise from many different sources and that they are treatable. In addition, recent research has shown that it is pos-

---

[8]Louis Kaplan, *Education and mental health* (New York, Harper and Row, 1971), p. 64.

[9]*Ibid.,* p. 67.

sible to identify potential emotional disturbances among young children and through a comprehensive program to improve their adjustment and achievement.[10] Kaplan suggests that supportive intervention be used with children who are most vulnerable to emotional stress rather than waiting until they manifest overt signs of maladjustment. Similarly, some parents should be given psychological help with their problems before they psychologically damage their children.

The type of professional help given in tertiary prevention is seldom undertaken by the school. Treatment is usually given in mental health clinics or institutions. In some instances public schools have provided special classes for the emotionally disturbed. For the most part, since the treatment requires a long duration of time and special facilities, schools have not become involved too extensively in this type of treatment process. A few large school systems operate their own child guidance clinics.

From a guidance point of view, the help available to parents can be classified into three categories: remedial, preventative, and promotional.[11] Remedial assistance is similar to secondary prevention in that its focus is on the identification and treatment of problems. The nature of the problems identified and treated varies because public opinion as to what is deviant varies. The prevention concept of guidance differs from the primary prevention concept of mental health in that its focus is on the school rather than the home. Parents are shown how to help their children become effective students but are given little help in how they and their children can live in harmony at home. The promotional approach is somewhat unique in that its focus is the development of skills, attitudes, and habits that will facilitate the pupil's quest towards self-actualization. The goal of most programs for parents is to demonstrate to them how they can help their children in their quest for self-actualization. Again the focus is the child, not family.

The major difference between mental health and guidance

---

[10]*Ibid.*, p. 67.

[11]Lawrence H. Stewart and Charles F. Warnath, *The counselor and society* (Boston, Houghton-Mifflin, 1965), pp. 35-43.

viewpoints in work with parents is that the latter's focus is restricted to the child and the school while the former places emphasis on the entire family. The professional practices used by the two orientations are very similar. In some school districts the counselor who follows the developmental model of counseling relies heavily on the mental health orientation. He works with the entire community, not only with the child. The advantage of this practice is that the counselor sees the child as moving about his total environment rather than just the school. As a consequence, he makes use of the various community agencies in helping the child rather than restricting himself to the resources of the school.

The elementary school counselor is concerned with the prevention of maladjustment by helping the school and the home institute practices that promote and enhance the well-being of the child and his family. With the assistance of other school personnel, he conducts a program of early identification of children who may have emotional problems. The treatment of these problems is variable in that the goal may be remediation, amelioration, or reassurance.

DEVELOPMENTAL APPROACH IN WORKING WITH PARENTS

The developmental approach in guidance is very similar to the preventative practices of mental health. The term "developmental" is used because it gives a positive thrust to the work of the counselor rather than the negative connotation that surrounds the word "prevention." In previous chapters we have discussed how the counselor works with the developmental aspects of the curriculum and of the teachers' behavior. This section will review some of the practices in helping parents provide opportunities that enhance the child's development.

Three basic methods have been used in educating parents about how to bring up their children: group programs for parents, literature and other mass media, and counseling. Tasch suggests that each of these approaches has the same general objective in that each tries "to increase the parent's competence in dealing with his children through heightened self-awareness, an improved understanding of the parental role, and a better understanding of the process of child growth."[12] Bettelheim believes that the goal of parent education should be to help parents "find a way of living more at ease with the children in their care."[13]

There have been some questions as to whether the school should offer a formal program of parent education. The lack of qualified personnel and resources limit the activities of the school in parent education. Dinkmeyer and Caldwell suggest that child study groups should be organized through the school's parent-teacher association.[14] The counselor would serve as a catalyst and facilitator of group discussion. They recommend that printed material be used to stimulate discussion and to provide guidelines for the counselor. The value of the printed material is that it provides a focal point for discussion and prevents the group from developing into just a sharing of experiences by parents.

Child Study Association[15]

Parent group education has been sponsored by the Child Study Association of America since 1888. This organization conducts a program of parent education by means of conferences and large meetings and through the publication of books and pamphlets.

> Basic to the Association's program is the concept that increasing parents' competence will help them help themselves to understand and deal with their children's problems; to understand more fully the impact of parent-child relationships on the total development of the child; to understand and cope with the forces in the community which interplay with those within the family. Concurrently, as new knowledge and experience has been gained from small-group research and practice, the use of continuous small-group discus-

---

[12]Ruth J. Tasch, "Guidance at the preschool level" in Glen D. Mills (ed.), *Elementary school guidance and counseling* (New York, Random House, 1971), p. 45.

[13]Bruno Bettelheim, *Dialogues with mothers* (New York, Free Press, 1962), p. 216.

[14]Don Dinkmeyer and Edson Caldwell, *Developmental counseling and guidance* (New York, McGraw-Hill, 1970), p. 226.

[15]This section is based on the book written by Aline B. Auerback. *Parents learn through discussion: Principles and practices of parent group education* (New York, John Wiley, 1968).

sions under professional skilled leadership has become the major method utilized by the Association in its educational programs.[16]

Parent group education is not the same as formal academic teaching about child development. The basic difference is that the group leader serves as a facilitator while the teacher is an authority on the subject of child development. The function of the group leader is to help parents arrive at their own answers through the interaction of other parents. The stress is on feeling responses rather than intellectualization of material. The small-group discussion helps the members validate their opinions. Parent education differs from group counseling in that its focus is on the need to understand the meaning of behavior within the family rather than on helping the individual parent to understand and resolve his particular problem.

Parent education groups are formed at the request of the community. Day-care centers, churches, schools, family or social centers, PTA's, welfare departments, and housing projects are among the organizations that have requested help in forming parent education groups. Since each organization has its own reasons for requesting assistance in forming groups, the content of the discussions and their tone and intensity differ among the various parent education groups. Some groups are formed to meet special situations (e.g., unwed mothers, parents of physically handicapped children, and foster parents) while most groups are organized around some particular age level of children. Parents join these groups in order to improve their functioning in the family. Research conducted by the Child Study Association has shown that the small group discussion method is effective in increasing parental competency.

Parent Education in California[17]

Since 1926, parent education has been an integral part of many school systems in California. The State Department of Education

---

[16]*Ibid.*, vii.

[17]Based on Evelyn Pickarts and Jean Fargo, *Parent education* (New York, Appleton-Century-Crofts, 1971), pp. 137-222.

and the California Congress of Parents and Teachers have cooperated in establishing classes. Both organizations have been instrumental in publishing a variety of materials that facilitate the conducting of classes. The Los Angeles program of parent and family life education has been one of the most extensive programs conducted in the state.

The goals, content, and methods used in the program are determined by the kind of parents who enroll in the classes. Usually, the classes are designed to meet the needs of parents at various points in the life cycle. Thus, the topics range from how a child learns, to how to deal with the teenage subculture. Most of the instruction takes place in small groups where the interaction among the parents helps in validating opinions held by the parents.

The Parent Preschool Child Project conducted by the Los Angeles School District is an example of a project designed to meet the needs of parents in poverty areas. The goals of the project were twofold: first, to help parents become aware of how their attitudes affect the behavior of their children and to provide parents with skills in helping them guide their children; secondly, to help children develop a set of skills which would help them meet the demands of the school. The teaching tactics used in the project were similar to those used in other parent education groups. An evaluation of the project showed that most of the goals of the project were reached by the parents and their children.

The Role of the School in Parent Education

In recent years a combination of factors has forced schools to evaluate, or reevaluate, their position towards parent education. Traditionally, parent education was seen by the school as being the responsibility of other service organizations. The federal government, through its involvement in poverty programs, mental health programs, and community action programs, has given impetus on the state and local level for parent education programs. Some of the poverty programs made parent education an integral part of their activity. Head Start and other compensatory programs called for parent involvement in the classroom and in parent discussion groups. Although the overall results from these programs have been mixed, there is evidence to suggest that these programs do promote a better family life.

The basic premise that underlies parent education is the idea that parents are the principal teachers of their children. The goal is to help their children become self-sufficient in a constantly changing world. Parents must be competent enough to foster in their children a skill that will enable them to make sense out of a world that refuses to stand still. In addition, the parents must be skillful and resourceful in promoting harmony within their own home. Parents need to be taught the knowledge and skills needed to reach these objectives.

What role should the school play in education of parents to become teachers of their children? No ready answer can be given because the school's task has not been defined nor its objectives clarified. In addition, many different organizations and agencies are involved in helping parents function more effectively as parents. Although in the past the school has helped parents in a variety of ways, it usually was in response to a request for help. To initiate a program of parent education would break with tradition and cause resentment among some other community agencies and organizations. The school could develop a program for parents through which they could help their children meet the challenges of school life. For example, a topic like "readiness for school" would have wide appeal because most parents like to have their children obtain the maximum benefit from their stay in school. The Head Start project had this topic as one of its main objectives. These types of programs would also influence family living in that a young child's concern about school and his progress in school are topics for discussion at home.

It should also be apparent that the responsibility for conducting a parent education program should not be that of the counselor alone. Although he is the most logical person to do it because of his expertise in group work, the parent education program calls for a wide knowledge of child development. Someone other that the counselor should have the major responsibility for the program because the counselor has many other special tasks within the pupil personnel program.

The success of a school oriented parent education program depends to a large extent on having a qualified individual conducting the program. Pickarts and Fargo suggest that a parent educator have interdisciplinary training.

> To function effectively, a parent educator needs a working knowledge of the institution of the family and the impact of social change on its function; an awareness of the variability of parenting patterns and of the effect of socio-economic and cultural factors on attitudes, values, behaviors, and skills; an understanding of the community's role in meeting individual needs and a facility for connecting families with community resources. . . . A solid understanding of the learning process and the function of leadership, of the communication skills that nurture individual growth are all integral parts of the parent educator's knowledge.[18]

At the present time very few individuals have met the criteria for a trained parent educator developed by these two writers. They are of the opinion that those who are engaged on a part-time basis with parent education programs should avail themselves of the training program offered by the Child Study Association of America. Trained personnel are needed if parent education is to become a significant aspect in the education of adults in their life roles. School social workers currently have some of the preparation suggested by Pickarts and Fargo.

The school should become interested in parent education because children through their parents can be helped in their quest for self-actualization. Parents who establish the appropriate family atmosphere give their children a distinct advantage in life over those who fail to do so.

PARENT COUNSELING AND CONSULTATION

Some children cannot be helped solely by the process of child counseling. In these situations it becomes apparent that, if the child is to change his behavior, some changes must be made in his relationship with significant others. These individuals— parents, teachers, or siblings—must alter the manner in which they interact with the child. For example, parents who demand

---

[18]Pickarts and Fargo, *op. cit.*, p. 121.

too much or too little in the way of school achievement may be the source of an inadequate self-concept in that they fail to provide the necessary social reinforcements to maintain the child's sense of self-worth. To help the child with this kind of problem, the counselor must work with the parents.

The counselor's work with parents can be divided into two broad categories. First, the counselor may enter into a counseling relationship with parents so they may resolve some of their personal concerns. This procedure assumes that the parents' personal concerns are interfering with the manner in which they interact with the child. Secondly, the counselor may consult with the parents about the child's problem and discuss with them the modifications in the child's environment that may enhance his well-being. This procedure assumes that the difficulty that the child is having is due to some factor or factors in the environment and that if they were modified in some manner, the child's behavior would be altered.

Counseling Parents

Should a counselor help parents with their problems? This is a difficult question to answer because the frame of reference for responding to the question is rather vague. What problems are we referring to? Many laymen would say that a counselor should help parents who feel that their child's difficulty is a problem to them. However, should a counselor help parents who are the cause of the child's difficulty in school? In this situation, the answer may depend on the nature of the parental problem. Does the mother have an intrapsychic problem that is chronic in nature? Is the father's difficulty precipitated by some interpersonal issues? In other words, many counselors would restrict their help to parents who do not have chronic or serious emotional disturbances and whose difficulty could be resolved in a few contacts.

This approach creates a problem for the counselor for this procedure requires that he have a set of diagnostic skills that can be used to delineate the type of problem that the parent possesses. Most counselors lack the competencies required to perform an adequate psychological evaluation of adults. In addition, parents would object to being evaluated by the counselor for fear that the community would know that they require psychological assistance.

If we assume that parents can only be counseled after an appropriate diagnosis, then the complexity of diagnostic classification becomes a problem. Those engaged in family psychotherapy have evolved a rather complex classification system. Acherman's psychotherapeutic program for mothers can be used to illustrate this point.

1. Therapy for deviations in the mother role, deriving mainly from conflict in a particular family pair.
2. Therapy for deviations in the mother role, which are in main consequences of distortion in the psycho-social structure and mental health of the family as a whole.
3. Therapy for deviations in the mother role, related in the main to clashes between requirements of the mother role, and other significant familial and extrafamilial roles.
4. Therapy for deviations in the mother role, related in the main to long-standing individual pathology of the mother's personality.[19]

Perhaps with the exception of the first type of diagnosis where the mother is in conflict with the pupil, most of the other categories require a number of contacts to resolve. In addition, they also require that various levels of therapeutic approaches be combined to help the mother. The process of helping the mother can be complex and time consuming.

Generally speaking, the counselor should not provide individual counseling to a parent who has personal problems because he usually lacks a mandate from the school board to provide this type of service. From a professional point of view he should not provide the parent with individual counseling, especially if the parental difficulty disturbs the entire family, because the process of helping a conflicted family requires special skills and competencies.

A therapeutic approach to the emotional disturbances of family life must begin, therefore, with a psycho-social evaluation of the

---

[19]Nathan W. Ackerman, *The psychodynamics of family life* (New York, Basic Books, 1958), pp. 283-384.

family as a whole. Next must come the application of appropriate levels of social support and educational guidance and a therapeutic approach to conflicted family relationships. Only then is it possible to consider individual psychotherapy for selected family members, and this therapy should initially be oriented to the specific dynamic relationships of personality and family role and to the balance between intrapsychic conflict and family conflict. Thus, in a very real sense, individual psychotherapy is auxiliary to and dependent upon an integrated therapeutic program for the family as a social unit.[20]

If the counselor accepts Ackerman's point of view, then he would not provide individual counseling to parents but he would become involved in the second phase of the treatment in which he would give support and guidance to the family as a unit and to the parents. Parent education, Adlerian family counseling, and Slavson's child-centered group guidance are examples of the kinds of help that the counselor can offer parents in this phase of treatment. Individual counseling for the various young members of the family can be provided not only by the counselors but by other pupil personnel staff members and community agencies. However, providing individual counseling for parents by the school should only be undertaken when the ramifications of this procedure are fully understood by those who will be involved. In most instances it would be best to refer the parent to a community or private agency for help.

Parental Consultation

The process of parental consultation is very similar to that of any other type of consultation. However, parental consultation can be approached as either working with the parents or through the parents. The latter procedure, working through parents, has the parents working as instruments of change. That is to say, parents administer the treatment program that has been developed by the counselor. For example, the parents of an acting-out child may be asked to cooperate in a behavior modification program whose goal is to curtail the frequency of the acting-out behavior. In this procedure the counselor does not attempt to modify the parents' attitudes towards the child in any manner. The counselor

---

[20]*Ibid.*, p. 304.

advises the parents about the nature of the treatment and asks their cooperation in administering it.

Parental consultation whose goal is to help the child with the parents as part of the treatment process assumes that the child's difficulties stem, at least in part, from the family situation.

> There is an increasing awareness by clinicians dealing with children that the behavior of the child is to be understood fundamentally only in the context of the intrafamilial interpersonal relations. Pathological relationships between mother and father and child play a great role in helping maintain the distorted and unintegrated tendencies in the child.[21]

This procedure assumes that both the child and his parents must make modifications in their behavior in order for the child to be helped. This approach differs from teaching parents on how to be effective parents in that it deals with the parents' emotions about their children.

Szurek labels this approach as collaborative or concomitant therapy.[22] He is of the opinion that many parents who want help for their children also would like some help for themselves. He suggests that the parents and the child each have their own therapist. The reason is that he believes that it is not the parent alone that fosters the behavior of the child but that the child stimulates certain responses in the mother. The techniques used in the interaction by the parent and child may tend to be mutually self-defeating. The two therapists can observe better than one how mutually gratifying to all is the interpersonal behavior, no matter how distorted or chaotic it may appear. After interviewing each separately, the therapists discuss their individual experiences with each other.

Collaborative therapy is not the same as providing individual therapy for the parent. The latter's goal is to help the parent with his concerns without specific regard for the welfare of the child.

---

[21]S. A. Szurek, A. M. Johnson, and E. I. Falstein, "Collaborative psychiatric therapy of parent-child problems," *American Journal of Orthopsychiatry*, Vol. 12 (1942), p. 512.

[22]S A. Szurek, "Some lessons from efforts at psychotherapy with parents," *American Journal of Psychiatry*, Vol. 109 (1952), pp. 296-310.

In collaborative therapy the goal is to help the parents provide a facilitative atmosphere within the home. Its purpose is to help the child by helping the parents with their concerns about their children.

Child-Centered Group Guidance of Parents

S. R. Slavson describes this process of child-centered group guidance for parents as being similar to that of parent education discussion groups.[23] It is offered to parents who come together usually under clinic-agency auspices and who have some understanding about the nature of their problem. Child-centered group guidance for parents is not a form of psychotherapy in that it does not attempt to change the psychic organization of the personality of the parents. It is a professional service offered to parents who wish to change their relation with their children.

> In guidance the aim is to affect specific attitudes which do not pro ceed from strong neurotic and compelling needs to behave in a particular manner; rather the behavior is a result of misconceptions of what the function of parenthood is, what the parent's role is in the development of the child, and of the rather universal lack of knowledge or misunderstanding of the needs of young children.[24]

Group guidance differs from analytical group psychotherapy, according to Slavson, in that the five dynamics of psychotherapy (transference, catharsis, insight, sublimation, and reality testing) are either absent or substantially different. For example, in child-centered guidance groups the aim is not to gain insight but to sensitize parents to their children and help them understand their needs. Although both rely on reality testing, the sole concern in child-centered guidance groups is the reality of the child-parent relation and the actuality of their current acts and behavior.

The child-centered guidance group usually consists of eight mothers or fathers who are assigned to separate groups and meet on alternate weeks for approximately two hours. Slavson suggests that the participants in the groups have children who are nearly the same age and of the same sex. The task of the group

---

[23]Slavson, *op. cit.*, viii.
[24]*Ibid.*, pp. 15-16.

322 Counseling and Psychology in Elementary Schools

is to concern itself with actual situations as they occur in the lives of the parents and only those that relate to their children. The group process consists of the following three features:

1. The subjects for discussion are the children and the way parents deal with them.
2. Free participation by all without formality, routines or organization of the discussion.
3. The leader is not a pedagogue, an authority or a sole source of information to whom the members have to turn.[25]

The leader's main task is to encourage the group members to express themselves freely about their relationships with their children. The group provides parents an opportunity to search for a solution to their child-rearing problems in a manner that meets their particular needs at their own levels and circumstances. The key aspect of this group experience is to help parents gain a better understanding of their relationships with their children by helping them arrive at them through their own efforts and reflections.

Fullmer's Family Group Consultation

Daniel Fullmer has developed, in conjunction with Harold Bernard, a group process whose general goal is to help family members to live in constructive ways with one another.[26] The specific goal of family group consultation is to help to improve the learning environment for the child in the educational setting. It assumes that part of the child's difficulty is due to emotional concerns generated by inadequate family communication. The group process intervenes directly in the family message systems. By clarifying the family message system, each member of the family has a better understanding of one another.

The family group consultation method can be used with only one family at a time or with a group of families. The focus in the group is on the "here and now" rather than on past experience

---

[26]D. W. Fullmer, "Family group consultation," in George M. Gazda (ed.), *Theories and methods of group counseling in the schools* (Springfield, Thomas, 1969); D. W. Fullmer and H. W. Bernard, *Family consultation* (Boston, Houghton-Mifflin, 1968); D. W. Fullmer, *Counseling: Group theory and system* (Scranton, International Textbook Company, 1971), Chapter 13.

of the family. The counselor and the family examine the "here and now" experience from the standpoint of identifying a set of common meanings that members of the family attach to a given experience. Fullmer recommends that at least two counselors work with a group, for at one point in the session the group divides into adult and child sections. The purpose of the sub-grouping is to further examine the meanings attached to certain message systems. Through the process of examining the various message systems, the family discovers that in order for harmony to be achieved within the family, its members must unlearn certain methods of speaking and listening. By clarifying the message systems, each member of the family will have a greater understanding and empathy for all other members of the family.

Fullmer and Bernard have provided a detailed outline for conducting family group consultation sessions. They believe that most families can be helped in about twelve meetings. The first three sessions are used to help the group become oriented to the family group consultation procedures. The next two sessions are used to teach the group how to use some of the counseling skills demonstrated in the earlier sessions. Both the orientation and the teaching aspects are undertaken by examining the conflicts that exist in the family. The rest of the sessions are designed to help the family develop alternative ways of behaving. This is done through a procedure that is labeled "event analysis." In this procedure a significant family incident is evaluated from several different perspectives with the purpose of helping the family gain insight into handling similar events in the future.

Fullmer and Bernard believe that family group consultation should be practiced by the school counselor because it is easier for the school to influence the family rather than some agency. In addition the school can use other personnel (e.g., social worker and school psychologist) in helping the counselor with his work. They believe that the school cannot ignore family problems because children bring them to school. The problems of the child to a certain extent then become the problems of the school because how the child behaves affects the school environment. They do suggest that the school staff must be trained to carry out this type of group work with the family.

Adlerian Family Counseling

Adlerian family counseling is a system of helping parents to alter their patterns of family relationships by providing them an opportunity to observe a family receiving counseling and to participate in group discussions about principles that are useful in helping the family with its specific concerns.[27] The procedure helps the parents to gain an understanding of principles that are helpful in enhancing the development of the child and of the family. In addition, the children become aware of the reasons they act the way they do in the family. Even though the parents and the children are present, the focus is on the parent. The goal is to educate parents and not to treat them.

The Adlerian family counseling process differs from Slavson's child-centered group guidance of parents and Fullmer's family group consultation in that teaching plays a more important part in the process. It is based on the writings of Alfred Adler and Rudolph Dreikurs. Both of these men believed that the family atmosphere and the family constellation play a vital role in shaping the life style of the child. They suggest that the child's ordinal position in the family influences certain types of behavior. It is important for the parents to have an understanding of these principles so that they evolve a family atmosphere that is both democratic and orderly. Failure to use the appropriate training methods leads to family conflict and misbehavior by the children.

The first step in helping the family is to interview the parents utilizing a structured outline. The value of using a structured outline such as that developed by Sonstegard is to evaluate the quality of the family relationship and the role that the family constellation plays in it.[28] The outline is used as a frame of reference for identifying the sources of conflict within the family. Essentially it tries to establish the purposes the child has for doing what he does. This type of interview can be conducted in private or in front of an audience. After the structured interview

---

[27]Rudolph Dreikurs, "Psychotherapy through child guidance," *The Nervous Child*, Vol. 8 (1949), pp. 314-318; Rudolph Dreikurs, *The challenge of parenthood* (New York, Duell, Sloan, and Pearce, 1959); Manford Sonstegard, "A rationale for interviewing parents," *The School Counselor*, Vol. 12 (1964), pp. 52-56; Dinkmeyer and Caldwell, *op. cit.*

[28]Sonstegard, *op. cit.*

the counselor tells the parents some of his hunches about the source of conflict in the family. In particular, the counselor emphasizes the role that the child's purposes play in structuring his behavior in the family. If the interview is conducted in front of an audience, the members are asked to make recommendations as to procedures that could rectify the situation and to offer an explanation of the dynamics that underlie the family conflict. Usually the audience is made up of parents who are in the process of receiving help by this method. It has been found that insights communicated by other parents tend to be accepted more than those given by an expert. This is also the fundamental treatment formula used by Slavson in his work with parents.

The general goal of Adlerian family counseling is the reorientation of the family towards procedures that enhance the welfare of all of its members. By understanding the nature of human behavior, they can employ procedures that can be substantiated by psychological principles. The parent, instead of acting in a haphazard manner, can move purposefully towards a predetermined goal.

It is apparent that a counselor who is to engage in family counseling must have had appropriate training. Although the counselor's many skills and knowledges would facilitate the development of this competency, it would be foolish for the counselor to engage in it without appropriate preparation. In addition, the counselor would have to arrange his school schedule in a manner that would permit him to engage in this activity. Most school administrators would examine this request with care because the counselor would have to take time from working with children and teachers and devote it to parents. They would point out that many public and private agencies in the community specialize in this type of service. To provide family counseling is a duplication of effort.

It should be noted that there are some instances in which the child's school problem is so related with his family life that the counselor is probably the best person to provide family counseling. It is our position that this should occur infrequently and that the majority of problems that require family counseling should be referred to the appropriate agency.

In the matter of consulting with parents the issues are somewhat different. Here, the focal point is the child, not the parent. As such, the counselor can legitimately utilize his time in working with parents. If common problems arise, then he can evolve some type of parent group that can help resolve the concerns. Again, he should feel free to refer parents to appropriate sources if they already exist in the community.

THE TEACHER'S WORK WITH PARENTS

The school and the home must work in collaboration with one another if the child is to have a meaningful experience in school. The parents assume that the school will provide their children with a set of experiences which will enhance their development. On the other hand, the school assumes that the parents are responsible for preparing the child for school. According to Grams, parents have a major responsibility for supplying a sound emotional base, providing adequate social skills, stimulating special abilities and talents, and transmitting values to their children.[29] It is necessary for the school and the parents to communicate their expectations to one another. The school, through orientation meetings, open-house, and teacher-parent conferences, provides means by which the school and parents can exchange ideas.

Communication between parents and teachers has been affected by several factors. One of the biggest obstacles to meaningful communication is the parents' fear that the school will change the behavior of their child. Many parents associate the need for change in their child's behavior with inadequate child-rearing practices. Parents of primary level children usually believe that one of the purposes of parent-teacher conferences is to communicate an evaluation of their child-rearing practices. They seem to forget that one of the principal contributors to the change is the child himself. An exposure to a new environment plus maturational changes are bound to influence the child's current modes of behaving.

In recent years the communication process between teachers and parents has been affected by the lowered status of teachers

[29]Armin Grams, *Facilitating learning and individual development* (St. Paul, Minnesota Department of Education, 1966), Chapter 3.

in many communities. This has led to the questioning of the value
of what is said by the teacher, and has affected the degree to
which parents listen to what is said. Some parents adopt the attitude that, since the school has nothing worthwhile to say, there
is no point in attending meetings or conferences. They would
rather exert pressure on the school board than express themselves
to school personnel.

The school has used a variety of procedures in trying to facilitate cooperation and understanding between parents and teachers.
Orientation meetings, open house, and PTA meetings are the
more general ways by which the school tries to bridge the gap
between the home and the school. The most specific way of facilitating cooperation and understanding is the parent-teacher conference.

The parent-teacher conference can be used for such different
purposes as orientation, information giving, interpretation or exchanging ideas. The teacher's goal is to gain a better understanding of the child by knowing the parents better. On the other
hand, the parent wishes to be informed about his child's achievement and behavior so that he can validate his expectations. Parents are interested in the child's academic progress because they
would like to know something about the child's general learning
potential, his educational development, and any special talents
or deficiencies he has. Their concern about classroom and social
behavior is somewhat different. They are not only interested as
to the degree to which the child has adjusted to the school but
how well they have helped their child to relate to other children.
Specifically, they are concerned about whether the attitudes and
values taught at home have been helpful in the child's interpersonal relations. Some parents fear coming to school because they
are of the opinion that they will be told some negative things
about their child which may reflect on them. There is an element
of truth in this observation for, other than having parents come
in for a report on their child's academic progress, parents are
seldom asked to come in and hear something positive about their
child. Usually the teacher asks a parent to come for a special conference when the child has been exhibiting some type of deviant
behavior.

No matter what the purpose of the parent-teacher conference, the teacher should practice good human relationships during the interview. This includes showing positive regard or respect for the parent, empathy and understanding of the parent and being genuine and honest. The teacher should be aware that the conference has both a cognitive and affective component. She should not ignore the latter for the parents' attitudes and values affect how well they listen to what is being said. Successful conferences require that the teacher have a definite purpose for calling the meeting and that she have the necessary material that would facilitate the discussion. Physical comfort of the parents should be kept in mind when choosing the location of the conference. It would be helpful if the counselor or some staff member who has skills in interviewing could develop an in-service training program whose goal would be to enhance the efficiency and effectiveness of parent-teacher conferences.

It should be pointed out that a parent-teacher conference is not the same as a consultation with a parent. Although both use many of the same procedures, they do differ in their goals. Essentially, the consultation is concerned with some specific aspect of behavior that is usually seen as a problem to the consultee, who desires some type of help with it. The parent-teacher conference has as its goal the more general aspects of the child's behavior. Although the focus is on specifics, the end goal is some type of statement about the child's progress or development.

The teacher's role in working with parents can range from mere information giving to working towards modifying the parents' attitudes towards their child. In a broad sense, the full range of activities engaged in by the teacher can be seen as enhancing the child's self-concept, for their goal is to provide a milieu that is relatively free of needless conflict. For a teacher to provide effective help, she must have a knowledge and understanding of human relationships. Through the medium of the parent-teacher conference, the teacher can discuss matters that can help the parent to better understand his child. This teacher activity should not be construed as being the same as counseling. Its intent is to help the child, not the parent.

SUMMARY

The school provides many services whose goal is to help the child to function more effectively. Parents need help in bringing up their children because they not only lack knowledge about child development but, more important, they do not know how to cope with the child's emotional concerns. If the parents are to help the child in his quest for self-actualization, they must understand the factors that affect it. Parents should be aware that expediency and authoritarianism lead to conflict and tension.

Parents may be helped in a variety of ways. If the school has a developmental approach to guidance, the staff provides assistance through conferences and small group discussion. In some school districts parent education is provided through the school or the school supports or encourages private sources such as the Child Study Association. Occasionally parents may obtain help by means of family counseling. This may be offered through the school, the local mental health clinic, family service agencies or other private agencies. In some instances, the treatment may be broad enough to include collaborative therapy. In other cases the helping relationship may include consultation with the parents. A major issue is that of the degree to which the school should become involved in the affairs of the family. The question is not whether the family should be helped but who should provide the helping relationship. The welfare of the child should guide the selection of the helper.

SUGGESTED READINGS

Auerbach, Aline B.: *Parents learn through discussion: principles and practices of parent group education.* New York, Wiley, 1968.

Dinkmeyer, Don and Caldwell, Edson: *Developmental counseling and guidance: a comprehensive school approach.* New York, McGraw-Hill, 1970.

Fullmer, Daniel W. and Bernard, Harold W.: *Family consultation.* Boston, Houghton-Mifflin, 1968.

Pickets, Evelyn and Fargo, Jean: *Parent education.* New York, Appleton-Century-Crofts, 1971.

Slavson, S. R.: *Child-centered group guidance of parents.* New York, International Universities Press, 1958.

PART IV

RESEARCH AND
EVALUATION

Chapter 14

RESEARCH AND EVALUATION IN COUNSELING AND STUDENT PERSONNEL WORK

T HIS IS THE AGE OF ACCOUNTABILITY. The public wants to know what progress the school is making in reaching its objectives. It wants the strong programs maintained and the weak programs either strengthened or eliminated. Evaluation provides a means for appraising the direction and the quality of services provided by the school. It helps the administrator see the relationships among various facets of the school's program.

The counseling program as one of the many activities within the school should be subject to evaluation. Only through systematic evaluation can the counselor ascertain the efficiency and effectiveness of the program. The counselor cannot use the notion that "elementary school guidance is too new to be evaluated." The program should be tested by acceptable standards as should any other program within a school district. If an evaluation shows that certain objectives are not being reached, then the counselor can use this information either to eliminate this particular phase of the program or to develop different means to attain it. Problems are better developed and appraised by means of appropriate data rather than by sheer guess work.

It is the purpose of this chapter to review the various evaluative procedures as they relate to the elementary guidance program. Through the study of the process of evaluation the counselor can better understand the need for developing a program

333

that has some tangible goals, and how information can be utilized in resolving some of the problems that confront him. In this respect, some attention will be given to research and how a counselor can conduct studies within his own school which will facilitate his professional development.

EVALUATION OF ELEMENTARY GUIDANCE

Evaluation is the process of appraising an existing program so that the counselor can answer the question of "What progress am I making?" Since evaluation has a value aspect, it has the connotation of goodness or badness about it. Many counselors fear evaluation because they are of the opinion that they must continually justify their program to their administrator and any "bad" results will lead to its termination. They fail to realize that only through evaluation can the guidance program be improved. Downing believes that failure to conduct an evaluation of the guidance program will lead to the following four undesirable conditions:

> (1) a weak or mediocre service at a level of quality far below the possibilities; (2) an apathetic, indifferent staff and a student body with little motivation for improvement; (3) a general failure to provide and utilize the proper activities, tools, and procedures essential to the educational progress of youth; and (4) inefficiency in the use of staff members and the school's resources.[1]

The evaluative process essentially consists of making judgments or inferences from observed data. This requires the counselor to obtain information that can be expressed quantitatively. The measurement phase of the evaluative process consists of gathering quantified descriptions of some empirical fact. A variety of instruments can be used to gather this information. Tests are but one of many different techniques that can be used to evaluate a program. Once the information has been gathered, the counselor can make some inference as to the quality of the program. It should be noted that although the counselor uses information to reach some of his conclusions, the inferences he

---

[1]Lester N. Downing, *Guidance and counseling services: An introduction* (New York: McGraw-Hill, 1968), p. 361.

draws basically represent a value judgment. Measurement devices can describe but only human beings can make statements regarding the worth of something.

Research is a method or technique of evaluation. It is concerned with determining whether or not certain results have been achieved. The research process is neutral in respect to its methods and results. It is primarily concerned with finding answers to questions. Evaluation is concerned with the progress that is being made towards some objective.

Essential elements of a program of evaluation

Any program of evaluation must consider the following questions: What is to be evaluated? What are the purposes of evaluation? What do we use? Can we do it ourselves?[2] The first question, What is to be evaluated?, suggests that the counselor must decide what of the many aspects of the guidance program will be evaluated. Hansen and Stevic suggest that evaluation can be concerned with the foundation, direction, scope, adequacy of service, and personnel aspects of the program.[3] Each of these aspects can be related to the general and specific objectives of the program. The counselor in cooperation with other school personnel determines which objectives have priority in the evaluation. This is not an easy task for at different stages of development of a guidance program the counselor has a different perspective of the progress he is making. For example, in the initial phases his concern may focus on his personal adequacy while in latter stages he may wish to know if the activities of the program have deviated from their philosophical base.

The second question, What are the purposes of evaluation?, is concerned with the mode in which the report will be used. Will the report be used to defend or justify the existing program or will it be used as a benchmark to gauge the quality and effectiveness of the program? In a general way, the evaluation

[2]H. H. Remmers, N. L. Gage, and J. F. Rummel, *A practical introduction to measurement and evaluation* (New York: Harper and Row, 1960) pp. 9-32.

[3]James C. Hansen and Richard R. Stevic, *Elementary school guidance* (New York: Macmillan, 1969) p. 256.

should enable the staff to better adapt the program to the individual needs of the pupils. Since every guidance program is based on reaching some goals, an evaluation can identify those areas that require more effective methods for reaching the goals. In some instances it may not necessarily mean changing of the activities but giving the activities better direction. The evaluation report can also serve as a basis for informing the public as to the progress the guidance program has been making in reaching its objectives.

The third question, What do we use?, is concerned with the methodology of evaluation. The type of instruments used in the evaluation to a large extent depend on being able to establish a logical relationship among the objectives of the program, the activities of the program, and the criteria of evaluation. There are a number of problems that arise when a meaningful relationship among the three areas is attempted. First, the goals of guidance and in particular counseling must be stated in concrete terms. Many of the goals of guidance are stated in general terms and it is difficult to translate them into operational terms. Second, the activities used to explicate the specific goals may not necessarily be directly related to the general goals. For example, what activities can be used to foster better self-understanding in an elementary school pupil? A number of activities could be assumed to enchance a child's self-understanding but a counselor would be hard pressed to identify a specific activity that unequivocally contributes to the child's self-understanding. This leads also to the third problem, that of identifying criteria that can be used to gather evidence which may be used to assess the degree to which the objectives have been reached.

The typical evaluation of a guidance program is concerned more with the outcomes of the program than it is with the process by which the goals were reached. However, a professionally oriented counselor should be concerned with the means by which the goals have been reached. The counselor should concern himself as to whether he has used the most effective and efficient methods of reaching a specific objective. However, it is difficult for a counselor to measure both the product and process with the same instrument. In the current state of the art of constructing evaluative instruments it is easier to measure the process than it is to measure the behavior changes which have occurred in the children.

It is rather difficult to establish a list of criteria that would be useful in evaluating specific outcomes that are associated with a particular procedure. For example, if the counselor used a task-oriented group activity for the purpose of facilitating better peer relationships, pre-established criteria would be of little help to him especially if they were based on counseling groups, which are not task oriented. There is no doubt that a listing of criteria may help a counselor to gain a better understanding of how to establish a logical relationship among objectives, activities, and criteria. In this respect the counselor should consult some of the references listed below so that he may have a further understanding of the criterion problem.[4]

The fourth question, Can we do it ourselves?, is concerned with the counselor's skills and competencies to conduct an evaluation study. Most programs of counselor preparation require the trainee to take some work in the area of evaluation and research. As a consequence, the counselor is familiar with many of the evaluation techniques and procedures, and should be able to select or construct instruments that are appropriate to his purpose. In addition he should be familiar with the basic statistical procedures that he may use to analyze his data in a meaningful manner. The statistical procedures should be used in order that the conclusions reflect some degree of objectivity. They do not have to be of a complex nature.

An important source for gaining an understanding of how to conduct an evaluation of an elementary guidance program are

---

[4]Donald H. Blocher, *Developmental counseling* (New York: Ronald, 1966) pp. 222-236; George E. Hill and Eleanore B. Luckey, *Guidance for children in elementary schools* (New York: Appleton-Century-Crofts, 1969), Ch. 13; B. T. Jensen, G. Coles and Beatrice Nestor, "The criterion problem in guidance research," *Journal of Counseling Psychology*, Vol. 2, (1955), pp. 58-61, reprinted in C. H. Patterson, ed., *The counselor in the school: Selected readings* (New York, McGraw-Hill, 1967), pp. 425-431; Merle M. Ohlsen, *Guidance services in the modern school* (New York: Harcourt, Brace and World, 1964), Ch. 17; and C. H. Patterson, "Methodological problems in evaluation," *Personnel and Guidance Journal*, Vo. 39, (1960), pp. 270-274.

the bulletins published by various state departments of education. Hill and Luckey list a number of bulletins that contain evaluation standards.[5] The bulletins can serve as a basis for developing the school district's own analysis of its guidance program. From them the staff can learn how to relate their goals to outcomes, identify appropriate criteria, and gain an awareness of methods that can be used in evaluating their programs.

An effective evaluation program can only be achieved if the counselor has established a specific set of objectives for his program. Evaluation is concerned with the progress that the counselor is making towards his objectives. It helps him decide whether the activities he has selected help him reach his goals in an effective and efficient manner. The instruments used to measure progress should not dictate the type of evaluation that is made. This type of approach to evaluation negates the fundamental purposes of evaluation since most instruments of evaluation can be used for many different purposes. It is essential that the counselor use objectives as his starting point in evaluation rather than the instruments that are available to him. In this way the counselor is in a position to answer some questions about his program rather than seeing how much he has of something.

Program evaluation

Recent federal legislation has required that recipients of federal grants under the Elementary and Secondary Education Act evaluate the effectiveness of their programs. The evaluation requirement has forced school districts to look at the total program rather than some specific aspect of it. Many of the problems encountered by evaluation teams are similar to the ones we have discussed. However there is value in reviewing some of the problems of program evaluation in that the counselor may gain additional understanding of how his evaluation can be related to the total program evaluation of the school.

One of the basic problems of program evaluation is to determine what is meant by the terms. Provus states that there are at least five different definitions of the term:[6]

---

[5]*Op. cit.*, p. 532.
[6]Malcolm Provus, *Discrepancy evaluation* (Berkeley, McCutchan, 1971), p. 10.

1. The judgment of authorities about a program
2. The opinions of program staff
3. Opinions of those affected by a program
4. A comparison of actual program outcomes with expected outcomes
5. A comparison of an executed program with its design

In the first approach use is made of either some set standards or personal opinions as to the quality of the program. Each of these procedures has some difficulties in that the latter would reflect the personal bias of the evaluators while the former may involve differences of opinion. The second and third approaches, although useful in that they reflect the personal experience of those associated with the program, are subject to bias and misunderstanding.

The fourth approach, evaluation of program outcomes, reflects the traditional approach to evaluation. This approach has been discussed in some detail above. Provus believes that this type of evaluation is better suited for conducting experiments than it is for evaluating the program.[7] He feels that a microanalysis of a student's behavior before and after being exposed to some type of treatment is of little use to a staff which has just initiated a program and wishes to use its experience to make alterations that would enhance its functioning. By its very nature, an experimental design cannot be altered during the period of its execution.

The fifth approach, comparison of an executed program with its design is favored by Provus in that it is concerned with every aspect of the program rather than just its outcomes.

> This comprehensive comparison of many aspects of actual events with expected events therefore requires the explication of a detailed picture of an entire program at various points in time as the standard for judging performance. These program standards may arise from any source, but under the Discrepancy Evaluation Model they are derived from the values of the program staff and the client population it serves.[8]

---

[7]*Ibid.,* p. 11.
[8]*Ibid.,* p. 12.

Provus believes that his Discrepancy Evaluation Model is superior to the traditional model in that it helps a counselor or administrator (1) to produce a quality product, (2) at a minimal cost, and (3) helps to make decisions as to what should be produced and how.

The Discrepancy Evaluation Model is useful for programs that have just been initiated. The process consists of "(1) defining program standards; (2) determining whether a discrepancy exists between some aspect of the program performance and the standards governing that aspect of the program; (3) using discrepancy information either to change the performance or to change program standards."[9] The model can be applied at any of four developmental stages of a program. When the program is being developed, the adequacy of the design is evaluated. When the program is introduced, the fidelity of installation is tested. As the program is carried out the various activities are evaluated in terms of the adjustments that have been made to reach the goals of the program. In the final stages of the program an assessment of the product is made. Provus suggests that in some cases a given program can be compared with other types of programs to determine the cost-benefits of the program.

The Discrepancy Evaluation Model has great utility in evaluating guidance programs that have just been initiated. It provides a framework through which a counselor can resolve some of the problems he has encountered in administrating the program by helping him identify alternative ways of coping with the difficulties. The model does not make decisions for the counselor but helps him put into perspective the elements that are required for the decision.

Community interest in evaluation is somewhat different from that of the professional staff. It is primarily interested in outcomes and cost of the program. What was accomplished by the program? What was the cost of that accomplishment? The criteria used by the community are somewhat different from those used by the staff. Parents are not interested in the technical as-

[9]*Ibid.,* p. 183.

pects of evaluation but in tangible evidence of accomplishment. The school may feel proud that a given program raised a child's IQ by ten points but the parent looks for overt signs of improvement in his child's reading. The counselor may rate a child as showing improvement in his social behavior but the mother looks for evidence in his relationship with his siblings. The community also examines the cost of the program in relationship to its accomplishments. In many respects the community is willing to spend money on a program if tangible results can be demonstrated. On the other hand poor outcomes will not be tolerated no matter what the cost of the program.

One of the basic responsibilities that the counselor has to the community is to show what goals have been achieved by the guidance program. His explanation should be given in a manner that can be readily understood by a lay person. He should point out to parents perceptible achievements. In order for a counselor to do this he must be in a position to translate his technical data into observations that can be readily understood by parents. This means that he must continually be sensitive to situations that may be used to demonstrate the highlights of his program. Failure to do this will lead to a misunderstanding of the goals and outcomes of a guidance program. This is a very difficult task, but one that must be done to some degree at least if the program is to gain community and parental support.

RESEARCH IN ELEMENTARY GUIDANCE

It was stated earlier in this chapter that research is a method or technique of evaluation. The basic difference between the two terms is that evaluation has a value aspect while research is neutral in respect to its methods and results. Rushong notes that "evaluation is the process of making a subjective judgment on the basis of objective evidence of the extent to which the objectives of the educational program are being reached."[10]

Helmstadter defines research as "the activity of solving prob-

---

[10]H. D. Rushong, "Present status and trends in the evaluation of counseling." *Educational and Psychological Measurement*, Vol. 13, (1953) pp. 418-430.

lems which leads to new knowledge using methods of inquiry which are currently accepted as adequate by scholars in the field."[11] Essentially evaluation is concerned with progress or achievement while research is concerned with testing generalizations or solving problems.

Another fundamental difference between the two terms is the use of research findings. Since the evaluation process is concerned with the goodness or badness of a program, rarely is there a rigorous investigation made as to why the program succeeded or failed. On the other hand research is always concerned with testing the generalizations that underlie a given operation. Once the variables which directly affect a given process are identified then the next step is to discover methods by which they can be controlled so that specific outcomes can be achieved. Research findings are used to make predictions while evaluation reports are used to make judgments about the effectiveness of a program.

Research activities in the school

A school district should become involved in conducting research for the explicit purpose of testing the generalizations which underlie the guidance program. One should not infer from this statement that research findings should be used only for substantiating a program. The research process can be used to identify those procedures that can effectively be used to reach a given outcome. For example, in our discussion of consultation it was pointed out that the research techniques used to compare the effectiveness of counseling with consulting are inadequate because inappropriate measures were used. It would be better for a researcher to identify those situations in which consultation is more appropriate than counseling, thereby enhancing the work of the counselor in terms of time and effort. Similarly, a counselor may investigate the conditions under which group counseling may be more appropriate than individual counseling in helping students with their relationships with peers.

The general thrust of the above suggestions is not to "prove"

---

[11]C. C. Helmstadter, *Research concepts in human behavior* (New York, Appleton-Century-Crofts, 1970), p. 5.

something but to establish a degree of effectiveness between goals and procedures. What contributes to what, how, and at what cost? By establishing a relationship between process and outcome the counselor is in a better position to control events. If the goal of counseling is to help pupils in their quest for self-actualization and there are different ways of achieving this goal then it is incumbent on the counselor to be prepared to offer different types of help to those who are at different stages in their journey towards self-actualization. Although the counselor cannot investigate all aspects of human development, he should be in a position to test some of the generalizations as they are used in his program. For example, if school readiness is used as a criterion to place a child from kindergarten to the first grade, then the staff should spend some time in validating the procedures used in making this judgment. The focus of this type of research is to validate a procedure or generalization for a given situation.

There are a number of areas that can be investigated by a school district. The topics should be selected in terms of importance to a school district rather than because of their novelty. The impact of organizational change, educational methodology, or modifications in family living, are some topics of interest to a school district. A teacher who is concerned with the reading achievement of her pupils may test an Adlerian generalization that the child's position in his family and his sex affect how well he performs in school. The point of this type of research is not to add to existing information about a topic but to gain insight into the underlying variables so that one may better discharge his professional responsibilities. For example, if the teacher in this example validates the Adlerian generalization then she will use it more effectively because of her internalization of the idea. One of the values of conducting research is that of identifying the scope and limitations of a generalization.

In addition to promoting the professional development of an individual, the school should be aware of other advantages of conducting research at the local level. The increased number of innovations in educational methodology have raised more problems than they have solved. A typical school administrator is usually frustrated when he turns to the research literature to discover the efficacy of a given procedure for he usually finds conflicting evidence. As a consequence the school conducts pilot programs in order to make its own assessment of new techniques and procedures in its setting. In a similar manner, the counselor must conduct his own exploratory studies in order to keep current. Many individuals implement procedures they have heard about at a professional meeting or read about in a journal without understanding their limitations or the ramifications that the practices will have on their own program. In many instances an exploratory study can prevent much professional distress.

A school district should encourage the conducting of research for it benefits in three ways. First, it benefits from the findings in that they help to identify more effective ways of reaching an objective. Secondly, it benefits in that the person conducting the research grows professionally by gaining a better understanding of himself and of the way he conducts himself in his professional activities. In reality the true benefactors are the children in that they function in a better milieu.

THE COUNSELOR'S ROLE IN RESEARCH

It has been suggested that if the counselor is to enhance his professional functioning he must engage in research, and he must be familiar with current research results. If the counselor fails to keep abreast of the developments and advances in his field, he is short-changing his clients in that he may be using obsolete methods when more efficient ones are available. Thus he must become a consumer of research if he is to remain a viable counselor.

When an individual is preparing to become a counselor, he becomes aware in many of his courses of the relationship between theory and research. To facilitate a better understanding of this relationship he takes courses in statistics and measurement. For the most part, this training only provides a minimal competency in understanding some of the research and as a consequence he relies on his instructors for the meaning of some of the research findings. This dependency on others for interpretation of research results is most unfortunate because it leads to a mental set that tends to reject research at any level, because of a fear of being exposed as inadequate.

A counselor who operates on a professional level realizes that he cannot function at this level without becoming an intelligent consumer of research. He has perceived that in order to read research articles he must have an understanding of the research process. Failure to have this competency will minimize the amount of information he can obtain from journals, monographs, books, and professional meetings. An understanding of the research process will enable the counselor to better relate theory and research to his own personal experiences.

We are not suggesting that an individual be a researcher first and a counselor second but that he have a minimal understanding of the research process. He should have some skill in basic statistical procedures and a knowledge of tests and measurements. Also important is that the counselor have an understanding of how the generalizations about the guidance function and process can be translated into operational research. For example, a counselor should have some idea as to how a general objective like "self-actualization" can be translated into a research question and the type of instruments that could possibly be used in the investigation. This type of skill would enable a counselor to evaluate research findings in a meaningful manner while possessing only a minimal understanding of statistics. In addition this skill will enable the counselor to formulate his own research projects in a manner that would meet professional standards.

The counselor is in a favorable position to conduct research because of his awareness of the problem areas of counseling. During the course of his work he encounters problems whose resolution could best be obtained through research. Skill in formulating questions and identifying problems is as important as expertness in analyzing data. Research is nothing more than a systematic, objective attempt to obtain answers to questions. An experimental design demands that the counselor clearly define the problem and specify the treatment process which he thinks will produce the answer. A basic knowledge in designing experiments and analyzing data can be obtained from the books listed below.[12]

Since the first step in conducting research is to define the problem, the counselor may not necessarily find agreement among his colleagues that his interests merit an investigation. Different perspectives give rise to different problems. A counselor whose focus is self-theory may focus on problems dealing with acceptance of self while a social worker who has a strong psychoanalytical background may wish to investigate the impact of a technique of a client's ego strength. The school phychologist who uses behavior modification techniques with pupils who have learning disabilities may wish to investigage the impact of a procedure on the acquisition of a response. It should be apparent that different conceptual orientations will give rise to diffuse research interests. Some of the bias can be controlled by following the basic elements of the research process: clean definition of the problem, definite hypotheses, explicit experimental procedures, and appropriate analysis of data.

The counselor who conducts research in his school district should be more concerned with finding answers to his problems rather than verifying elements of a theory. Some counseling theories are rather complex and require sophisticated experimental designs to substantiate some of their elements. Most school districts do not have the money or the resources to conduct an intensive research project. An additional concern that a counselor should be aware of is the impact that any experiment has on the outcomes of the total program. For example, a counselor who has a strong interest in play therapy may find that some of his primary level pupils who are in the control group may fail to interact with him because they want to play with dolls like the other children in their class. On the other hand, some upper grade pupils may not refer themselves to the counselor because they

---

[12]James L. Bruning and B. L. Kintz, *Computational handbook of statistics* (Glenview, Scott, Foresman, 1968); Donald T. Campbell and Julian C. Stanley, *Experimental and quasi-experimental designs for research* (Chicago, Rand McNally, 1963), C. C. Helmstadter, *op. cit.;* Stephen Isaac and William B. Michael, *Handbook in research and evaluation* (San Diego, Robert R. Knapp, 1971).

feel that they are too mature for most of the play media. The counselor should examine those things he is doing so that he knows what the effects are on his clientele. However, before he attempts a new procdure he should reflect on the possible consequences of his actions.

Approaches to research in counseling and guidance

It is not our purpose to present an extensive outline for conducting research at the local school district level. We will, however, present a summary of some of the approaches that are found in the research literature. Most of the research approaches have been categorized so that they show a relationship between the treatment process and outcomes.

Studies that examine the outcomes of counseling and guidance investigate the degree to which a goal was achieved or the amount of change or improvement in a student. Usually it is better for the counselor to measure the degree of change rather than to measure success for the latter term is value judgment which reflects a conceptual bias. For example, a passive child whose behavior has been altered by counseling so that he is more assertive with his peers may be seen as a problem by his teacher because he is getting into fights. She may feel that the counselor was not too successful with this boy. The counselor should be rather explicit as to the type of change that will be exhibited by the pupils. Improved grades, changed attitudes, better personal adjustment, and increased self-understanding are among the many different outcomes that can be selected as indicators of change. More often than not the availability of instruments affects the choice of outcomes. This is unfortunate because some of the answers to the problems encountered by the counselor can only be obtained by novel rather than standardized testing instruments. The counselor should also measure change in terms of what he expects his techniques or activities to accomplish rather than some general goal. "Better grades" is a general statement which can be improved by an explicit goal such as that the pupils will be able to read at a certain level of comprehension. This outcome would be inappropriate if the activity was a task oriented group whose focus was on behavior problems that arise during recess. In outcome studies the counselor must establish a logical relationship between what he does and what he expects. He should be more concerned with change in behavior rather than in "success."

Research whose focus is on the process of counseling or guidance concentrates on the components of various procedures. A counselor who uses play therapy may wish to know if there is any difference in preference in toys selected by boys as compared to girls, or if children with different types of problems select different types of toys. A counselor may appraise his own counseling to see if there is any relationship between the amount of time the pupil talks and the degree of change in him. The basic thrust of this approach is to have a better understanding of how the various sub-parts in a given activity function in relationship to the total procedure. For example, if the counselor found that children with different types of problems select different types of toys in play therapy, he may wish to increase the number of toys available to the children. He may also conduct further experiments to see if he can judge the effectiveness of play therapy by the sequence of toys a child selects. In a general way, the counselor's familiarity with process research enhances his understanding of the relationship between outcome and procedure. This is to say that the counselor's focus should not be just on outcomes for in many instances the degree of change in a pupil is directly related to some specific element of the treatment process.

Some studies originated as an afterthought rather than as a planned experiment. This usually comes about when a staff member exhibits some curiosity about information that has accrued in the field. The validation of many appraisal instruments comes about in this manner. A teacher may wish to know if there is any relationship between a reading readiness test and performance on a standardized achievement test. The school psychologist may perform an item analysis of some of his test data to see if specific items are related to certain learning disorders. This approach cannot be adversely criticized for several reasons. First, in many instances it takes time to accumulate sufficient cases so that an adequate analysis of the data can be made. Secondly, the counselor may not be aware that he is faced with a problem and must use hindsight to identify early manifestations of the difficulty. Third, the counselor is primarily a helper and as such devotes most of his time to this activity. The time he spends on research must be carefully allotted so it does not jeopardize his primary function, and research such as this may be of less importance than that considered above.

A type of research that is seldom conducted by the local school district is one that investigates the influence of variables such as counselor attributes (i.e., age, sex, socioeconomic background) or situational artifacts (i.e., size of counseling room, color of the wall) on the process or outcome of counseling and guidance. This type of study requires a sophisticated design and considerable amount of time. Since the schools get a limited benefit from it they are reluctant to fund this type of study.

PROBLEMS ASSOCIATED WITH RESEARCH

Many of the problems associated with evaluation can also plague research procedure. This should not be surprising in that research is but one aspect of evaluation. The major difficulty in studying counseling is the establishment of criteria of counseling effectiveness. In many instances the conceptual base determines whether the counseling process was successful with a pupil or not. Such general criteria as personal adjustment, academic achievement, and personality measures cannot be used as direct measures of change but only indirect evidence of the impact of counseling. It is an unwarranted assumption that a change in the self concept will lead to better academic achievement. Yet such a change may be desirable for other reasons. Perhaps the school's interest with this type of criteria stems from the fact that it is receiving tangible benefits from the work of the counselor. In the same vein it influences the selection of criteria because of its interest in "successful programs;" the school demands justification of its expenditures. The subtle difference between "success" and "change" escapes most school personnel and as a consequence causes needless problems.

A second difficulty which a counselor encounters is the use of statistical procedures. It has been suggested that a counselor can have a reasonable skill in designing experiments without becoming an expert in statistics. The use of computers in analyzing data has complicated the research done at the local school district level. More often than not the counselor would like a rather simple analysis of his data but the computer consultant suggests esoteric procedures that only a few can understand. This needless complication condemns many studies to oblivion. The counselor should use only those procedures with which he is familiar and let the professional researcher use the more sophisticated techniques.

It also has been suggested that the amount of time to do research and the impact of an experimental design can be considered as problems associated with research. These two problems are similar in that they both affect the work of the counselor. Each takes something away from the student and as such influences the effectiveness of the total guidance program. A counselor's awareness of these two difficulties should help him set realistic limits as to the type and scope of research that he undertakes in the school district. A professionally oriented counselor recognizes that in order to enhance his functioning he must solve some of the problems that confront him in his work; however, he also realizes that there are times when the needs of the pupils supercede his personal needs.

STUDIES OF ELEMENTARY SCHOOL GUIDANCE AND COUNSELING

In 1967 Cottingham's review of literature revealed only limited research dealing with the basic areas of elementary guidance. Deficiencies were found in the following: (1) theoretical formulations of the nature of elementary guidance; (2) the guidance function within instruction (the teacher's guidance responsibilities) and beyond (the counselor's role); (3) unmet needs of elementary pupils.[13] Cottingham outlines a series of research proposals that would fill the research voids that he discovered. He suggests that a formulation of a theoretical foundation of ele-

---

[13]Harold F. Cottingham, "Research voids in elementary school guidance." *Elementary School Guidance and Counseling*, Vol. 1. 1967.

mentary guidance would facilitate the development of appropriate research designs.

Six years later, Miller, Gum, and Bender, in their review of literature report on the results of hundreds of reports that evaluated and studied the guidance process.[14] For the most part, the gap reported by Cottingham has been partially filled at least. They summarize their observations in the following manner:

> The studies to date for the most part have been descriptive in nature, finding out about counselor characteristics and how estimated counselor time is distributed over a set of functions. Most doctoral studies have been on perception of counselor role by teachers, counselors, principals, and counselor educators . . . More recently attention has turned to demonstrating the effectiveness of behavioral counseling, client-centered counseling, and the use of the counselor in a consultative role with teachers and parents, especially in the area of behavior modification. Studying the effectiveness of classroom group guidance is another recent interest of researchers and one which seems increasing.[15]

They also note that the staff within a school has difficulty comprehending what the counselor is attempting to do within their building. In spite of the fact that principals tend to provide insufficient administrative support and teachers have inadequate perceptions of the functions, many outcomes studies indicate that children are helped by the guidance program. Generally speaking, great strides have been made in evaluating guidance programs and studying its specific functions.

The Minnesota Department of Education sponsored a study conducted by Miller, Gum, and Bender who investigated, among other factors, the inter-relationships among guidance variables and role and model aspects. This report should be read by all who are associated with elementary guidance because of its comprehensiveness. Their basic conclusion was that "attention to the development of the self-concept is an important purpose of the school worthy in its own right and should not be justified

---

[14]Dean Miller, Moy F. Gum, and Donald Bender, *Elementary school guidance: Demonstration and evaluation* (St. Paul: Minnesota Department of Education, 1972)

[15]*Ibid.*, pp. 36-37.

primarily on the basis of its relationship to school achievement although such a significant link should not be treated lightly."[16] They found that pupils could be helped by counselors although each counselor had his unique way of using his time to serve various functions. It is suggested that it is impossible for a counselor alone to contribute effectively to all important outcome variables. It can be inferred that the counselor needs the assistance of other qualified personnel if the guidance program is to be successful. In this respect the effectiveness of the counselor as a consultant was related in part to staff openness. However, the counselor's total effectiveness was related to the number of buildings he served. They recommend that, whenever possible, a counselor should serve only one building because as the number of buildings he serves increases the less likely he is to be known to the staff.

A study sponsored by the Office of the Superintendent of Public Instruction of the State of Illinois and written by one of the authors complements the Minnesota study cited above.[17] It investigated the pattern of counselor behavior for a two year period. The counselors recorded their daily activities on forms designed to cover all functions of elementary guidance. Most of the counselors' time was devoted to counseling, with consulting a distant second. In the opinion of their teachers, 325 of the 429 counseled pupils showed some degree of improvement. In addition teacher ratings of pupils' behavior characteristics showed marked improvement. It was concluded that counselors can help most pupils with their concerns but those who have a complexity of problems require additional help from qualified professional help.

The above two studies were cited for several reasons. First, they demonstrate that state departments of education can assume a leadership role in helping school districts become involved in research. By providing assistance in the form of consultants they can enhance the professional development of the school district

---

[16]*Ibid.,* p. 248.

[17]Henry Kaczkowski, *An appraisal of the elementary school counselor's role behavior* (Springfield: Office of Superintendent of Public Instruction, 1971).

staff by helping them examine the relationship between functions and outcomes. Secondly, studies that examine the relationship between functions and outcomes should be conducted for at least two years because of the tendency of the staff to change tactics from one year to another. In our comments about evaluation we suggested that one of its functions is to help the staff in modifying its programs so that the desired outcomes could be reached. Third, the results suggest that most counselors initially attempt to reach too many goals and as a consequence must make adjustment in terms of the needs of the pupils and their teachers. Fourth, each report indicates that if all the children are to be helped the school district requires a diversity of professional helpers. Last of all, the studies point out that different counselors in a school district have different impact on their clientele.

In recent years the *Elementary School Guidance and Counseling* journal has been devoting more space to research articles. This thrust reflects the need for studying the relationshp between functions and outcomes. However, there has been only a limited attempt to examine the relationship between the functions and the needs of the children. To a certain degree, this type of research requires an interdisciplinary approach in developing an adequate research design and execution. All in all, the field of elementary guidance has progressed more rapidly than most experts anticipated in the early 1960's.

REPORTING TO THE COMMUNITY

Most of the studies and reports are written to be read by other professional personnel. Seldom are reports written for the general public. However, in the age of accountability, the public is demanding to know more about what is going on in their schools. It is incumbent on the school district to give more information about programs and their outcomes.

Prior to the implementation of the guidance program in a school district, the administrative and counseling staff should inform the public about the nature of the program. The orientation report should focus on what is being done, why it is being done, how it will be done, and the personnel associated with it.

The report should relate the general goals of the program with activities and some of the anticipated outcomes. Much time and energy should be devoted to this orientation phase because it helps in the development of acceptance of the guidance program by the community. Community support is needed if the program is to be maintained for any period of time. Parents, by talking about the guidance program to the principal and teachers, may influence the degree to which the staff accepts the program. Like any innovative idea, a newly implemented guidance program faces a period of time where it struggles for acceptance by the staff. Parental acceptance helps create a facilitative climate in the community. The guidance staff may generate this facilitative climate by attending meetings of various organizations in order that they may clarify any misconceptions and answer questions about the program.

After the program has been operational for some time, the counselor should make periodic reports to the school board and the community. The report should be written in layman's language and when necessary, have a technical supplement that supports the generalizations made in the body of the report. Essentially the report should be written from a cost-benefit perspective That is to say, who was helped by whom and with what effectiveness. An analysis of the distribution of the counselor's time in respect to functions is helpful in that it helps to establish in the public's mind the relationship between functions and outcomes. As suggested earlier the report should place more emphasis on changes made in behavior rather than on success of the program because this approach will imply the complexity of measuring the outcome of the program. As with the orientation report, the counselor should make himself available to various organizations so that he can explain and clarify elements contained in the evaluation.

SUMMARY

This chapter has reviewed the role that evaluation and research play in the development of a guidance program and those associated with it. Evaluation was seen as a process whereby a judgment is made about a set of observations that were made in a systematic manner. Research was seen as a technique of evaluation whose primary interest is to find answers to problems. It was noted that one of the chief problems associated with evaluation and research is that of establishing criteria for assessing outcomes. Without suitable criteria it is impossible to measure the progress of a program or the degree of change in a child. It was suggested that a counselor gain some competency in research so that he may become a more effective producer and consumer of research. Without this competency his professional development will be restricted. The review of studies sponsored by two state departments of education indicated that local school districts can conduct quality research if they are given appropriate assistance. An examination of the research and evaluation conducted in the past six years indicated that many aspects of elementary guidance are being studied and that information obtained from them has enhanced the professional development of the staffs. More important, many of the findings point out that children do benefit from guidance services. As more knowledge is gained about the process of guidance and counseling the degree of benefit will increase even more.

SUGGESTED READINGS

C. C. Helstadter: *Research concepts in human behavior.* New York, Appleton-Century-Crofts, 1970.

George E. Hill and Eleanore Luckey: *Guidance for children in elementary schools.* New York, Appleton-Century-Crofts, 1969, Chapter 13.

J. W. Hollis and L. U. Hollis: *Organizing for effective guidance.* Chicago, Science Research Associates, 1965, Chapters 20 and 21.

Henry Kaczkowski: *An appraisal of the elementary school counselor's role behavior.* Springfield, Illinois: Office of Superintendent of Public Instruction, 1971.

G. Dean Miller, Moy F. Gum, and Donald Bender: *Elementary school guidance: Demonstration and evaluation.* St. Paul, Minnesota Department of Education, 1972.

Merle M. Ohlsen: *Guidance services in the modern school.* 2nd Ed. New York, Harcourt, Brace, and World, 1974, Appendix B.

NAME INDEX

SUBJECT INDEX

A

Adlerian family counseling, 324-326
Affective education, 276-277
American Personnel and Guidance
    Association, 16
American School Counselor
    Association, 25
Appraising students for instruction,
    257-263
Arizona State University, 10
Association for Counselor Education
    and Supervision, 25
Authenticity (see Genuineness)

B

Behavior modification, 22, 226-236
Bureau of Child Study, Chicago
    Public Schools, 75-76

C

Career education, 267-271
Child development specialist, 15-17
Child Study Association of America,
    312-313
Classroom
    as a social system, 218-226
    groups, 117-120
Client
    perception of counselor conditions,
        101-102
    self-exploration, 102
Concreteness, 93-94
Consultation
    and the counselor, 198-205
    definitions of, 185-187
    evaluation of, 192-198
    mental health consultation, 183-
        184, 190
    roles and functions in, 191-192
    types of, 189-191
Counseling
    and teaching, 102-104

conditions of, 90-96
    implementing, 96-102
developmental, 10, 19-20
early beginnings, 6-7
future of, 11-12
goals of, 88-90
groups, 148-158
in the 1950's, 7-8
in the 1960's, 8-10
models of, 13-25
neotraditional, 10
problems in, 107-110
traditional, 8
Counselor
    and consultation, 198-205
    and parents, 301-328
    and research, 344-349
    and the curriculum, 244-271
    as child development specialist,
        15-17
    as consultant, 17-19
    as coordinator, 14
    as counselor, 22-23
    as data handler, 13-14
    as developmental specialist, 19-21
    as facilitator of personal
        development, 38-44
    as psychological educator, 23-24
    as social engineer, 21-22
    developmental, 10
    early concepts of, 6-7
    in the 1950's, 7-8
    in the 1960's, 8-10
Curriculum
    and instruction, 247-250
    and learning, 247-250
    and teaching, 247-250
    and the self-concept, 263-267
    nature of, 244-247

D

Discipline, as limits, 49-53

361